Curriculum Development for Intensive English Programs

This book provides a comprehensive, contextualized approach to curriculum creation, design, development, and evaluation for Intensive English Programs. The book starts by guiding the reader through the important but often overlooked steps of contextualizing their current or future language curriculum to give decision makers the full picture of what their curriculum is intended to accomplish. Subsequent chapters break down the popular ADDIE (Analyze, Design, Develop, Implement, and Evaluate) model of curricular design into meaningful units focused on learner and context analysis, learning outcomes, assessments, materials, and implementation and evaluation processes. Accessible and engaging chapters include a variety of prompts, activities, and summaries to support learning and implementation.

With instruction on how to build a language curriculum from scratch and insights for changing or improving an existing curriculum, this book is a key resource for instructors and program administrators in language programs as well as essential reading in TESOL methods and language curriculum design courses.

Grant Eckstein is Associate Professor of Linguistics and an academic coordinator at the English Language Center at Brigham Young University, USA.

Norman W. Evans is Professor of Linguistics and former director of the English Language Center at Brigham Young University, USA.

K. James Hartshorn is Assistant Professor of Linguistics at Brigham Young University, USA.

Benjamin L. McMurry is Administrative Coordinator of the English Language Center at Brigham Young University, USA.

Curriculum Development for Intensive English Programs

A Contextualized Framework for Language Program Design and Implementation

Grant Eckstein, Norman W. Evans,
K. James Hartshorn, and Benjamin L. McMurry

Routledge
Taylor & Francis Group

NEW YORK AND LONDON

Cover image: © Getty Images

First published 2023
by Routledge
605 Third Avenue, New York, NY 10158

and by Routledge
4 Park Square, Milton Park, Abingdon, Oxon, OX14 4RN

Routledge is an imprint of the Taylor & Francis Group, an informa business

© 2023 Grant Eckstein, Norman W. Evans, K. James Hartshorn and Benjamin L. McMurry

The right of Grant Eckstein, Norman W. Evans, K. James Hartshorn and Benjamin L. McMurry to be identified as authors of this work has been asserted in accordance with sections 77 and 78 of the Copyright, Designs and Patents Act 1988.

All rights reserved. No part of this book may be reprinted or reproduced or utilised in any form or by any electronic, mechanical, or other means, now known or hereafter invented, including photocopying and recording, or in any information storage or retrieval system, without permission in writing from the publishers.

Trademark notice: Product or corporate names may be trademarks or registered trademarks, and are used only for identification and explanation without intent to infringe.

Library of Congress Cataloging-in-Publication Data
Names: Eckstein, Grant, author.
Title: Curriculum development for intensive English programs : a contextualized framework for language program design and implementation / by Grant Eckstein, [and 3 others].
Description: New York, NY : Routledge, 2023. | Includes bibliographical references and index.
Identifiers: LCCN 2022025562 (print) | LCCN 2022025563 (ebook) | ISBN 9781032306599 (hardback) | ISBN 9781032287379 (paperback) | ISBN 9781003306122 (ebook)
Subjects: LCSH: English language—Study and teaching—Foreign speakers. | Curriculum planning.
Classification: LCC PE1128.A2 E273 2023 (print) | LCC PE1128.A2 (ebook) | DDC 428.0071—dc23/eng/20220531
LC record available at https://lccn.loc.gov/2022025562
LC ebook record available at https://lccn.loc.gov/2022025563

ISBN: 978-1-032-30659-9 (hbk)
ISBN: 978-1-032-28737-9 (pbk)
ISBN: 978-1-003-30612-2 (ebk)

DOI: 10.4324/9781003306122

Typeset in Palatino
by Apex CoVantage, LLC

Printed in the United Kingdom
by Henry Ling Limited

Contents

1 A Metaphor for Curriculum and Curricular Design	**1**
Introduction	1
House-Building Metaphor	2
A Contextualized Approach	4
A Principled Approach	5
Curricular Level: Program, Course, Class	8
Curricular Components	11
Putting It All Together	12
2 Defining Curriculum	**18**
Introduction	18
Curriculum	19
Governing Documents and the Essential Curriculum	21
Envisioning the Essential Curriculum	26
Variations in Curriculum	28
Locus of Curricular Control	29
3 Context and Contextual Analysis	**35**
Introduction	35
Context	36
Contextual Analysis	41
Methods for Contextual Analysis	52
Articulating Your Assumptions	53
4 Governing Documents: Mission, Goals, and Objectives	**59**
Introduction	59
Mission Statements	59
Program Outcomes	65
Course Goals	67
Class Objectives	73
Guiding Principles: Stability, Responsiveness, and Cohesion	75
5 Learner Analysis	**79**
Introduction	79
Learners in the House Metaphor	80
Learner Analysis	82

Needs Analysis	86
Resources for Conducting a Learner Analysis	92
Using a Learner Analysis to Solve Programmatic Problems	94
Evaluating the Learner Analysis	96

6 Contextual Synthesis — 101
Introduction	101
Contextual Synthesis	102
Sample Contextual Syntheses	105
Planning a Contextual Synthesis	118
Addressing Challenges Identified in the Contextual Synthesis	121

7 Learning Outcomes: Design, Develop, and Implement — 127
Introduction	127
The House Metaphor	129
From Contextual Synthesis to Learning Outcomes	129
Learning Outcomes for Virtual, Hybrid, and Distant Learning	130
Learning Outcomes	130
Designing Program Learning Outcomes	132
Developing Program Learning Outcomes	138
Implementing Program Learning Outcomes	143
Designing Course Learning Outcomes	144
Developing and Implementing Course Learning Outcomes	147
Developing and Implementing Class Learning Outcomes	149
Overall Implementation	150

8 Assessment and Feedback: Design, Develop, and Implement — 153
Introduction	153
The House Metaphor	153
The Nature of Assessment	154
Tests	154
Tests and Assessments: The Program Level	161
Designing, Developing, and Implementing Tests and Assessments	162
Additional Considerations	170

9 Learning Experiences: Design, Develop, and Implement — 174
Introduction	174
Building a House	175
Learning Experiences: Design, Develop, and Implement	175

10 Program-Wide Implementation — **197**
Introduction — 197
Building a House — 198
Building Facilitator Competency — 200
Building Learner Competency — 204
Delivery of the Product — 206
Strategic Implementation — 207
Understanding Personal Strengths and Weakness
   as an Implementer — 216

11 Evaluation of Process and Product — **223**
Introduction — 223
Building a House — 224
What Is Evaluation? — 225
Evaluating the Product — 229
Evaluating the Process — 236
Process of Evaluation — 241

Index — 252

1

A Metaphor for Curriculum and Curricular Design

Introduction

Any educator, regardless of responsibilities or position, is impacted by curriculum. Administrators, materials developers, supervisors, and classroom teachers all interact with curriculum in one way or another on an almost daily basis. Despite its centrality in education, however, it is amazing how little is known about curriculum—what it means, what it includes, and how it is developed and designed (Tyler, 2013; Christison & Murray, 2021; Macalister & Nation, 2020; Richards, 2001; Brown, 1995; Allen & Sites, 2012).

Having worked as language program administrators in various contexts over a number of years, we have had many opportunities to interact with colleagues in other programs who are struggling to establish an effective curriculum. For instance, it is surprisingly common to hear of programs in which a teacher is handed a class list, a textbook, and a well-wish as they start a new course. Alternatively, we have interacted with colleagues who have been given released teaching time in order to develop or redesign a curriculum. However, too often, these individuals have had little, if any, experience developing curricula. Our aim is to provide a clear understanding of what curriculum means and how it can be designed, developed, implemented, and evaluated within the framework of a contextualized curriculum development model.

Several key elements of this book need to be noted at the outset. First, much of what we present here is based on our own experiences and the work of many scholars who will be noted throughout the book. In particular, Tyler's (2013, p. 1) *Basic Principles of Curriculum and Instruction* poses four central questions to curriculum development. These questions are:

> what educational purposes should the school seek to attain, what educational experiences can be provided that are likely to attain these purposes, how can these learning experiences be organized, and how can we determine whether these purposes are being attained?

Our aim throughout this book is to provide answers to these questions.

A second important consideration is the book's intended audiences. We have principally designed the book for language program administrators, teachers, and language professionals who are often asked to design curriculum, even without much (if any) formal schooling or training in this area. In addition, it is intended for instructors and their students in BA, MA, PhD, and Teaching Certificate programs who are taking materials and methods and curriculum design classes. While our primary focus is curriculum for intensive English programs, as indicated in the title, this is a principle-based text; as such, it is applicable in many contexts. For instance, we do not focus specifically on K–12 curricular examples, but the principles presented here could easily be adapted for just such a context.

Finally, curriculum design models can be categorized as either process-oriented or product-oriented. ADDIE and SAM (Allen & Sites, 2012) are process-based models that outline the steps in curriculum design. Other models, such as Backward Design (Wiggins & McTighe, 2005) or Design Layers (Gibbons & Rogers, 2009), focus on the structure of the end product. The organization of this book is based on the ADDIE model, and the curricular components resemble Tyler's model and that of Wiggins and McTighe.

House-Building Metaphor

In order to deconstruct and simplify the unwieldy concept of curriculum, we have adopted a metaphor that we will refer to frequently in this book. The metaphor compares curriculum design and development with the construction of a house. In many ways, the two processes are analogous. Building a house requires vision, foresight, planning, resources, and careful execution. A house is built for a general purpose, such as to provide shelter, house a family, or offer privacy. It is designed with the local geography, climate, available resources, and laws in mind so that a house in a cold climate in the mountains will be unique in significant ways from a beachfront home on a tropical island.

In spite of any obvious differences in the final look and feel of a home, the process of building a house is essentially consistent, regardless of construction methods and materials. There is initial conception, site development, architectural design, hiring of contractors and laborers, material purchasing and delivery, building, inspection, and ultimately moving in. Then come years and years of maintenance, improvements, additions, and so on. Of course, there are variations of this building process. Most obvious is the case of a family purchasing an existing home; in this case, the family sees none of the initial building process but enters the picture at the maintenance and improvement stage. Other variations might include situations in which initial building stages are done irregularly or informally, such as with haphazard construction or makeshift and temporary dwellings. Setting up a tent, for instance, doesn't require an architectural firm, though it can be argued that even sleeping under the stars requires some level of forethought, planning, site development, and set-up, however minimal and informal that might be.

Turning this metaphor to curriculum, it is easy to pick out relevant similarities. Designing a curriculum requires vision, foresight, and planning. Without these, an educational program will devolve into a collection of inconsistent activities and time fillers, rather than evolving into a cohesive curriculum. As Richard-Amato (2003, p. 195) has noted, "A hodgepodge of activities thrown together does not a curriculum make". Like a house, a curriculum is built for a general purpose. In the topic area of English language teaching, a curriculum is primarily designed to teach students English. But some English programs are built to simultaneously turn a profit, prepare students for future/concurrent university work, or serve the acculturation needs of a particular learner group. And just like a house, a curriculum must be sensitive to the local geography, climate, and laws where it is built, though these concepts may be less tangible for a curriculum. For instance, a curriculum is not necessarily impacted by its placement on a mountain or a beach, but it is affected by environmental considerations, such as the political, social, and economic forces that determine what the curriculum can and cannot offer.

The process of curriculum development is one area where our metaphor can be particularly instructive. Although there are industry standards and regulations for home construction in most countries in the world, the same is not necessarily true for the construction of a curriculum. Some schools seem to reinterpret the adage, "Throw enough dirt, and some will stick," to suggest that enough language teaching (however random or unplanned) might eventually result in a reasonable curriculum. We recommend, however, a principled, contextualized approach to curriculum design and development. Such an approach does not include every step used in home construction, but it does recognize five essential components of curriculum creation: analysis, design, development, implementation, and evaluation. These five components come from the ADDIE model of curriculum design.

A Contextualized Approach

Our purpose in this book is to articulate an efficient approach to curriculum design and development. We feel that such an approach should be contextualized and principled. By contextualized, we mean that a curriculum should be understood within its unique context. Designers should consider why the curriculum exists or why it needs to be developed. They should also consider where it will be implemented, by whom, and what it will do for the target language learners (see Box 1.1).

Box 1.1   Contextual Questions

To understand a curricular context, use the basic journalism questions as illustrated in Figure 1.1.

The most essential question is that of *why*. Why does the language program exist? A very thoughtful and thorough answer will provide important insights into the purpose of a particular curriculum. From there, additional questions can help clarify what should be taught, to whom, when and where, and how this will all be done.

This information is meant to give a small introduction to the contextual elements of curriculum development. The concept is developed further in Chapters 3, 4, and 5.

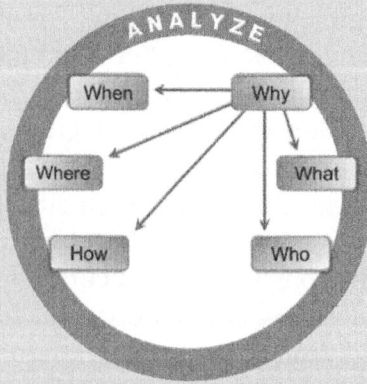

Figure 1.1 Basic journalism questions used for curricular context analysis.

A Principled Approach

By *principled*, we mean that curriculum development should not be haphazard; rather, it should be guided by a set of actions. In our view, the best actions include those already mentioned of *analyzing* the curricular context and learner needs and then *designing*, *developing*, and *implementing* all the curricular components in a relatively orderly fashion. Throughout all this, curriculum designers should *evaluate* both the curricular components and the entire process, as shown in Box 1.2.

The result of a principled, contextualized approach is a cohesive curricular product that is tailored to the needs and constraints of a learning environment. It is a unique curriculum by design, not by accident or happenstance. And, of course, it takes time to properly analyze and design. But ultimately,

---

Box 1.2   Principled Curriculum Approach

The ADDIE model of curricular development involves five principles of action: Analyze, Design, Develop, Implement, and Evaluate. The five steps are meant to be both recursive and overlapping, as Figure 1.2 indicates.

The starting point for creating or improving a curriculum should always be analysis. For major changes, or when starting a curriculum from scratch, the analysis phase may need to be thorough and relatively formal. For small changes, such as adopting a new textbook, the analysis phase may be rather simple.

Following analysis, curricular innovation should proceed in a principled manner, with attention to all stages of the ADDIE model. We discuss applications of ADDIE in the second half of this book.

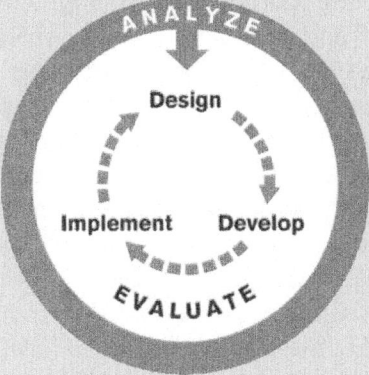

Figure 1.2 Graphic representation of the five steps of the ADDIE model.

it is a well-wrought and justifiable curriculum since stakeholders understand why the curriculum exists, what it is designed to accomplish, and how it works to accomplish those goals (see Christison & Murray, 2021; Macalister & Nation, 2020). See Box 1.3.

Box 1.3   Extending the Metaphor to Context

House Context

A comparison of different international homes illustrates the importance of context in building design. Several contextual factors must be considered. First, the availability of resources will determine how a house can be built. Second, the climate in a specific location predetermines certain characteristics of building construction. A Samoan *fale* and a Mongolian *ger*, for instance, have a number of similar characteristics. They are rounded, contain supporting posts, and have domed roofs. Their purposes are similar, too: they both provide shelter and offer living space. In spite of their visual similarities, the two structures display some very different characteristics, which can be traced back to the environmental contexts of Samoa and Mongolia. The Samoan *fale*, for instance, has no walls and is made of plant materials. The Mongolian *ger*, on the other hand, is made of animal skins or fabric and is completely enclosed, with the exception of an open circle at the top of the roof. The reasons for these differences are obvious. The tropical weather in Samoa would make a walled-in structure too hot, and plentiful *lau* or palm leaves create thatching to cover the roof. But in Mongolia, an open-walled structure would be too cold, and the hole in the top of the roof allows for the smoke from an internal fire to escape.

Curriculum Context

The metaphor of context can be extended to curricular decisions as well. Take, for example, the situation of English language teaching in a foreign language environment and compare it with second language teaching. An EFL classroom is a little island of English language teaching in a sea of another dominant language. An ESL environment is just the opposite: a student can be immersed in English inside and outside of the classroom.

There may be some similarities in both teaching environments. For instance, teachers in both contexts will likely encourage extensive reading in English, a task that could take place anywhere. But there are salient dissimilarities, too. An ESL teacher can assign students to interact with the community, read street signs, go to the movies, attend parties, and shop at a local supermarket; all of these activities will naturally involve English. An EFL teacher, however, cannot assume that English is everywhere outside of the classroom. Instead, he or she must plan activities carefully and find

> ways to expose students to English. However creative, these activities are virtually guaranteed to be more contrived and less authentic than activities in an ESL setting.
>
> The same could be true of countless other contexts. Consider the differences between independent language programs and programs situated within a university. Even in sponsored programs, the difference between an intensive English program at a university and one at a community college will be vastly different. Other contextual factors include student demographics, teacher skills and backgrounds, financial strength of the program, government regulations and restrictions, cultural constraints, a school's charter, and so on.

In our experience working with language programs all across the world, we have found that most people involved in curricular change do not have a contextualized and principled approach. Often, they are eager to implement changes that they are sure will solve the most pressing problems, but they later become dissatisfied with the results.

In one particular program we observed, the curriculum coordinator (who was also teaching a 15-credit load of ESL classes and balancing other administrative duties) wanted to improve students' language proficiency gains by adding one more level of classes to the current five-level language program. Only after a careful and thorough analysis of the program's context did it become apparent that adding another level of instruction was just one part of a balanced solution. In fact, adding a level in isolation would likely have resulted in little improvement at all. Instead, the contextual analysis showed that many teachers felt disenfranchised from the language program, graduates of the English language program were dissatisfied with their speaking classes, and a small number of key administrators were ill equipped to handle the needs of an adult ESL population.

There were many other revelations that the administration found just as startling. Merely making this analysis available to teachers and administrators breathed new life into the curriculum. Eventually, another level of classes was created, but in the process, the learning objectives for all classes in the program were reviewed, made more rigorous, and coordinated among all the courses and all the levels. Once this was accomplished, new curricular materials could be designed, developed, and implemented.

Without a contextualized and principled approach, though, this language program would have fallen headfirst into yet another round of expensive Band-Aid approaches, or, as suggested earlier, more rounds of throwing dirt and hoping it sticks. See Box 1.4.

> **Box 1.4 House Metaphor Using a Contextualized, Principled Approach**
> *Building a Language Learning Curriculum: Plan, Process, Product*
>
> **Context**
>
> **Why** is the curriculum being designed?
> **What** is the principal purpose it will achieve? (Mission of institution, goals)
> **Where** will the curriculum be implemented with what resources, and for whom?
> **What** will it do for our language learners? (Purposes and learning outcomes)
>
> Illustration 1.1 The W questions for the house metaphor.
>
> (House diagram: Why is the house being built? What is its principal purpose? Where, for whom, and with what resources will it be built? What do we want it to be/do for us?)
>
> **Principles**
>
> **How** will we achieve these purposes and learning outcomes?
> **What** process will we follow to design this curriculum?
> **ADDIE** is initiated.
> Analyze, Design, Develop, Implement, and Evaluate all curriculum components: learning outcomes, assessments, feedback, and learning experiences
>
> Illustration 1.2 The H question for the house metaphor.
>
> (House diagram: How will we achieve these purposes and learning outcomes? Given the general concept outlined in the plan phase, we now go to work in blueprinting the construction of the desired house. Much detail goes into this process including site inspection, soil testing, materials selection, timelines, sequencing charts, etc.)
>
> **Product**
>
> The result is a product that reflects the decisions previously made in the plan and process steps. Furthermore, the curriculum is unique to the plans and processes involved in its creation. However, careful planning and construction should always result in a curriculum that is responsive, cohesive, and stable (see Chapter 4).

Curricular Level: Program, Course, Class

So far, the discussion of curriculum has focused mainly on the big picture of program creation and development. We have mentioned adding a new bank of classes or revising learning objectives for the entire language program. But assuming that curriculum is only changed at this level would be incorrect. In reality, curricular design or revision can be accomplished in at least three areas: the program, the course, and the class (see Box 1.5).

Box 1.5 Program, Course, and Class Diagram

Figure 1.3 is a simple program diagram. There are only two skills taught in this program (reading and writing) and only two levels (beginning and advanced). At the beginning level, there is only one section of each course, but at the advanced level, there are two sections of each course.

The **program level** encompasses everything in the chart. Both the reading and writing classes, the two levels of proficiency, and the multiple sections are all part of the program level. A change in the program mission or the addition of another level would affect the entire program.

The **course level** encompasses all the sections of a particular level in just one skill area. This program has four courses: 1) Beginning Reading, 2) Advanced Reading, 3) Beginning Writing, and 4) Advanced Writing. A change in textbooks for the beginning reading course would certainly affect that course in a substantial way, but its effect on the other courses would be less dramatic.

The **class level** is illustrated by the round circles below each section of each course. A change in one day's instruction would certainly affect that day and perhaps the days surrounding it, but it would have a minimal impact on class instruction in a different course.

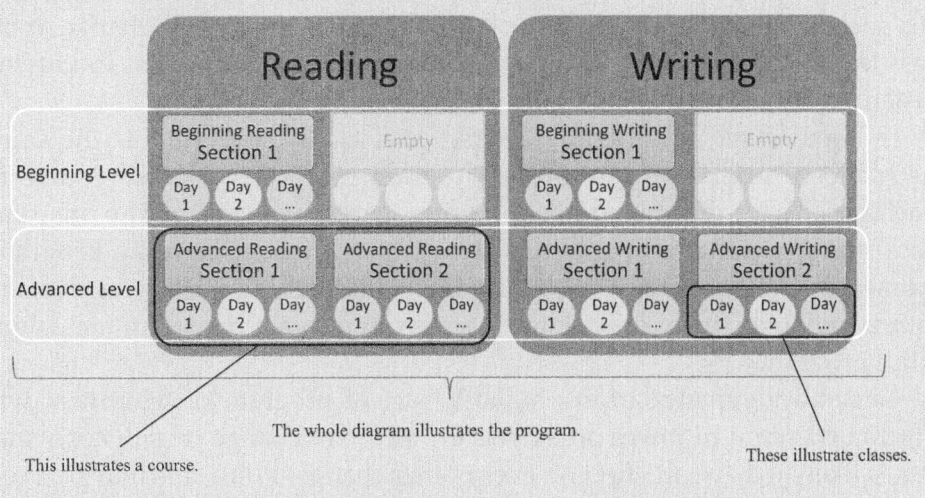

Figure 1.3 A program diagram featuring program, course, and class level coordination of curriculum.

Program

The program level is made up of all the sub-programs, levels, courses, and classes that take place at an institution. For example, in an IEP, the program includes all the courses at each proficiency level and in each skill area. This encompasses the mission of the program, any standardized placement, proficiency, and advancement tests, and program-wide activities or sub-programs.

Course

A course is a set of instructional and evaluative sessions that are specific to a proficiency level and skill. An IEP may have courses such as Intermediate Reading, Advanced Writing, or Novice Grammar. In small schools, there may be only one section of each course, but in larger programs, there may be multiple sections taught by either the same or different teachers. A course includes any associated sections and encompasses all the standardized objectives, tests, and activities that go with them. Curricular changes at this level might include creating a standardized test for all sections of a given course or adopting a new textbook in a grammar course.

Class

A class refers to a set of instructional activities in a single day's instruction. But a class can also be more and less than this: a single class could be just a few minutes during a class period (sometimes called *a lesson*) or could span multiple days of related instruction (sometimes called *a unit*). The notion of class is highly variable because classes can be dynamic and resist conforming to a specific time limit or a specific kind of routine. Curricular change at the class level might include adding a new homework assignment or modifying an activity that students are unprepared to complete.

In some cases, a program, course, and class may refer to the same instructional unit. For example, a program may offer a crash course in teaching EFL for those interested in going overseas to teach. The one-time class may be eight hours of instruction on a weekend, so the program, course, and class would all be the same. In other situations, a program and course may overlap. If only one course is offered in a program, the course is the program.

Generally, a change at the highest level of program development will affect curriculum in lower areas, too. In fact, any change in any curricular area is likely to have an effect on every other change. While this may be overwhelming to consider given the numerous and often tiny changes that take place in classes daily, such a perspective can also be heartening. For instance, any positive change in a single class can have equally positive ripple effects elsewhere. Including a new learning outcome in a particular course and coordinating this with other courses in the program will amplify the benefits of that learning outcome. A well-coordinated curriculum, therefore, has the potential to magnify positive changes exponentially.

Curricular Components

In addition to its levels, every curriculum has three essential internal components. These are 1) learning outcomes, 2) assessments and feedback, and 3) learning experiences that lead to language improvement. A curriculum may have other features, but no curriculum can have fewer than these. Although we briefly introduce these concepts here, we will discuss and describe them in detail in Chapters 7, 8, and 9.

Learning Outcomes

Learning outcomes are statements of student ability. They should answer the question, "What should students be able to do as a result of the instruction?" (For example, an outcome statement for an intermediate speaking course might read: *Students will be able to correctly pronounce words from the academic word list.*)

Learning outcomes should be developed at all levels of instruction. At the programmatic level, outcomes are extremely general and hardly measurable at all. In fact, the mission statement is the top governing learning outcome and may only reference specific language skills vaguely by stating that students will develop English language proficiency in reading, writing, listening, speaking, grammar, and pronunciation. It may or may not indicate a specific proficiency range for enrolled or prospective students. From such a statement, increasingly numerous, specific, and measurable outcomes can be drafted at the course and class level. Courses usually have up to a dozen learning outcomes, and every class might have between one and five very detailed and measurable outcome statements—for example, *By the end of this class, students will be able to correctly pronounce 10 unfamiliar words from sub-lists 1 and 2 of the Academic Vocabulary List.*

Assessments and Feedback

Assessments are used to measure students against the intended outcomes designated for a program, course, or class. Possible forms of assessment include tests, quizzes, exams, writing samples, portfolios, performances, and oral interviews. At the program level, assessments could be standardized tests. The TOEFL is often used programmatically to determine whether students are prepared to enter a content curriculum in college. At the course and class levels, assessments and feedback are usually tailored to the instruction they are meant to test.

Assessments can also be *formative* or *summative*. Formative assessments are used to inform instruction. Summative assessments are used to determine student learning at the completion of an instructional unit. Sometimes an assessment can be used for both formative and summative purposes, such as pre- and post-tests.

In addition to these assessments lies an oft-overlooked component: feedback. Feedback is the data returned to students that were collected through assessment. In some cases, feedback may be as simple as a letter grade. In other cases, especially with formative assessments, detailed feedback about the language proficiency of the learner is needed in order to inform and improve instruction.

Learning Experiences

Learning experiences are the activities that students engage in to help them meet learning outcomes. Although common learning experiences include worksheets, textbook pages, lecture slides, discussion notes, activities, and such, a comprehensive list is impossible. Teachers are constantly designing ways to engage students in meaningful learning experiences.

Learning experiences can also happen at all three levels of instruction. A programmatic learning experience might be a program talent show or assembly. A course experience may occur when students from all sections of a reading class visit a local museum. Class experiences fill up the bulk of instructional time and can include homework assignments as well. Learning experiences should be equitable, flexible, simple and intuitive, perceptible, and error tolerant. Learning experiences should require little physical exertion and provide appropriate size and space for their use.

Putting It All Together

This chapter has introduced a number of intertwining ideas related to curriculum design. We have briefly discussed the role of a contextualized and principled curricular approach that acknowledges three levels of curriculum and three essential components of any curriculum. Arranging all this into one comprehensible model for the benefit of seeing the 'whole picture' is a formidable task. Box 1.6 attempts to illustrate this big picture from start to finish, with all concepts included. We call this all-in-one model the *Contextualized Curriculum Model*. We also spend the remaining chapters of the book dissecting every component of this model and explaining how to accomplish a thorough curriculum design, renovation, or remodeling project. We do this through the use of direct instruction, examples, anecdotes, and reflection tasks at the end of each chapter.

Box 1.6 The Contextualized Curriculum Model

Figure 1.4 illustrates how the curricular levels and components filter through a contextualized, principled approach. Curricular design is a complex system with interdependencies and numerous connections.

Many processes happen concurrently and recursively, although others are dependent upon the outcome of other processes. For instance, notice that the output from the analysis phase provides essential data to inform the rest of the design process.

At each level, curriculum designers consider each curricular component and do so as they go through the design, development, and implementation stages. An ambitious curriculum designer could theoretically investigate all three curricular levels and all three curricular components at every stage of the ADDIE model in one massive curriculum project. A more sensible approach, however, might be to look at just one square on the matrix (e.g., course-level assessments and feedback [the center square]), follow it through the designing, development, and implementation stages before choosing another square on the level/component matrix to address.

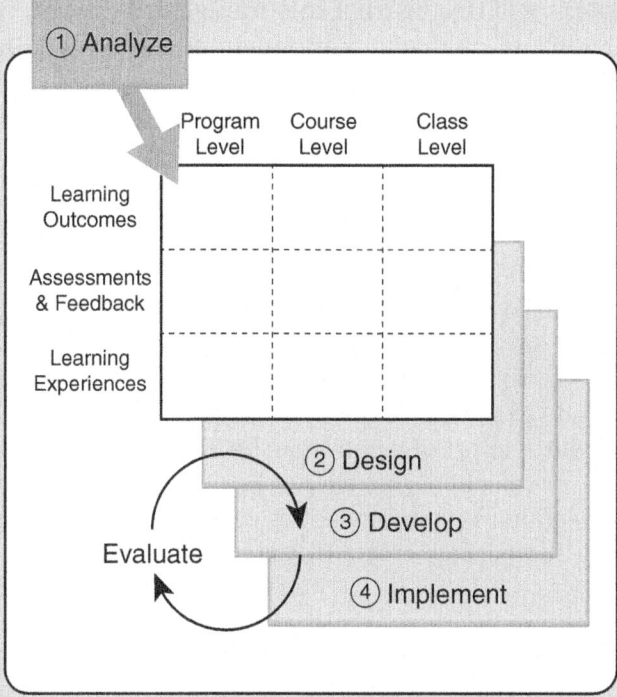

Figure 1.4 Curricular levels and components filtered through a contextualized, principled approach.

Chapter Summary

In this chapter, we introduced the complex notion of curriculum design and change in terms of house construction. Long before any cement is poured or wooden framing is erected, designers need to carefully consider the context of the future house. This includes such factors as geography, climate, and purpose. From there, a principled approach can be followed to ensure the house is built to necessary specifications. This same combination of context and principles informs curriculum design. Before any changes are implemented, the curricular context should be analyzed. Only when designers understand the context can they apply principles for designing, developing, and implementing curricular change.

To deconstruct the curriculum briefly, we explained the three levels of curricular change and the three components of any given curriculum. Change can occur at the program, course, or class level, and components essential to any curriculum include learning outcomes, assessments and feedback, and learning experiences. Put together, our Contextualized Curriculum Model illustrates the entire curriculum development process from start to finish. The remaining chapters will deconstruct this model and explain how to create, improve, or change any curricular component at any level of instruction in a contextualized, principled way.

Activities

Activity 1.1: Similarities among Language Programs

Think of two language programs you have taught in or are familiar with. The more similar they are to one another, the better. Once you have these two programs in mind, identify as many of the similarities between them as you can. Both programs, for instance, probably seek to teach English, both might be associated with a university, both may be self-funded, and so on. Given the similarities you identified, determine the contextual features that have led to these similarities. Which similarities do you suppose are universal and common among all language programs, and which do you think are context-specific?

Activity 1.2: Reverse-Engineering Two Curricular Contexts

Using the same two language programs as those in Activity 1.1, identify obvious differences between the two. These differences might include location, size, purpose, governing agencies, and so forth. Trace each difference back to its contextual origins. You might ask yourself questions such as "Why is program X smaller than program Y?" or "Why does program X focus on preparing students for university study, while program Y focuses on university *and* survival skills English?" This activity allows you to reverse-engineer two curricular contexts and thereby gain insights into the contextual analysis process.

Activity 1.3: Curricular Principles Applied to House Design

The five principles of curriculum change are:

1. Analyze
2. Design
3. Develop
4. Implement
5. Evaluate

Overlay these principles on the concept of constructing a house. How might a housing company follow these steps to construct the place where you live? Explain the process in your own words.

Activity 1.4: Curricular Principles Applied to a Course Change

Consider a potential change you would like to make in a language course in which you teach or study. The change could be big, like the addition of one new learning objective, or it could be smaller, like the inclusion of an additional reading passage in a particular class unit.

With this curricular change in mind, think through how you would analyze the context to ensure that your change would fit with the purposes of your course or class. Next, think through the remaining four principles of curriculum change.

- What would the ideal change look like (design)?
- How would you create, purchase, or select the new materials (development)?
- How would you introduce the changes and train students to work with them (implementation)?
- How would you ensure that the curricular change met your expectations and remained effective throughout this process (evaluation)?

Activity 1.5: Mapping a Program

Think carefully about a program in which you teach or study. Using Box 1.5 as an example, visually outline the organization of your program. Identify all skill areas, instructional levels, and courses (don't worry about including the classes). Since this can quickly become an unwieldy graphic, choose a small program to outline or choose only one or two skill areas.

Activity 1.6: Evaluating Curricular Components

Obtain a copy of the learning outcomes for a class in which you have taught or studied. If you can't access the learning outcomes, think about what one of the outcomes of the class might be. Choose just one outcome, and think of the assessments used to measure student progress on that outcome. Think about the kind of feedback students received to help them improve, either before or after the assessment. Next, think of the learning experiences used to prepare students for the assessment. Are the learning objectives sufficiently clear and obvious? Are the assessments or feedback effective in measuring student ability? Are the learning experiences crafted to ensure that students develop the necessary knowledge or skills to succeed in the class? Would you make any changes to improve the curricular components you analyzed in this activity?

Activity 1.7: A Full Refugee Curriculum Project

Suppose you were contacted by the local government to address a recent immigrant problem in your community. Dozens of refugees from another country have been sent to your town and are in immediate need of both survival language skills and important information about the local culture that would allow them to better assimilate into the community. Given what has been discussed in this chapter, articulate a brief explanation of all the steps you might take to develop a refugee curriculum from scratch. Use the Contextualized Curriculum Model illustrated in Box 1.6 to help you visualize all the major curricular decisions and processes you should think through. Starting with the analysis step, think through the entire process. For an additional challenge, try writing down your process and creating a final outline of what your curriculum would entail.

References

Allen, M., & Sites, R. (2012). *Leaving ADDIE for Sam: An agile model for developing the best learning experiences.* American Society for Training & Development Press.

Brown, J. D. (1995). *The elements of language curriculum.* Newbury House.

Christison, M. A., & Murray, D. E. (2021). *What English language teachers need to know volume III: Designing curriculum* (2nd ed.). Routledge. http://dx.doi.org/10.4324/9780429275746

Gibbons, A. S., & Rogers, P. C. (2009). The architecture of instructional theory. *Instructional-Design Theories and Models, 3*, 305–326.

Macalister, J., & Nation, I. P. (2020). *Language curriculum design.* Routledge. http://dx.doi.org/10.4324/9780429203763

Richard-Amato, P. A. (2003). *Making it happen: From interactive to participatory language teaching*. Longman.

Richards, J. C. (2001). *Curriculum development in language teaching*. Cambridge University Press. http://dx.doi.org/10.1017/CBO9780511667220

Tyler, R. W. (2013). *Basic principles of curriculum and instruction*. University of Chicago Press. http://dx.doi.org/10.7208/chicago/9780226086644.001.0001

Wiggins, G. P., & McTighe, J. (2005). *Understanding by design handbook* (2nd ed.). Association for Supervision and Curriculum Development.

2

Defining Curriculum

Introduction

Before deconstructing and explicating the Contextualized Curriculum Model that will be used throughout this book, we must articulate two key points. First, we need to note that we describe how to construct our model in an ideal setting. Few of us will find such a setting. It is often the case that we step into a situation that does not allow us to start at a logical beginning. We may have to hit the ground running and work our way back. This is certainly possible and should be kept in mind as you work on developing a curriculum using our model. Second, we need to clarify just what we mean by curriculum. This is no easy task, since there is little consensus among theorists and practitioners regarding the actual nature of curriculum.

Furthermore, there is no shortage of terms used to describe various components of a curriculum. Most of the terms are used either interchangeably or inconsistently by various practitioners and writers. It is beyond the scope of this book to explain these inconsistencies. Instead, we will simply define the terms as we use them and then use them consistently throughout the chapters that follow. The terms of most importance in this chapter include *Curriculum*, *Mission*, *Goal*, *Objective*, and *Learning Outcome*. Part of the challenge of using these terms is that they all seem very similar and perhaps synonymous. While each has a sense of looking forward to an end result, we use them to reference different levels of abstractness and specificity.

Curriculum

Originally, the word *curriculum* derived from Latin. It meant *to run*, or *a course*. Modern definitions used in educational settings may be narrow, such as "a course of study in one subject" (*Collins English Dictionary*, 2003) or broader, such as "the aggregate of courses of study given in a school, college, university" (*Random House Dictionary*, 2013). Other definitions may encompass even more, such as "the totality of the experiences the pupil has" (Kelly, 2009, p. 13).

In light of the obvious diversity in the foregoing definitions, we have chosen to adapt a rather lengthy one to guide us in our institutional thinking about curriculum. We will use this definition as the basis for what is presented hereafter.

Curriculum is a carefully structured framework of theories, methodologies, assessments, resources, facilities, people, and experiences that functions as a dynamic, working instructional plan. It consists of the why, what, where, when, how, and who of instruction. Its purpose is to orient teachers and staff so that they can guide and support learners in achieving individual and program objectives. A curriculum should be tailored to fit a specific context rather than being imposed upon it, and it must respond to local needs, customs, and constraints (McMurry & Evans, 2023; also see Christison & Murray, 2021; Macalister & Nation, 2020; Rodgers, 1989).

This definition basically means that everything a student comes into contact with during the learning experience (not just the key experiences) is part of the curriculum. A textbook, therefore, would not qualify as 'the curriculum' alone, but it would certainly be part of it. So would field trips, learning outcome statements, homework assignments, programmatic tests, and so on. Even the desks and chairs would be part of the curriculum. The approach teachers take to teaching (e.g., communicative methods, total physical response, genre-based language teaching, project-based learning) would also fall under the umbrella of curriculum. We have seen cases in which teachers have arranged their classrooms and office space to be conducive to student inquiry, and these designs would also be part of the curriculum. A major advantage to such a broad definition is that it may prevent important factors that affect learning from being lost from the purview of those with the responsibility to maintain the curriculum.

In our view, a program's curriculum is larger than a single person, and no single person can fully dictate a curriculum either. Since teaching and learning are dynamic processes that frequently defy tidy, linear progression, a curriculum is always in flux. In an ideal setting, a program's curriculum would be guided by the vision of a small group of teacher-leaders and improved through the steady innovations of exceptional teachers and the evolving needs of the students. In reality, though, a curriculum might be 'established' by an external authority such as a national or state government, a board of directors, or a business executive. But even in these cases, teachers generally have some latitude to flavor or even modify the curriculum by making intentional decisions about when, where, and how they will introduce materials, organize their time, and arrange their teaching spaces.

Although we see curriculum as encompassing *everything* a program does, we recognize the need to break a curriculum into conceptual units in order for it to be understood and ultimately improved. This is why we introduced the three levels of curriculum earlier: program, course, and class. Each level can be thought of as having its own curriculum with its own set of governing documents.

Program Curriculum

The *program* curriculum is what we have been discussing so far in this chapter, and the governing curricular document at this level is the program's **mission statement**. It provides the vision for the program-wide curriculum by explaining what students are to learn and how they are to learn it. This vision is operationalized through a small number of **program-level learning outcomes** that explain what students should get from the program by the time they graduate. Usually, the primary end goal is to develop English proficiency, but this goal might be more specifically to use English effectively in a particular industry or to have sufficient English skills to warrant admission to a university.

Course Curriculum

The *course* curriculum covers decisions and experiences for a particular course, and the governing principles of a course are articulated in **goal statements** that are operationalized in a small number of **course-level learning outcomes**. These outcomes are generally listed on a course syllabus and explain what students should know or be able to do after taking the course.

Class Curriculum

The *class* curriculum is governed by **learning objectives,** which are operationalized as **class-level learning outcomes**, or things which students will be able to do by the end of a class period. Students usually don't get a list of class outcome statements, and many experienced teachers do not bother to write them down. Nevertheless, class-level learning outcomes are essential for day-to-day student learning.

Governing Documents and the Essential Curriculum

The concept of curricular governing documents that we introduced earlier, is probably fairly intuitive for most language teachers. In fact, it is rather common for teachers to receive some of them, such as a list of course goals or objectives, as part of their teaching assignments. In some cases, teachers might think of these documents alone as the curriculum and assume that all other materials, resources, and activities are just peripheral. See Box 2.1.

In truth, the governing documents cut to the very heart of any curriculum and are invaluable planning tools. Often, they represent the only consistent part of a program's curriculum, since teachers, textbooks, theories, and methods change on a fairly regular basis. These documents are also the primary clues a new teacher has to the larger context of the program, since the mission

---

Box 2.1 A Curricular Metaphor

Although it may be a stretch, it is possible to see the essential curriculum in terms of our house metaphor. Think of the process for building a house in the United States. Various design documents, such as initial sketches, lead to more detailed blueprints and finally individual instructions on the day-to-day construction.

Program: Generally, the process starts out because of a specific need. Perhaps the family is growing and needs more space, or the house is a financial investment meant to be rented out or sold. Whatever the purpose, someone needs to have an initial vision for the process, and that works as a mission statement at the program level.

Courses: The family who wants the house built then has a number of routes for completing the construction. A traditional route is to hire a builder who knows all the big steps leading to a completed home. The builder has blueprints made and hires subcontractors to manage all the major steps, which would represent the various classes in a program.

Classes: The subcontractors bring in crew members and assign them parts of a big-step task; these represent the individual classes. The crew might represent teachers or students (or both) in this metaphor.

statement is usually found on a program's website and most programs want their teachers to be aware of what each course is supposed to cover. Although they are more fully discussed in Chapter 4, we will briefly introduce the governing documents and illustrate how they are related to the overall curriculum in this chapter (see Box 2.2).

Mission

The mission statement is the most general of the governing documents. It is a short document (usually one or two paragraphs) that explains why the language program exists and what it intends to accomplish. It is often a unifying statement of purpose that guides all subordinate goals and objectives.

A very simplified mission statement may be something like this: "Our program provides adult immigrant students with literacy resources for survival and occupational communication." In this case, all goals and objectives of such a program should somehow lead back to furthering this mission. Any goals and objectives that detract from the mission should be reevaluated and potentially eliminated (or the mission should be expanded). Additional information about how to develop a mission statement is discussed in Chapter 4.

Box 2.2   Visualizing the Essential Curriculum

Figure 2.1 illustrates the essential elements of a curriculum. Each curricular level has a governing document. These documents are the mission statement, goal statements, and objective statements. They correspond to the program, course, and class levels respectively. These are treated more extensively in Chapter 4.

So how do the governing documents and learning outcomes relate?

Governing documents are written for a program's faculty and staff. They are vision statements that ensure that the curriculum is cohesive and comprehensive. They help everyone who works with students move in the same direction.

Learning outcomes are written for the students in a program. They should be written in plain language so that teachers and students can understand them. There may be less oversight of learning outcomes, particularly at the course and class levels, because individual teachers often decide how to translate course goals and class objectives into actual instruction.

Ideally, everything that is part of a curriculum can be subsumed into three broad categories of learning outcomes, assessments and feedback, and learning experiences. Learning experiences are by far the broadest curricular component and cover such diverse experiences as in-class instruction, field trips, homework assignments, office-hour conversations, group activities, and so on.

Some areas of curriculum, such as the facilities (desks, chairs, building features) and methods of instruction (communicative approach, genre-based language teaching), are not always spelled out in one of the three essential curricular components. They are, however, reflected in the types of learning experiences teachers design for their students. For instance, a school with rich technology resources can plan digital learning experiences, while a school with strong connections to a university might plan learning experiences that involve auditing a university course. Likewise, a program that embraces communicative language teaching might emphasize learning outcomes that prioritize fluency over accuracy and production over reception.

Governance	Program Level (Mission)	Course Level (Goals)	Class Level (Objectives)
Learning Outcomes	(Program Outcomes)	(Course Outcomes)	(Class Outcomes)
Assessments & Feedback			
Learning Experiences			

Figure 2.1 Essential elements of a curriculum.

Goals

Goal statements govern each course in a program. These statements collectively describe what a course should accomplish. An intermediate reading course might state the following as one of its goals: "Immigrant ESL students will be able to read a variety of authentic texts in English."

Goals, in contrast to objectives, are still fairly general and usually require several steps or a substantial amount of time for students to accomplish. The ability for immigrant ESL students to read a variety of authentic English texts, for instance, may come gradually over the duration of multiple assignments and numerous class days, so curriculum designers use objectives to scaffold the attainment of goals. Further discussion on how to draft goals is provided in Chapter 4.

Objectives

Objectives are used in a very specific sense in this model. These statements describe the elemental, day-to-day steps that teachers take in order for the goals of the course to ultimately be accomplished.

Following from the goal for immigrant ESL students to read a variety of authentic texts in English, one objective might be for the teacher to provide students with a simplified 300-word newspaper clipping in English each day and have students practice reading it. Another objective might be to provide 12 new vocabulary words in English for students to study as homework. Once all the objectives are met, a student should theoretically have also attained the associated goal. Additional discussion of objectives is also presented in Chapter 4.

Learning Outcomes

Outcomes are statements of measurable accomplishment that accompany a governing document. While the governing documents provide an ideal about what should happen in the curriculum, the associated outcomes describe the achievement criteria or what evidence will be used to determine that learning has taken place. Learning outcomes are discussed at length in Chapter 7, though we introduce them briefly here.

Box 2.3   Trickle-Down Curricular Governance

In our estimation, the most influential document in a curriculum is the mission statement. Ideally, this statement informs the kinds of courses to be taught in the language program and their goals. The goals then inform the day-to-day objectives of a class, as illustrated in Figure 2.2.

In addition to this trickle-down governance, the mission statement also informs the program outcomes or things students need to complete in order to achieve the mission. Meanwhile, goal statements inform the course outcomes, or things students need to complete in order to pass the course. Objective statements inform the class outcomes, or things students need to do as part of their class duties for the day.

Is it possible to have a curriculum without all of these documents? The short answer is yes. We have seen curricula with only course outcomes written down. However, the long answer is no, in that the curriculum will not be as effective as it should be with these documents. Someone or some group of people ultimately needs to know what is in each box. If these documents aren't written out, chances are they still exist, but that they reside in the minds of different people in the program. It is dangerous to rely on 'mind documentation' since people's memories are subjective and unreliable. Furthermore, there is no way to view, evaluate, edit, update, standardize, or coordinate these documents unless they are written out.

This is not to say that the documents have to be long. In fact, we are proponents of short and easy-to-understand missions, goals, objectives, and outcomes. A mission statement and its outcomes might be less than a page long. All the goal and outcome statements for an entire course could also be written in less than a page. Objectives and outcomes for a single class might be just a couple of lines.

Finally, we restate what we noted in the introduction of this chapter. There may be situations where you will have to "hit the ground running" with existing curricular components and work toward establishing the elements outlined in Figure 2.2. In many instances, curriculum is developed in a spiraling manner.

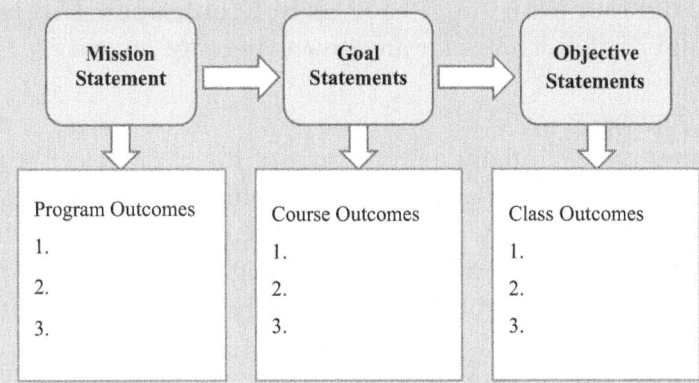

Figure 2.2 Interaction of mission statement, courses taught, and class objectives.

Since each governing document provides the framework for subordinate learning outcomes, a curriculum should have program learning outcomes, course learning outcomes, and class learning outcomes. To be sure, class-level learning outcomes tend to get the most attention in teacher development courses and in-service training because these statements are essential in lesson planning. Teachers usually do not get trained to write program outcomes, since these are usually done at an administrative level, nor do teachers often write course outcomes unless they are developing a course from scratch. See Box 2.3.

Program Learning Outcomes

Program outcomes are generally three or four statements that expand on the mission statement. For instance, a program that focuses strictly on literacy might have an outcome that specifies that students will take and pass reading, writing, and vocabulary courses. If students successfully pass these three courses, then this is the evidence that the program outcome was completed.

Course Learning Outcomes

Course outcomes are fairly specific statements about what students in a course should expect to know or do as a result of successfully completing a course. They essentially unpack the goal statements for students. For instance, in a reading course, students may be expected to be able to identify main ideas in level-appropriate texts. Such an outcome is student-centered and easy to measure. It is also a course-level outcome because it is not sufficient evidence to graduate from a program, nor is it something students could accomplish in a single class period.

For each goal statement, there are usually one to three course outcomes, so a course with four goals could have up to 12 outcomes. That is usually a sufficient number of outcomes for any given language course.

Class Learning Outcomes

Class outcomes are essentially a rephrasing of the class objectives in a way that is student-centered and measurable. A reading class might have a class outcome in which students will locate three books that match their interests and proficiency level by learning how to navigate the Lexile.com website. Once students identify three books that match these criteria, the outcome will have been achieved.

Envisioning the Essential Curriculum

The essential curriculum was described previously as the governing documents and their associated outcomes. Figures 2.3 and 2.4 allow the reader to envision a portion of an essential curriculum. They draw from two different hypothetical scenarios: an intensive language program and an adult language program.

Although this has been our focus in this chapter, a comprehensive curriculum is more than just a well-reasoned series of classes and courses. It is more than just objectives leading to goals and then to an overall mission. A comprehensive curriculum involves considering this structure, to be sure, but also involves all other school-sponsored activities, including associated materials, resources, and facilities. These should all be maximized for meaningful student participation. Ideally, this student participation inside and outside the classroom leads to the ultimate fulfillment of layers of objectives, goals, and mission statements at all the levels of instruction from class to program. See the examples in Box 2.4 and Box 2.5.

Box 2.4 Intensive English Writing Program for International Students

	Program	Course	Class
Governing Documents	**Mission Statement:** Provide international students the highest quality teaching of academic English writing in preparation for college courses.	**Goal Statement:** After this course, students will be able to persuade an audience by using appropriate rhetorical conventions, clear organization, and appropriate vocabulary.	**Objective Statement:** Students will be introduced to and practice using phrases that introduce a personal opinion.
Outcomes	Students will develop academic writing skills appropriate for university study in the United States. Students will develop strategies and skills to efficiently read university-level texts. Students must complete or test out of all three courses (College Writing I, II, and II) before matriculating into university coursework.	Students will write three multi-draft essays of at least six pages and nine or more paragraphs. Students will demonstrate the use of four rhetorical moves, including 1) defending an opinion, 2) synthesizing research, 3) arguing a position, and 4) proposing an explanation.	Students will be able to correctly recognize two effective and two ineffective ways of introducing a personal opinion in a short quiz at the end of class. Students will be able to correctly introduce two personal opinions in their upcoming essay drafts.

Figure 2.3 illustrates the essential curriculum documents as they might appear on Day 22 of an advanced, pre-university writing course in a writing-only ESL program.

28 ◆ Defining Curriculum

Box 2.5 Adult Language Program for Immigrant Students

	Program	Course	Class
Governing Documents	**Mission Statement:** Provide adult immigrant students with literacy resources for survival and occupational communication.	**Goal Statement:** After completing this course, immigrant ESL students will be able to read a variety of authentic texts in English.	**Objective Statement:** Students learn the meaning of 12 new vocabulary words in English as homework.
Outcomes	Students will develop essential language skills for navigating their social environment in English. Students will develop essential employment language skills in English. Students who miss fewer than 15 days of instruction in the program will receive a certificate of program completion.	Students will score 80% or higher on a newspaper reading comprehension test at the end of the course. Students will use safety guidelines to identify three major hazards or violations in a hypothetical workplace environment.	Students will be able to correctly match 12 vocabulary words to their dictionary definitions in class tomorrow. Students will be able to correctly use eight new vocabulary words in semantically accurate sentences.

Figure 2.4 An illustration of the essential curriculum documents as they might appear on Day 5 of an occupational reading course in an adult education literacy program.

Variations in Curriculum

Although a language program encapsulates all instruction and relevant support services in a given environment, there is room for some interpretation for individual contexts. For instance, an intensive English program might be very clearly defined in that all of its associated classes are taught in a restricted number of classrooms in one or more localized buildings close to its own administrative offices. Other programs are more complex, such as a Writing Across the Curriculum program in which classes overlap with other programs and instruction happens in only a portion of each class, which itself may be taught in any number of buildings across a college campus or even across a state.

Locus of Curricular Control

The big-picture view of the essential curriculum presented in this chapter tends to simplify the actual messiness of real-life curricula. One area that is often overlooked when describing curriculum is a question of authority: who has the power to create, change, or improve a program? Often the assumption is that a high-level administrator has the authority, but in many cases, we have seen that curricular power can reside at any level within a program's hierarchy.

As noted in Box 2.6, multiple people are generally involved in any given curriculum, from administrators to curriculum coordinators down to teachers and students. Their roles in the curriculum inherently impact their degree of control over curricular changes. Thus, a classroom teacher may have greater control over curricular aspects in the classroom than at a program level. But this is not always true.

Since programs vary greatly, the locus of control could be held by a single individual at one level in the hierarchy or by a group of individuals spanning multiple levels. It also may be at the top or toward the bottom of the hierarchy. For example, in some programs, the curriculum is carefully controlled and dictated from the highest level. Box 2.6 suggests that the Higher-level Administrator is the ultimate voice. In some programs, there may in fact be voices that are even higher. In other programs, the teacher may have much more autonomy. She might be given a book or simply asked to teach a particular skill to students at a particular proficiency level. In such cases, much of the locus of curricular control may reside with the teacher to make decisions that are good for the whole program. In some situations, the teacher may allow the students to identify what needs to be taught and learned. In such cases, the students may also share in the locus of curricular control.

While the graphic in Box 2.6 provides a visual representation of individuals and entities that oversee curriculum development, it also provides a visual of those that might be involved in a co-constructed curriculum. Each individual represented in this graphic might be included in designing aspects of the curriculum. For instance, the language learner might be asked to contribute ideas on a curriculum intended for adult language learners' needs.

Box 2.6 Power and the Locus of Curricular Control

In addition to identifying the locus of curricular control itself, it is important to locate yourself within the program hierarchy as well.

Figure 2.5 presents several levels of a hypothetical program hierarchy (you may substitute hierarchical labels appropriate to your program). Using this figure, identify the locus of curricular control in your program by marking the appropriate box in the middle column. For each level, you can indicate the degree of influence by marking the high, medium, or low box.

Where Are You?

Also identify your position in the program hierarchy by marking the appropriate box in the right-hand column. Regardless of whether you find yourself above, below, or somewhere in the middle of the locus of curricular control, or whether you feel you have a great influence or very little influence on the curriculum, locating yourself in this way will help contextualize your potential opportunities to influence the curriculum.

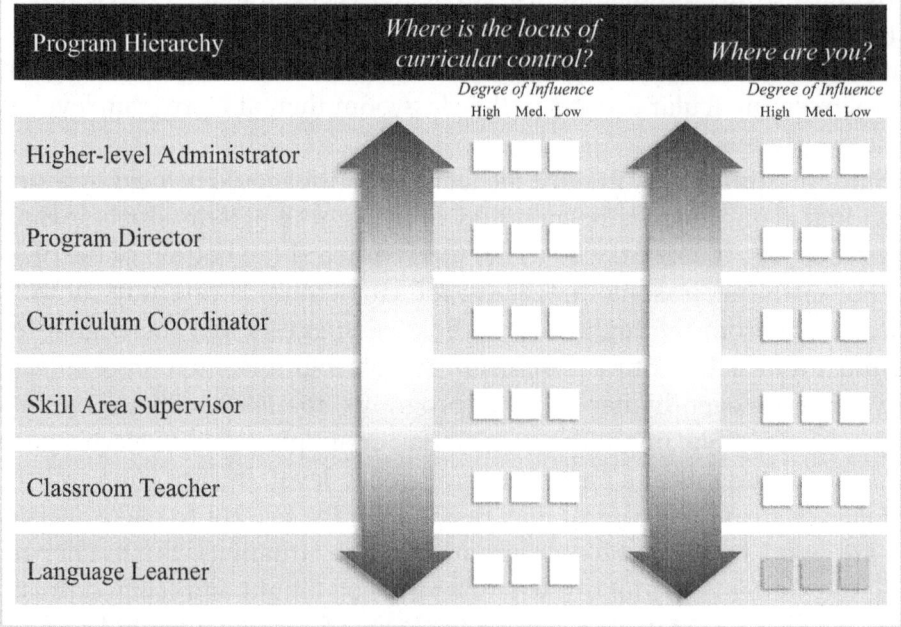

Figure 2.5 Identifying the locus of curricular control.

Mott and Lohr (2015, p. 1073) support this notion, "One strategic approach to curriculum development is to derive programs, courses, and syllabi from adult learners themselves. . ... [T]raditional curriculum development can be adapted to support significant learner involvement in a wide variety of learning contexts and environments".

Recently, a community adult language program for immigrant students was redesigned using a co-constructed model. Individuals from each of the categories in the graphic were interviewed and contributed suggestions on how the existing curriculum might be improved from their perspective. The final product was positively impacted by each of these voices.

The ideas presented in the subsequent chapters will not only assist those with direct responsibilities for curriculum development, but they will also be helpful for those seeking to make improvements from any location in the program hierarchy. Though some programs may utilize a rigid, top-down approach of curricular change, most programs will benefit a great deal from co-constructing the curriculum by carefully gathering and evaluating input from all segments of the program hierarchy, especially from the teachers and the students. While some programs systematically gather feedback from teachers and students to help inform administrators regarding how well components of the curriculum are functioning, others may be less systematic or may not elicit any input that could benefit the program.

Chapter Summary

In this chapter, we defined our curriculum as a carefully structured framework of theories, methodologies, assessments, resources, facilities, people, and experiences that functions as a dynamic, working instructional plan. It consists of the why, what, where, when, how, and who of instruction. Its purpose is to orient teachers and staff so that they can guide and support learners in achieving individual and program objectives. A curriculum should be tailored to fit a specific context rather than being imposed upon it, and it must respond to local needs, customs, and constraints. McMurry and Evans (2023). (Also see Macalister & Nation, 2020; Rodgers, 1989.) This broad statement encompasses everything within a language program. We then took a closer look at the essential curriculum by dividing it by levels and introducing the notion of governing documents. The mission statement provides an overall vision for the program and informs the goal statements for each course.

The goal statements inform individual class objectives, which in turn determine how each class lesson will proceed. Each of these governing documents informs curricular outcomes at the program, course, and class level. Having these documents in place makes it easier to see, evaluate, and revise the essential curriculum. In future chapters, we will further delve into each of these governing documents, as well as the broad concept of learning outcomes.

We also discussed the notion of curricular control. Each program has a locus of control; for some, it may be in administrative hands, but for others, that locus could be among the teachers or even students. Locating the locus and one's position relative to that locus can help individuals in a program better understand and navigate the power structures in order to make positive change.

Activities

Activity 2.1: Definition of a Curriculum

Consider our definition of curriculum offered at the beginning of this chapter. What are some school-sponsored activities that might be considered part of a curriculum? In what ways might such school-sponsored activities illustrate *how* and *what* students are to learn in a language program?

Activity 2.2: Who Dictates a Curriculum?

We made the argument that no single person can dictate a curriculum. However, we have also met many instructors who felt helpless to change or improve their program's curriculum because it was controlled by a state agency or a language program franchise. How might you reconcile these two beliefs? Is it possible even for disenfranchised educators to impact or even dictate curriculum? On the other hand, is it possible for a single governing body to dictate all levels of curriculum?

Activity 2.3: The Essential Curriculum

The essential curriculum structure that most people think of as 'the curriculum' is a series of governing documents at the program, course, and class levels. Consider a language program that you are familiar with. Which of these governing documents have you seen or worked on? Are these documents publicly available and easy to find? Are they current—that is, recently modified—or do they truly reflect what happens in your language program? Who is in charge of updating or revising these documents?

Activity 2.4: Governing Documents

Consider a language program that you are familiar with. Locate the mission statement and the course goals for one course. What connections do you find between these documents? Do the expectations of the course seem to contribute to the mission of the program? If not, what might need to change in order to bring the two governing documents better in line with one another? How long are these documents? Are they written in language that is easy for you and for students to understand?

Activity 2.5: An Essential Curriculum Project

Return to Activity 1.7 in the first chapter and think about the refugee curriculum described there. Take the next steps in curriculum design by drafting some governing documents. Specifically, articulate a brief mission statement. For some of the courses in the program, try drafting two or three goals you would want students to accomplish at one proficiency level.

Activity 2.6: Seeing an Essential Curriculum

Following your own creation of an essential refugee curriculum, go online and search for other refugee language programs near you. Skim their webpages to get a sense of their essential curriculum. Look for a mission statement and some kind of course goals (you might find only course titles or short descriptions). Evaluate the strengths and weaknesses of various refugee curricula based on your internet search.

Activity 2.7: Your Relationship to the Locus of Curricular Control

Take a moment to briefly describe how frequently and how thoroughly your program solicits input related to the curriculum from all segments of the program, including from teachers and students. How open is the program to unsolicited input? Are there adjustments that could be made to improve the flow of information sent to the decision makers that could help improve the curriculum? If so, what are they?

References

Christison, M. A., & Murray, D. E. (2021). *What English language teachers need to know volume III: Designing curriculum.* Routledge. http://dx.doi.org/10.4324/9780203072196

Collins English Dictionary. (2003). www.collinsdictionary.com/us/dictionary/english/curriculum

Kelly, A. V. (2009). *The curriculum theory and practice* (6th ed.). Sage.

Macalister, J., & Nation, I. P. (2020). *Language curriculum design.* Routledge. http://dx.doi.org/10.4324/9780429203763

McMurry, B., & Evans, N. W. (2023). Language program administrators' roles and responsibilities. In M. A. Christison, & F. Stoller (Eds.), *A handbook for language program administrators* (3rd ed.). Springer.

Mott, V. W., & Lohr, K. D. (2015). Co-constructed curricula: An adult learning perspective. In V. Wang & V. Bryan (Eds.), *Andragogical and pedagogical methods for curriculum and program development* (pp. 1073–1092). IGI Global.

Random House Dictionary. (2013). Curriculum. *Random House Dictionary*. https://www.penguinrandomhouse.com/books/7841/random-house-websters-dictionary-by-random-house/

Rodgers, T. (1989). Syllabus design, curriculum development and polity determination. In R. K. Johnson (Ed.), *The second language curriculum* (pp. 24–34). Cambridge University Press.

3

Context and Contextual Analysis

Introduction

We feel that contextual awareness is an often-overlooked prerequisite to effective curriculum development or change. In fact, when we talk with teachers or administrators who bemoan aspects of their current curriculum, we often find that their predecessors made some curricular decisions without sufficient thought for the curricular context. Incidentally, we find that the educators doing the complaining are usually *en route* to making similarly short-sighted curricular decisions. When teachers or administrators begin tinkering with a curriculum without considering the full curricular context, their adjustments tend to be haphazard or insufficient to address problems fully. Viewing the whole context in advance of any change, therefore, permits strategic and inclusive decision-making. Moreover, when it comes time to convince lawmakers, board members, and funding agencies to support a particular curricular change, it is much easier to win the argument by including a well-articulated (and concise) contextual analysis with the proposed solution.

Another major reason to analyze the context of learning relates to what Phillip Jackson in 1968 termed *hidden curriculum*. A hidden curriculum refers to behavior, values, and other features of school life that are implicitly reinforced in the social relations of schooling (Margolis et al., 2001; see also Apple, 2018). Behaviors implicitly communicated might include pro-social activities, such as waiting in line, turn-taking, or keeping busy. Hidden values might include undesirable sexist or racist ideologies reinforced by peers or teachers.

Such behaviors and values are part of a hidden agenda because the curriculum itself does not overtly teach or measure them, but students nonetheless pick up on them and teachers reinforce them.

While the term *hidden curriculum* is often used negatively, Gable (2021) argues that by probing and understanding it, school leaders can better support teachers, staff, and learners. Martin (1976) offered four options for action once stakeholders learn of a program's hidden curriculum. First, they can do nothing and thus re-hide the hidden curriculum; second, they can change practices and processes to eliminate unwanted curricula; third, they can abolish the hidden curriculum, though this may mean abolishing the entire school; fourth, they can embrace the hidden curriculum and thus make it overt curriculum. It is important to note that none of these actions can really be taken until the hidden curriculum is discovered.

The process of articulating and discovering both the overt and the hidden curriculum is the process of contextual analysis. It is the process of understanding the constraints placed upon a program and fully understanding the purpose and content of that program along with the target learners, instructional approaches, and assumptions about learning. It requires asking teachers and students about their experiences with the curriculum. It also involves documenting this information so that all stakeholders understand the overt curriculum and can make decisions about how to respond to the hidden curriculum. This chapter explores all these issues and provides guidance on how to complete a contextual analysis.

Context

The notion of context can be understood broadly as encompassing all of the different circumstances and constraints associated with the intended teaching and learning in a curriculum. It also includes all of the connections among these circumstances and constraints. That is a lot to think about, especially given that our definition of curriculum includes theories, methodologies, assessments, resources, facilities, people, and experiences that support instruction. To understand the curricular context, then, is to understand the essential purpose of a curriculum: why it exists, what it intends to accomplish, who it is built to serve (and who will serve those individuals), where and when it will operate, and how it will accomplish all of this.

The house metaphor discussed previously is very appropriate for this chapter. Imagine an architect or planner preparing to design a house without knowing why the house will be built, who the house will be for, or where it will be located. Understanding such constraints will have a dramatic impact on preparations. For example, knowing whether the house will be for an individual, a couple, or a family could impact the size of the house, along with the function of particular rooms and their proximity to each other. Will part of the house be used for a small business? Will it be used for entertaining large groups? Will it need a music room or a space for exercise equipment? Will the house be temporary and offer only a place to sleep and store a few possessions for a couple of days or weeks? Answers to these questions are necessary so the house can be designed appropriately (and so the owners get what they want and pay for). Moreover, knowing where the house is to be built will impact how it is built and the materials that can be used. It will impact whether the water table is low enough to allow for a basement, whether the roof needs to be designed for heavy snow loads, whether extra precautions should be taken for potential flooding, earthquakes, or strong winds, or whether the planners just need to locate level ground to pitch a tent.

The same is true for a curriculum. It is vital to know why it exists, who will be studying, where and when it will operate, and how it will do all this work (see Box 3.1). Imagine a designer giving little forethought to the purpose of a curricular change. Such a scenario is problematic, yet often top-down curricular change seems more anchored in idealism than in reality. Understanding what the curriculum or the change is for, who it is meant to serve, where it will be implemented, and so on are essential to getting the innovation right.

Box 3.1   Context Determines Curriculum

In Chapter 1, we explained how homes in two different countries illustrated different contexts. A Samoan *fale* and a Mongolian *ger* have similar purposes, but understandably different construction materials and methods due to their respective climates.

Even in the same country (and city), homes can vary greatly in their shape, size, and construction. Most homes are built for shelter, security, and privacy. However, a modern mansion is also built for luxury, entertainment, and perhaps social status, while an apartment might cater to a different set of needs, including economy, proximity to work, and a more Spartan lifestyle.

These dwellings also reflect certain constraints. Mansions are usually built on sprawling estates where there is plenty of room; hence, they are often far from the city. Apartment buildings require a minimal building footprint, so they are ideal for the city. Other constraints, such as building codes, zoning regulations, and market value, can also affect the design and placement of housing structures.

> The difference in these kinds of dwellings makes up the essence of context. The structures have different purposes, different tenants, different geographic limitations, and so forth. Context, therefore, can be thought of as a pattern of constraints, imposed either by nature or by intention, which shape the final outcome of a home.
>
> The same is true for curricula. The constraints imposed by nature and intention shape the outcome of the curriculum. They also predicate the kinds of modifications that can take place in the future. A program with a small budget, few teachers, and limited physical space will necessarily have a curriculum that serves a relatively small number of students. Likewise, a program in a city with a highly multicultural population is likely to see students from a diverse number of backgrounds. In this sense, the context determines the outcome.

Curricular Constraints

The context of an unbuilt curriculum is no less real than that of an established one. When designing a curriculum from scratch, designers need to consider the purpose of their curriculum and think through all the other contextual questions presented later in this chapter. They also have to consider constraints that can limit (both positively and negatively) what can be done in a program (see Box 3.2).

An obvious and persistent curricular constraint is that of funding, since access to money often dictates whether and sometimes how a curriculum can operate (Blumenthal, 2002). Other constraints come from governing entities, such as national or local governments, accrediting agencies, and school boards. Zoning laws, for instance, may prohibit establishing a language school in a particular neighborhood. Accrediting agencies may require all teachers to have a particular level of education. Governing agencies may insist on a particular core curriculum, especially in early education settings.

Constraints can also be positive. Most notably, they may delimit what a program is meant to offer. By focusing on academic English, for instance, a program places a constraint on itself to offer only English instruction that will help students achieve academic success. Other types of English, such as workplace English or survival English, will have to be taught elsewhere. This constraint frees a language program to specialize and excel at one thing.

Constraints might also be thought of as opportunities. Many intensive English programs we are aware of are constrained by their self-funding status. Being self-funded means that tuition money goes directly to the school for its own maintenance and improvement, rather than paying into a parent organization that "gives back" sufficient money to keep the program running.

> **Box 3.2 Constraints in Context**
>
> The primary reason to think carefully about contextual elements is that they play a constraining role in curriculum design and instruction, so understanding contextual constraints early will help a developer narrow a curricular trajectory early on. If all the students are refugees, for instance, this may constrain the kind of cultural knowledge a curriculum developer can rely on or may necessitate a great deal of extra instruction that may have otherwise gone undeveloped. If all the students are interested in attending university next semester, the curriculum developer may be obliged to plan more university-level activities and materials. Online instruction highlights a number of constraints curriculum developers must work within. For instance, designers cannot rely on traditional face-to-face interactive activities and so must consider ways to provide instruction that either does not require interaction or uses novel approaches for engaging learners. But online instruction also brings with it some positive constraints. Developers may be able to assume that learners have access to computers and internet service and thus can prepare more technology-mediated instruction.

Self-funding generally means more freedom in the use of those funds and more latitude to adjust tuition according to surpluses or deficits. A program that enjoys the constraint of being a self-funded entity might, for instance, build an extensive computer lab with surplus tuition money.

Cultural Constraints

Established curricula also face curricular constraints, although some of these may be imposed just as much by culture as by governing agencies. Cultural constraints, which are often tied closely to the hidden curriculum, often come in arguments laced with comments such as "we've already tried that" or "the older teachers will never go for that."

While it is easy to dismiss these comments as complaining, we argue that they should be taken seriously (or, at least, the underlying concerns should be given thoughtful consideration). If a curricular innovation has indeed been tried and resulted in failure, the context surrounding it should be examined. It is possible that very real constraints—including the age or culture of the teachers—will stop an otherwise thoughtful innovation from taking root. Conversely, it may be that some constraints only exist in the minds of some people. In this case, a careful contextual analysis will reveal whether a constraint is real and must be worked around, or whether it is really just an impression that can be changed with a little persuasion.

When dealing with impressions that can be changed, a good approach is to openly communicate with others about their impressions. In one particularly effective meeting we are aware of, the supervisor of a program's ESL writing courses met with the director of the program's writing center. Both individuals had what were thought to be irreconcilable ideals. The writing supervisor, however, had prepared a document outlining what he saw as his own assumptions about the writing center, *as well as* what he viewed to be the writing center director's assumptions about the writing program. The intention of the meeting was not to accuse, but to communicate. By the end of an hour-long meeting, both individuals were aligned on a single purpose for helping the ESL students in the program. Not all conflicts involving constraints or impressions resolve so easily or quickly, but being open about assumptions and impressions is the right place to start.

Levels of Context

Although a curricular context is easy to understand at the programmatic level, there are also course-level contexts and class-level contexts.

Course Context

A course-level context can be shaped by the purpose of the course, the content to be taught, the relationship between the course and other courses in the program, the teacher(s) assigned to teach the course, the students in the course, the textbook and methods used in instruction, as well as location and time of instruction. Some constraints may include whether the course is taught in a computer lab, whether it lasts a semester or quarter or term, whether it is a feeder course for more advanced study or a specialty course, whether the teacher has specialized training in the material, whether the students are required to take the course, whether it is taught with online affordances, and so on. Courses that meet right after lunch in a poorly lit classroom with an unenergetic teacher have a vastly different context than classes right before lunch in bright classrooms with natural light, staffed by teachers with dynamic personalities.

Class Context

Individual class sessions also have contexts that are shaped by the purpose of the class, the teacher and student needs, the physical location of the classroom, and so on. Some adult education classes are designed with their specific student constraints in mind. For instance, one program we know encouraged teachers to teach stand-alone classes rather than classes that built on one another. That way, students who couldn't attend regularly because of work and family duties could still attend and fully participate despite their frequent absences. Online instruction has become increasingly possible and convenient, and so, depending on certain factors, classes may include students from different time zones with different levels of access to technology and computer skills, and diverse reasons for attending class.

Contextual Analysis

Chapter 1 included a brief introduction to the model of curriculum development used in this book. The first step included in the model is **analysis**. One vital purpose of this analysis is to help those involved in curricular decisions to understand the context in which the teaching and learning will occur. We explained the idea of context previously. Now we will turn to the process of analyzing a curricular context (see Box 3.3).

Box 3.3 Questions to Guide a Contextual Analysis

A contextual analysis can be performed by asking basic journalistic questions (*why*, *what*, *when*, *where*, *who*, and *how*), as illustrated in Figure 3.1.

The Why: Articulate the *why*, or the purpose of the teaching and learning.

The What: Based on the purpose of instruction, decide *what* material, processes, or information is to be taught.

The Who: Understand *who* the learners are, which refers to the students along with their abilities, interests, attitudes, ambitions, and motivations. Also understand *who* the teachers are with their training, skills, perspectives, personalities, assumptions, philosophies, and motivations.

The How: The reason for the instruction should directly affect *how* the language is taught, learned, and assessed, such as by lecture, group work, direct experience, etc.

The Where: Identify the specific geographic location of instruction with a particular landscape and climate, as well as a particular facility along with its classrooms, labs, resources, and materials. This may include the physical locations of online and distant learners, along with the physical location of instructors teaching from home or other locations. Also, identify the social, cultural, economic, and political environments of learners and teachers.

The When: Decide *when* to hold classes and their duration.

While we traditionally think of such an analysis being performed at the programmatic level, it is appropriate for individual teachers to analyze the context of their own course and even perform a mini-contextual analysis on individual classes. Contextual analysis can also be a helpful tool after a particular class ends, since these questions can help a teacher think through what conditions led to a lesson going especially well or poorly.

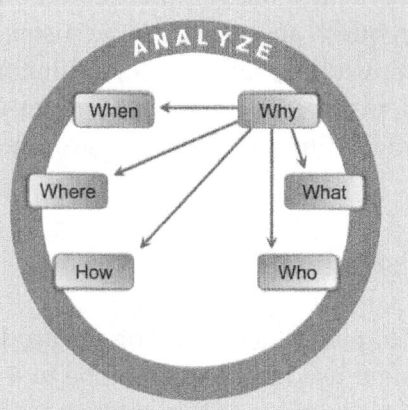

Figure 3.1 Basic journalism questions used for contextual analysis.

Purpose of a Contextual Analysis

Understanding a given teaching and learning context will bring needed clarity and focus to efforts to develop or improve curricula (see Box 3.4). While a thorough understanding of the context is essential to effective curriculum development, it usually requires diligent effort involving careful examination, investigation, and contemplation. Sometimes factors that should have the greatest influence on efforts to develop or refine curricula in a particular context may be overlooked without careful analysis. A greater understanding of these factors can come in the form of answers to critical questions, such as *why, what, who, how, where,* and *when*.

The Why

The initial step in contextual analysis is to understand the motivation for a program or the need to which it responds. For example, an adult ESL program might be responding to a need for local immigrants to improve their survival and occupational English. An academic IEP might be responding to the need of a local university for more English-proficient international applicants. A foreign language program in a university might be responding to the US military's need for more critical language experts to serve overseas. Oftentimes, this conceptual context, as well as a programmatic direction or purpose, becomes apparent when asking the core question of *why the program exists*.

The need for clear direction and purpose in any educational endeavor is essential to a successful outcome. Without a clear sense of destination, one might say, any train will do. In other words, a curriculum must have a clear

> **Box 3.4 Contextual Analysis Feeds into All Other Aspects of Curricular Change**
>
> Figure 3.2 illustrates our principled curricular approach. The analysis phase is done before anything else.
>
> A proper analysis is more than just a contextual analysis—it includes a learner needs analysis too, but this will be discussed in Chapter 5. The two parts of analysis (context and needs) precede and motivate the rest of the approach.
>
> A poorly done analysis may result in ineffective curricular change. The good news, however, is that once a contextual analysis has been performed, it can be revised and updated for future curricular change until the next time a major contextual analysis is needed.
>
>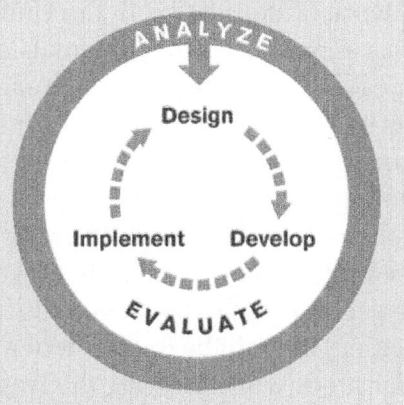
>
> **Figure 3.2** Graphic representation of the five steps of the ADDIE model.

purpose from the outset in order for all other subordinate teaching resources to have true curricular meaning. In a curriculum, each curricular component must somehow be tied back to the reason for a program's existence and purpose. Therefore, in each curriculum endeavor, perhaps the most critical step is to ask and answer a *why question*.

Sample *why* questions include the following:

- *Why* does this program, course, or class exist?
- *Why* is this program run this way?
- *Why* are we in business?

Answering one or more of these questions will establish both an initial context and a guiding purpose or mission for the curriculum. It will provide the rationale for all curricular material, while also justifying the removal of curricular material that does not lead toward that purpose.

Curriculum designers who use *why* questions to investigate the purpose of their institution can quickly start to develop a rough mission statement for the language program. Ideally, the mission statement will represent the collective thinking of several individuals all asking and answering *why* questions about the program. A fuller discussion of how to move from *why* questions to a complete mission statement will be addressed in Chapter 4.

Certainly, the most important purpose of a contextual analysis is to identify the *why* of the specific educational endeavor. For instance, as a consequence of World War II, the United States government concluded that there was a great need for diplomats and military personnel who were proficient speakers of a variety of languages. Subsequently, they established entities such as the Defense Language Institute (DLI Foundation, 2021). The way languages are taught and assessed in these institutions is closely tied to their underlying purposes. For every language-learning endeavor, we should be able to articulate the *why*, or the purpose of the teaching and learning. For example, in one setting, the intent of English language instruction might be to enable employment and reduce poverty in third-world nations. In another setting, it might be the result of a business model designed to generate financial profit while meeting the language needs of the clients. Or it might arise from a group of volunteers who see a need to help local migrant workers in their community to better function in society. The curriculum need not be designed solely by a group of top-down thinkers. Indeed, a co-constructed curriculum in which learners themselves have a voice in deciding content, course design, or learning outcomes (Bovill, 2013), can ensure that a program's *why* aligns with students' purposes for learning. Whatever the underlying reasons for the teaching and learning in a program may be, it is essential for those reasons to be clearly understood by those endeavoring to develop or improve curricula (see Box 3.5).

Box 3.5 Sample Why Questions and Hypothetical Answers

Question: Why does this program exist?
  Answer: To provide students with listening, speaking, reading, writing, and grammar support in order for them to matriculate into a US university.
  Therefore: If a curriculum component does not help students matriculate into a US university, it may need to be pruned.
Question: Why is this program run this way?
  Answer: We inherited a program that seeks to serve two very different populations: students who want to matriculate into a US university, and students who are studying abroad for one year (or less) and only want a US learning experience. Therefore, we must run the program in a way that accommodates both learning purposes in each class. Sometimes these purposes are at odds (i.e., study abroad students may dislike homework while US university-bound students often want more). So we work to continually balance this dynamic.

> **Therefore**: Curriculum components that teach US culture *and* prepare students for US university study should be privileged over components that do just one or the other. Components that do neither should be removed.
>
> **Question**: Why are we in business?
>
> **Answer**: We are in business to educate international students. However, we are funded almost entirely by self-generated tuition, and we only make that revenue when students get the kind of courses they want and need. Thus, we are in business to provide students with a valuable education *while* addressing their educational needs and interests.
>
> **Therefore**: All curriculum components should be aligned with core student needs and interests. Any component that does not meet one of these criteria should be removed, and components that only address student interests but not needs should be reevaluated to potentially address needs as well.

At the same time, it is vital that those involved in analysis recognize that the broader context of specific teaching and learning extends far beyond its basic purpose. They need to see the connections and interactions between the answers to the critical questions mentioned here. For instance, the *why* or purpose for the intended learning is closely associated with the answers to each of the other critical questions, such as *what* should be taught, *who* are the students and teachers, *how* should the teaching be done, *where* will it occur and when?

The What

Up to this point, our discussion on curriculum has dealt with important preliminaries. These are critical, foundational elements that often go overlooked, especially when a curriculum designer is expected to create a program quickly. Usually, curriculum designers jump right to this current section—asking w*hat* to teach. Indeed, the content of a curriculum is its most prominent feature because this is what teachers plan for and present, students are asked to successfully master, and administrators inevitably obsess about. Furthermore, a program in need of changing or updating already has historical content, so it does make sense to begin curriculum design by looking at what already exists; this is not entirely wrong, since curriculum design is inherently non-linear. It is possible to start by asking what the program hopes to accomplish and then work back to ask how well such content matches a program's population, purpose for existence, or relevance in a given conceptual context.

However, deciding what to teach should ideally flow directly from the reasons for the learning. For example, if the reason for the instruction is to help learners be able to conduct business in English, the instruction must include the vocabulary and grammatical structures needed to achieve its purpose. In addition, the learning might need to include information and insights about culture-specific business etiquette that could be taught and practiced along with the developing language skills. In this case, studying technical vocabulary associated with science, politics, space exploration, or pop culture may do very little to help the learner be empowered to conduct business in English.

So whether beginning with this section or moving through context and the question of *why*, the main question to ask now is this: What goals/outcomes does this program hope to accomplish? It is possible to answer this question from a top-down, authoritative position, where a program official creates a list of learning objectives. Other programs may use a bottom-up approach by asking students what they want to learn or noticing deficiencies in student learning, and thereafter designing curricula to address these interests or deficiencies. Most programs do a bit of both.

Regardless of approach, the actual answer to the question of what to teach should ideally come out of governing documents as well as outcome statements at the program, course, and, eventually, class level. If these don't exist, then curriculum designers may need to roughly describe a program's purpose and general course objectives before moving forward. While a rough description can be useful temporarily, curriculum designers should produce more formalized documents at some point, and this process is described in more detail in Chapter 4. But ultimately, a full context will include all of these governing and outcome documents eventually.

The *why* or purpose of the instruction should always inform *what* is taught. If the question of what to teach seems unclear, it may be because the purpose behind the teaching and learning has not been adequately clarified and understood.

The Who

The purpose of the instruction should also be closely associated with the answer to the question, *who*? It would make little sense to attempt to provide language instruction designed to help learners conduct business in English if the learners had no interest in business or if the teacher lacked an understanding of how to conduct business in the target language. Thus, a critical aspect of understanding the context of the teaching and learning is an understanding of *who* the learners are. This refers to the students along with their abilities, interests, attitudes, ambitions, and motivations. What are their ultimate hopes and aspirations for their language development? What in their educational or sociocultural backgrounds might facilitate or constrain their language development? For example, are the learners refugees who need basic communication skills to survive in a new linguistic and cultural environment? Are the learners prospective university students in North America who need the ability to effectively read and write academic language? Are the learners working in a remote village in Africa, studying online with the hope of getting a better job in a nearby city?

Understanding who the students are could also affect what is taught. For example, beginning proficiency students will need different instruction and materials than those with higher proficiency levels. In addition, students with special educational needs (SENs) will also need to be considered (see Chapter 8; Harmer, 2015). Students with limited technology skills will need different support than those who are technologically savvy. If the purpose of the instruction is to prepare students to conduct business in English, for example, some students may already have much of the social and cultural background needed to function successfully in an English context. Other students, however, may need to learn much more about social and cultural expectations and how they might apply when using English to conduct business in a particular setting (see Box 3.6).

Box 3.6 Who are the Learners?

The *who* question asks curriculum designers to consider the people involved in the program, including stakeholders, administrators, teachers, and specific kinds of learners who study in the program. Let us deconstruct what it means to investigate just learners in a program.

Thinking about demographics is a good place to start, including age, gender, nationality, native languages, and so on. But more specific and in-depth information may also be helpful since this information can affect what a curriculum is able to achieve. For instance, consider these questions aimed at a US English language program:

- What purposes do students have for studying? (Academic ambitions, survival language, training for specific tests, etc.)
- What is their educational background? (Well-educated in first language, some primary school, totally unschooled even in first language, etc.)

> - What is their previous language learning experience? (Years of formal study, years of informal 'conversation' study, no experience at all, etc.)
> - How long have they lived in the US? (All their lives but in linguistic enclaves, never lived in the US, in the US since junior high school, etc.)
>
> Obviously, there are other questions, but these examples illustrate that learners can come from a variety of backgrounds, and while many language programs do have homogeneous populations, others do not. These different populations often require subtle, and sometimes prominent, modifications in curriculum to make educating them successful.
>
> So-called Generation 1.5 learners who graduated high school in the US, for instance, often have advanced oral English proficiency and may need to have a slightly different educational experience than international students whose length in the US can be measured in days or weeks (Roberge et al., 2009). These students may have strong grammar knowledge but weak oral proficiency. These two populations are very different from refugees who may have recently gone through a traumatic relocation process and thus may still be coping with stress, anxiety, and cultural issues. They may also have limited literacy skills even in their native language, have difficulty using technology, or feel overwhelmed by education altogether.

The *who* also includes the teachers with their training, skills, perspectives, personalities, assumptions, philosophies, and motivation. It is helpful for those involved in analysis to understand who the teachers are, why they are teaching, and what they can offer their students. For example, are they volunteers who simply hope to help the needy in their community? Do they have facility with computer technology? Are they well trained? Are they paid for their work? Administrators of a program or institution will also influence the context in the applications of their policies, procedures, and leadership styles. Many other stakeholders could also be identified, such as parents or family, those in higher-level oversight of the program, prospective employers of the language learners and so forth. Each of these contributes to the larger context that curriculum developers need to understand in order to do their jobs effectively.

Understanding learners and teachers is not always as straightforward as it would seem. Many teachers assume that, because the administration hired them, the administration knows everything about them. In reality, administrators rarely have an overall sense of the strengths, weaknesses, abilities, backgrounds, education, and preferences of their teaching staff. How then can program directors learn this important information? The answer is to ask. We recommend sending out a survey to all teachers (and all learners) to ascertain pertinent aggregate information about them. See the Appendix to this chapter for an example of teacher and student surveys we have seen used as part of the contextual analysis. Information from these surveys should be gathered for a purpose, not just randomly collected. For example, by asking how long teachers have taught outside of the current program, administrators can quickly get a sense of the experience level of their faculty.

The How

The reason for the instruction should also directly affect *how* the language is taught, learned, and assessed. Not all teaching and learning activities are equally effective, and what may work well for one instructional purpose may not work well for another. For example, methods used for helping English language learners to write effective research papers may not be well suited to helping international pilots to use English to communicate effectively with air traffic controllers. Similarly, if the intent is to help the learner use the language to successfully negotiate or conduct various business transactions, merely being familiar with some business-related vocabulary may be woefully inadequate. The instructional methods, practice activities, and formative feedback need to result in the learner's ability to actually use the language in ways that are consistent with the purpose of the instruction. This may necessitate formative assessment that is as authentic as possible, along with systematic ways to evaluate the effectiveness of the teaching and learning.

A common approach in ESL teaching is Communicative Language Teaching, which has ties to interaction and sociocultural theories of language acquisition (Richards, 2005). The point of such an approach is to use interactions and realistic language to accomplish communicative tasks. While it has gained popularity in North America, this is not the only approach to language teaching for both historical and contextual reasons. Other approaches might include grammar-translation, audiolingualism, and situational and cognitive approaches (see Celce-Murcia et al., 2013). These differ and are broader than methods and techniques such as drills and memorization, providing enriched or modified input, or output and production, which may be specific activities used in various approaches. Although it is beyond the scope of this book to detail these language approaches and techniques, it is imperative that curriculum designers and classroom teachers think carefully about the approaches or instructional techniques they use or espouse in their curricular contexts.

Furthermore, online instruction has become widespread, particularly following the global COVID-19 pandemic. As a result, teachers have numerous online options available to them for instruction, but merely because technology is available does not mean that any and all instruction is improved through technology. Instructors and curriculum designers are still obligated to make thoughtful choices about how best to use learning management systems, websites, apps, and other online tools to best support student learning.

While deciding how to teach should be tied directly to the purpose of the learning, it will also need to be influenced by a clear understanding of who the students are and what specific learning needs they may have. For example, certain teaching methods may be highly effective for younger learners, but much less effective for adults. Though some of the decisions about how best to teach a specific group of students may need to be made by the teacher once the course has begun, there may be many factors about the prospective students that can be useful, if not essential, to the design, development, and implementation of curricula.

The Where
Similarly, *where* the learning occurs also needs to be consistent with its purpose. Traditionally, and in its broadest sense, the where includes a specific geographic location with a particular landscape and climate. The location could be rural or urban, sparsely or densely populated, surrounded by poverty or abundance. It also may include a particular facility along with its classrooms, labs, resources, and materials, each of which may impact the context in substantial ways. Physically, a program may be very wealthy and therefore situated in a clean, well-lit, carpeted building with wide halls, a large front office, multiple copy machines, a computer lab, technology-equipped classrooms, and integrated web cameras and internet in every learning space. On the other hand, a language program may be in an older building with limited or no internet connectivity, an aging or non-existent computer lab, and only blackboards and overhead projectors in each room. Whatever the physical space, this contextual constraint shapes what curriculum designers can do. For instance, if internet connectivity is spotty, it would be impractical for a curriculum designer to adopt online learning units to be used during class. Similarly, if each room has a computer projector, then a curriculum designer has the luxury of making more materials digital instead of paper-based. In some cases, learning may be enhanced through authentic practice experiences in specific locations. For example, if the class purpose is learning to conduct business in English, this might include engaging in purchasing negotiations at a factory or conducting financial transactions at a bank.

With online instruction, the *where* includes considerations such as where learners are located geographically as well as physically. Geographically, learners may be spread across the globe and span many time zones, cultures, climates, and political systems. Or they may be clustered in a small region and share similar local experiences. Physically, learners may locate themselves in quiet, study-friendly locations free from distractions, or they may be studying in bed, at a beach with spotty internet, or while riding in a train or car. Online instructors may similarly be dispersed across the globe or locally concentrated in one geographic location. They may provide instruction from home, a work office, a hotel room, or less ideal locations. All of this is important because learners and teachers are influenced by their environment. When that environment is shared and optimized for learning, students and instructors can draw on it as a resource. But when learners and teachers do not share environments, or when those environments are diverse and/or not optimized for learning, instruction must change to accommodate that reality.

We should note here that government regulations and programmatic restrictions may limit some online teaching options and therefore environmental factors. For example, some governments prohibit visa-holding international students from taking hybrid or distance ESL courses as a condition of their student status. Such a prohibition can keep certain language programs from developing and offering such courses. The effect is that learners in these situations are required to share a localized physical environment that, again, can impose a constraint on learning.

The *where* question may also be profitably applied to the political or metaphysical location of a program. This includes looking at a program's funding stream, its stakeholders, benefactors, and controllers, along with their ambitions for the program. Other information can be found by questioning a program's philosophical approach or where it is located in terms of theories of language acquisition. A program may also be bound by social, economic, and political influences, as well as cultural norms, local customs, or legal directives.

The When

The reason for the instruction may also influence *when* the learning needs to be conducted and how long it will last. Classes might need to take place in the evening after students get off from work or at inconvenient times for online learners in distant time zones. Or they may need to avoid summers when students are more likely to be away. The timing of classes aside, programmatic context can also inform when a particular course will be offered relative to a deadline or course sequence. For example, a language course that provides several levels of language instruction must decide which courses can be taken concurrently and which must be taken sequentially. Such constraints may further determine how much teaching and learning time is needed to make the intended progress according to a set timeline. Given a specific set of learners, one also might appropriately ask whether the students are likely to achieve the expected level of mastery within the duration allocated for the learning. For example, a couple of weeks of foreign language instruction might be enough to give students an introduction to a language or culture but completely inadequate for preparing most beginners for study at university in that language.

Deciding when to hold classes and their duration could be associated with other critical questions, such as where and who. For example, if the only available facility is shared with another entity, this might constrain when instruction and language practice can occur. In addition, if a particular group of students are highly motivated to develop their language skills as quickly as possible, they may be able to effectively engage in learning activities for longer periods than those who may be less committed to the learning endeavor.

Product of a Contextual Analysis

Oftentimes, the previously mentioned contextual questions are in the minds of curriculum developers, but they may remain implicit. When a curriculum is thus passed on to another generation of developers, much of this contextual knowledge must be rebuilt or guessed at. Thus, we recommend taking the time to articulate and write out a contextual description that will allow the description to be both distributable and durable. Those involved in compiling this description should ensure that contributions come from a variety of perspectives. Once a draft has been generated, key stakeholders should agree on a final draft that can remain in use until subsequent changes may be needed. The process of writing such a document, as well as the major contents, is discussed more fully in Chapter 6.

Methods for Contextual Analysis

The many journalistic questions posed previously suggest that a contextual analysis requires a lot of thought and work. And while that is true, we have found that the work can be greatly simplified if done by a group. In the case of an established language program, it makes sense to talk with some of the most senior teachers and administrators, who often know a lot about the purpose and content of the curriculum. Other questions can be answered by looking around or talking to the individuals who schedule classes or manage the school's physical space. It is also a good idea to collect data from students and teachers about their purposes and qualifications, respectively. A short electronic survey can quickly sample a school's student population by asking students about their language background, interests in future study, perceived language needs, and so forth. A survey sent out to teachers can also ask about their educational background, teaching experience, teaching preferences, and so on. The idea of surveying students and teachers will be addressed further in Chapter 5, but for now, it is worth considering a variety of data collection options.

Articulating Your Assumptions

In addition to thinking through the essential contextual questions outlined in the previous section, it is often vital to articulate relevant assumptions in the analysis phase that can form a philosophical framework for the subsequent design of a curriculum. Articulating assumptions about the best ways to facilitate language teaching and learning expands the *how* addressed previously and guides the design phase. It would make little sense to design a curriculum in a manner that was inconsistent with the key assumptions about language teaching and learning held by the major stakeholders.

For our purposes, an assumption is a brief written statement that captures a single institutional belief. Some statements may have a stronger empirical basis, while others may simply reflect the collective beliefs of those responsible for the curriculum. Though indisputable proof for specific assumptions is unnecessary, assumptions in general help guide curricular design in ways that place practice in harmony with beliefs. The following (partial) list of assumptions comes from a program we are familiar with. Each assumption is accompanied by potential implications or actions that might be appropriate for informing the design phase later.

Assumptions
1.0 Extensive language practice and feedback will facilitate language development
    1.1 Language use and feedback should be maximized in the classroom
    1.2 Homework should create appropriate opportunities for language use and feedback
    1.3 Language use should be encouraged outside of the classroom
    1.4 Well-designed extracurricular activities may effectively promote language use
2.0 Language learning can be undermined by a variety of affective factors
    2.1 We should provide support for students with mental, emotional, or physical issues

2.2 Teachers should be trained to identify needs and direct student to resources

2.3 Teachers should adapt teaching to meet student needs in the classroom

3.0 Acculturation is an important part of learning in our context

3.1 Culture should be integrated into all four classes

3.2 Students should be encouraged to participate in community activities that provide authentic opportunities to learn about culture

4.0 Self-regulated students will be the most successful learners

4.1 We should provide training to help students develop patterns of self-regulation

4.2 We should teach strategies for language learning and use and provide opportunities for learners to practice utilizing these strategies

5.0 Teachers can greatly influence student language learning

5.1 Teachers should maintain a positive learning environment

5.2 Teachers should facilitate student motivation with engaging learning activities

5.3 Teachers should be accessible to students

5.4 Teachers should communicate frequently and effectively with students

6.0 Teaching and learning can improve when student skills are effectively assessed

6.1 Teachers should regularly engage in formative assessment and feedback

Chapter Summary

This chapter presented the concept of context and then examined the importance of a contextual analysis preceding and informing any attempt to develop or revise a curriculum. This included an emphasis on answering critical questions, such as *why* a program exists, *what* will be taught, *who* the students and teachers are, *how* instruction will be delivered, and *where* and *when* the learning and teaching will occur. Finally, we touched upon the utility of articulating curricular assumptions. These statements can help individuals in a program understand the essential beliefs held by one another and articulate both the overt and the hidden curriculum.

Activities

Activity 3.1

Describe the *why* for your program or a program you are studying. Is there more than one purpose? If so, list as many as you can. If you list more than one purpose, which purpose or purposes are the most important?

Activity 3.2

Describe *what* is taught in the program. Is it well aligned with the purpose of the program? Are there any inconsistencies between what is taught and the program's purpose? Given the purpose of the program, is there content that is missing that should be added to the curriculum?

Activity 3.3

Describe *who* your students are. What do you know about their backgrounds, including nationally, educationally, socially, culturally, economically, politically, and so forth? Are they heterogeneous or more homogeneous? What are the aspirations and expectations for their language development? How might this information affect what or how they should be taught?

Activity 3.4

Describe *how* language is taught in the program. Which aspects of *how* are built into the program and affect all the classes, and which may be based on needs teachers perceive in their individual classes?

Activity 3.5

Describe *where* the teaching and learning occur, including the facilities and associated resources. Also describe the metaphysical context, including relevant social, cultural, economic, and political influences in the environment and at the institution.

Activity 3.6

Describe *when* the teaching and learning occur within your program. Do courses have a fixed beginning and end, such as with semesters? If so, when do they begin and when do they end? What time of day are class periods held and how long do they meet?

Activity 3.7

Articulate some of your own personal assumptions about language learning. Write down at least three and explain how they inform your approach to teaching in the classroom.

Chapter 3 Appendix

Sample ESL Student and Teacher Surveys for Contextual Analysis
Student Survey
1. What level are you currently studying in?
2. What country were you born in?
3. What is(are) your native language(s)?
4. How long have you studied English in the US at any school (including high school)?
5. How long did you study English in your native country at any school?
6. In what year were you born?
7. What was your age when you moved to the US?
8. How long have you studied in this language program?
9. How do you pay for school? Indicate the percentage of tuition that comes from each source:
    a. Personal funds
    b. Parents or family members
    c. Scholarships (such as SACM)
    d. Grant (such as from a FAFSA application)
    e. Money from a sponsor
    f. Other (please explain)
10. Outside of class, how many hours do you spend on these things most days?
    a. Job or work
    b. Caring for children or family
    c. Homework or studying
11. Why did you choose to study at this language program?
12. What are your future goals after finishing ESL classes?

Teacher Survey
1. What country were you born in?
2. What is(are) your native language(s)?
3. In what year were you born?
4. Please indicate the highest level of education you have completed and type in the degree field of your received degree (i.e., TESOL, Linguistics, English, etc.). If you have a double degree, please list both.
    a. BA
    b. Certificate

c. MA
   d. PhD
5. What skill area do you prefer MOST to teach?
   a. Reading
   b. Writing
   c. Listening
   d. Speaking
   e. Grammar
6. What skill area do you generally end up teaching?
   a. Reading
   b. Writing
   c. Listening
   d. Speaking
   e. Grammar
7. Which levels do you prefer MOST to teach?
   a. 1
   b. 2
   c. 3
   d. 4
   e. 5
8. Which levels do you generally end up teaching?
   a. 1
   b. 2
   c. 3
   d. 4
   e. 5
9. How have you developed as a professional teacher throughout your career? Rate the following from 1 (none at all) to 4 (extensive amount).
   a. Formalized teacher training (i.e., graduate classes)
   b. Incidental teacher training (i.e., pre- or in-service training)
   c. Professional learning (i.e., attending conferences)
   d. Self-study (i.e., individual readings, research)
   e. On-the-job learning (i.e., learning from teaching classes, reflecting on practice)
10. How long have you worked at this language program?
11. How long have you taught ESL at any/all institutions including this program?
12. At what other nearby institutions do you currently also teach?
13. Why did you choose to teach at this language program?
14. What do you think students generally want from ESL classes in this program?

References

Apple, M. (2018). *Ideology and curriculum* (4th ed.). Routledge. http://dx.doi.org/10.4324/9780429400384

Blumenthal, A. J. (2002). English as a second language at the community college: An exploration of context and concerns. *New Directions for Community Colleges, 117*, 45–54. http://dx.doi.org/10.1002/cc.52

Bovill, C. (2013). Students and staff co-creating curricula: A new trend or an old idea we never got around to implementing? In C. Rust (Ed.), *Improving student learning through research and scholarship: 20 years of ISL* (pp. 96–108). Oxford Centre for Staff and Learning Development.

Celce-Murcia, M., Brinton, D. M., & Snow, M. A. (Eds.). (2013). *Teaching English as a second or foreign language*. Heinle Cengage Learning.

DLI Foundation. (2021). *History*. https://dlif.org/home/history/

Gable, R. (2021). *The hidden curriculum: First generation students at legacy universities*. Princeton University Press. http://dx.doi.org/10.1515/9780691201085

Harmer, J. (2015). *The practice of English language teaching*. Pearson Education.

Jackson, P. (1968). *Life in classrooms*. Hold, Rinehart, and Winston

Margolis, E., Soldatenko, M., Acker, S., & Gair, M. (2001). Peekaboo: Hiding and outing the curriculum. In E. Margolis (Ed.), *The hidden curriculum in higher education* (pp. 1–20). Routledge. http://dx.doi.org/10.4324/9780203901854

Martin, J. R. (1976). What should we do with a hidden curriculum when we find one? *Curriculum Inquiry, 6*(2), 135–151. http://dx.doi.org/10.4324/9781315021553-11

Richards, J. C. (2005). *Communicative language teaching today*. Cambridge University Press.

Roberge, M., Siegal, M., & Harklau, L. (Eds.). (2009). *Generation 1.5 in college composition: Teaching academic writing to US-educated learners of ESL*. Routledge.

4

Governing Documents
Mission, Goals, and Objectives

Introduction

With a clear definition of curriculum and an understanding of how context is central to curriculum development decisions, we now focus on the governing documents that guide curriculum development. The concept of governing documents was introduced as part of the definition of curriculum in Chapter 2. As indicated in the present chapter title and elsewhere in this book, any language curriculum will benefit from three basic governing documents: A mission statement, goals for each course, and objectives for each class. Most people think of a curriculum as these documents and their associated outcomes, but there is often little teacher training devoted to writing mission and goal statements. The purpose of this chapter is to show the significance and nuance of governing documents and suggest ways to write them. We will also introduce the three interrelated principles of stability, responsiveness, and cohesion (Evans et al., 2010), which can preserve consistency in a curriculum amid curricular changes and development.

Mission Statements

Begin with the End in Mind
A mission statement is an organization's broad declaration of why it exists, what it does, how it accomplishes its work, and who it serves (e.g., Alegre

et al., 2018). Such statements have become a common feature of many entities in various contexts, including corporate, non-profit, religious, government, and educational organizations.

Quality mission statements in an educational setting should express why the institution exists. They come in various lengths and proportions: some are articulated in a single, concise sentence, others are written as succinct paragraphs, and yet others may be several pages in length. Because one of the primary purposes of a mission statement is to inform stakeholders of the broad purposes of an institution, we suggest that, generally, the more concise a statement is, the better. An ideal would be to have a statement that can easily be remembered or even recited by stakeholders.

While there is no standard length for a mission statement, certain elements should be included. These elements follow the journalistic question pattern we have already introduced. In relatively sparse language, a mission statement should answer the following questions:

- *Why* does the organization exist?
- *What* does the organization do to achieve that purpose (activities, resources, etc.)?
- *How* does it accomplish its purpose (values)?
- *Whom* does it serve?
- *Where* is the organization located?

As an example, one community adult education program states its purpose in these terms: "to provide support and instruction in the English language, and American culture." Its expression of *what* it does to achieve that purpose (activities, resources, etc.) is "by offering evening classes in English speaking, listening, reading and writing as well as culture." This program declares in its mission statement *how* it accomplishes its purpose (values): "high quality classes taught by TESOL trained volunteers." The context (for *whom* and *where*) in their mission statement is articulated in these phrases, "for non-native speakers in our community who are striving to integrate socially and economically into the community."

In Box 4.1, mission statements are analyzed for their essential components, as discussed previously. The first is drawn from an intensive English program at a major university in the United States. The second and third come from programs associated with different community colleges.

Box 4.1   Sample Mission Statements

Brigham Young University—English Language Center

Mission Statement

> "As a lab school, the English Language Center supports the Department of Linguistics by facilitating the teaching, learning, and research of English as a second language. The ELC achieves this mission by providing TESOL students with opportunities to apply university study in practical contexts and to develop excellence in English language teaching, and providing ESL students with the highest quality teaching of foundational and academic English in a research-based curriculum."

Key Elements

Why	Lab school for teaching English as a second language where TESOL students gain practical ESL teaching experience and ESL students learn English
What	Intensive English program that provides TESOL students ESL teaching, tutoring, and curriculum development opportunities; ESL students learn foundational and academic English
How	Excellence, high quality
Who	TESOL students, ESL students
Where	Department of Linguistics, ELC intensive English program

Northshore Community College—English Language Institute

Mission Statement

> "The central mission of the English Language Institute at Northshore Community College is to provide high quality English as a second language (ESL) instruction and orientation in US culture to international students, professionals and other non-native speakers by means of an intensive English program."

Key Elements

Why	English as a second language (ESL) instruction and orientation in US culture
What	Intensive English program

How	high-quality instruction
Who	international students, professionals, and other non-native speakers
Where	Northshore Community College

AB Community College—English as an International Language Program

Mission Statement

"The central mission of the English language as an International Language Program at AB Community College is to assist College students who are non-native speakers of English in accomplishing the goals envisioned by the College and the students when they enrolled by providing these students with English language proficiencies necessary for success academically and in later life."

Key Elements

Why	Accomplish the goals envisioned by the College and the students when they enrolled
What	English language proficiencies necessary for success academically and in later life
How	Necessary proficiencies for success
Who	College students who are non-native English speakers
Where	AB Community College

An early first step for any institution that does not have a mission statement is to create one. For those that already have one, an early step is to ensure it has all of the elements outlined here, especially if that mission statement has not been reviewed and possibly revised in several years.

The Process

The process of writing and revising a mission statement is every bit as important as the statement itself. Even though certain key elements are necessary, mission statements vary in length from program to program, and so too will the process of creating a mission statement differ. The best mission statements are crafted like any good piece of writing—through a careful process. Just as an essay is first brainstormed, drafted, reviewed, revised, and reviewed and revised again, a mission statement is created in the same way. In writing an essay, the author will typically talk to trusted peers or teachers for help to clarify the writing. Similarly, in crafting a mission statement, key stakeholders should be included in brainstorming, reviewing, and revising. In the case of a language program, key stakeholders would likely include teachers and administrators. Here is a general description of how this process could work.

1. Prepare
Perform a contextual analysis (as described in Chapter 3) in order to get a thorough understanding of your program, its purpose, demographics, and so forth.

2. Brainstorm
Consider the history and/or future direction of the program. Determine what the program does and does not (as well as can and cannot) accomplish. Given any obstacles that arose in the contextual analysis, identify possible ways to ameliorate those problems through curricular decisions. Be creative and avoid blindly following one particular solution because it "seems obvious" or is favored by an outspoken person or group.

3. Draft
Organize notes from the *prepare* and *brainstorm* stages into a single document that encapsulates the program's purpose of existence. Answer the journalistic questions at this time, referencing information from previous stages.

4. Feedback
Get insights from stakeholders to help mold the text of the mission statement. In early stages, this feedback might come only from the highest-level administrators. Eventually, though, everyone involved with the language program should at some point be given a chance to comment on the text. This might include students who could provide feedback to their teachers through formal surveys or focus groups. Usually, feedback comes a little at a time, either through informal chats and email conversations or through formal, in-person meetings.

5. Revise
Make changes to the mission statement draft based on each feedback session. Continue to receive feedback and revise until the mission statement perfectly resembles the program's purpose.

6. Edit

By the end of such a recursive feedback and revision process, there is often little need for formal editing. Any language errors usually work themselves out. However, it is still a good idea to ensure that the wording, punctuation, and formatting don't contribute to confusion. Also, it may be necessary to reflect on whether the mission statement is readable to an audience beyond the program's top administrators. A mission statement that is filled with jargon and acronyms will probably be inaccessible to students, new teachers, funding agencies, and just about anyone who lacks insider knowledge of language teaching, so some editing (or revising) for audience awareness might be necessary.

7. Publish and Improve

The temporary last step in drafting a mission statement is that of publishing it. Websites, front offices, and marketing materials are good locations for disseminating this information, as well as including it in regular teacher training sessions. It should certainly also be consulted regularly when making decisions that will affect the program's curriculum.

The reason publishing is a 'temporary' last step is that there will always be further revisions to the mission statement as contexts and purposes change. These may be subtle or dramatic, immediate, or distant. The point here is not to fall victim to the belief that, once drafted, a mission statement will never change.

A Source of Protection

So far, our argument for creating a mission statement is that it explains or justifies a language program's existence to students, teachers, administrators, funders, and other stakeholders. By consulting the mission statement, these groups will know what the program is all about. But the mission statement serves another, perhaps equally important, purpose, and that is clarifying for program administrators what the program is *not*.

We have observed in our language program that many groups want to take advantage of the program's resources. For instance, a community group at one time wanted to use empty classrooms to hold meetings and related activities. While innocuous enough, we considered the implications on students and teachers of renting out space to another group. Given that our mission statement enjoins us to use our curricular facilities to benefit university students, we felt that outside groups with no connection to the university and that offered no benefit to our target population failed to meet the purposes of our program, so the request was declined.

On the other hand, many teachers wanted funding in order to pay for registration and travel in order to present their teaching-based research at conferences. Our mission statement includes a directive to share our scholarship in presentations, so it was deemed appropriate to offer some limited funding to teachers actively engaged in scholarship. By judging every resource request according to our mission statement, we are able to quickly determine which requests to entertain and which to pass up.

Program Outcomes

Each governing document has associated learning outcomes. Although these will be discussed in more detail in Chapter 7, it is worth previewing them briefly here. Program outcomes are coordinated with the mission statement. While these are usually general and somewhat vague, they express what students will do to fulfill the mission statement. Much of this might be implicit or procedural, such as attending class consistently, passing all required courses with a C+ or higher, attaining individual educational goals established through the program, and so on. See Box 4.2.

Box 4.2 Our Mission Statement Process

A well-crafted mission statement has the potential to guide an organization for a long time, but occasionally, even the best mission statements deserve some tweaking or revising to represent changes in an organization's purpose, context, circumstances, or plans for the future. This happened in our program several years ago as our program evolved. After using the same mission statement for a decade, we realized that it needed to be updated. Here are the circumstances and processes surrounding our mission statement changes.

Through a contextual analysis, we recognized that our intensive English program had five major obstacles:

1) It did not effectively meet the needs of true beginning language learners.
2) It provided only academic English, even though some students wanted and needed survival, vocational, and interpersonal language skills.
3) Students were not gaining sufficient English proficiency in the five levels of English instruction; there was a proficiency gap between Levels 3 and 4 in particular.

4) The curriculum was not designed to accommodate students who repeated a level.
5) The content for the highest level of instruction was not focused and was therefore inconsistent; students who completed this level were not always well prepared for university instruction.

We saw two possible solutions to these problems. The first was to focus exclusively on just the advanced learners by cutting out any curriculum that focused on beginners. The second option (and the one we chose) was to expand the curriculum in order to offer more types of English instruction over more courses and levels of instruction.

At first, only a few individuals were involved with proposing changes to the mission statement. These included the director of the program, the curriculum coordinator, and a few administrators. Soon, the program director had a general idea of the direction he wanted the mission to go. He called a meeting of all administrators (some of whom were lead teachers in the various skill areas) to review the mission statement. Other meetings followed, including one in which all teachers were invited to give input on their vision for the language program. Over the course of subsequent meetings, emails, hallway conversations, retreats, and input sessions, a totally new mission statement was drafted. More meetings, emails, and hallway conversations resulted in fine-tuned changes to the language of the mission statement. Every word in every sentence was carefully chosen, debated, reconsidered, and finally changed and/or approved. From start to finish, the process took about 12 months. Here is the text of that revised mission statement:

The Mission of BYU's English Language Center

As a lab school, the English Language Center supports BYU's Department of Linguistics and English Language by facilitating the teaching, learning, and research of English as a second language. The ELC achieves this mission by:

1. *Providing BYU students with opportunities to apply university study in practical contexts and to develop excellence in English language teaching, tutoring, curriculum design, materials development, technology use, assessment, evaluation, and research.*
2. *Providing ELC students with the highest quality teaching of foundational and academic English in a research-based curriculum.*
3. *Sharing our scholarship by presenting and publishing our relevant experience, research, and resources for the benefit of others.* (BYU English Language Center, 2022)

Once this mission was in place, we began working with teachers to understand the new vision and to think of ways to support it in their classes. All

> teachers received a copy of the new mission statement, and copies were hung throughout the building to remind students and staff of the program's purpose. We then held program-wide pre-service and in-service meetings with all teachers to further explicate the mission. A year after adopting the mission, it was part of the culture and daily life of the program. During this year, we also began drafting course goals that were targeted to help fulfill the mission. Some of these needed only to be revised, while others had to be generated from scratch because new courses had to be developed.

Course Goals

Course goals represent the governing document at the course level, so each course has its own set of goals. These goals describe the purposes of a course and the expectations of what constitutes successful completion of the course.

Goal Statements

Simply articulated, goals are short statements that express what teachers expect of students in their classes. They articulate the central content or skills that students are expected to master. As such, they are unique to the course for which they are written, while being sufficiently general to give teachers some freedom in accomplishing the goals. Course goals should not be interchangeable among courses, nor should they be repeated in adjacent courses, except where content or skills are intended to be reviewed or practiced again. There is no standard on how many goals should be listed for any given course, though typically, we see between five and seven.

Sample Goal Statements

A goal statement for an intermediate ESL reading class might look something like this:

> *After completing this course, immigrant ESL students will be able to read a variety of simplified authentic texts in English.*

In this statement, the skill to master is reading simple, authentic English texts. The types of texts to be mastered are not explicitly identified here, but they might be included in the course outcomes, which elaborate on each goal. This goal is unique to a reading course, inasmuch as it would be unusual to see this exact goal in a traditional speaking or grammar course. Adjacent courses might have a similar goal, but with some different modifying adjectives. For instance, a higher-level goal might state that students should be able to read a variety of complex authentic texts; a lower-level goal might expect students to only read texts that have been modified for beginning ESL readers.

Obviously, goals need to reflect the most important content or skills to be mastered, but aside from this, there are a variety of ways to write them. For instance, they can be written in the present or future tense, in simple English or sophisticated jargon, and they can be long or short. Some course designers prefer to frame goals as statements of what *teachers* will do to facilitate learning in a given course. Others write them as general statements of what *students* will do (though caution should be exercised, since student-centered course goals can easily be confused with course learning outcomes).

Figure 4.1 illustrates a list of six course goals for an advanced ESL writing class in a program in which students earn college credit for completing the course. The goals are listed twice for illustration purposes; they are written as student-centered goals on the left and as teacher-centered goals on the right.

	Student-Centered Course Goals	*Teacher-Centered Course Goals*
	In this course, STUDENTS are expected to . . .	In this course, TEACHERS are expected to . . .
Writing	Write at least 2,500 words of polished academic writing in assignments that have real-world audiences and a defined genre (like a letter to an editor, a résumé, a scientific report, etc.).	Provide students with instruction, activities, and exercises to help them compose academic paragraphs and essays totaling 2,500 words of polished writing (consisting of final papers, a final exam, and revised short projects) composed for a real-world audience and a defined genre.
Writing process	Practice each step of the writing process and get different kinds of feedback to know what works for them.	Help students to develop strategies for each step of the writing process and to manage their revision processes by exposing them to various sources of feedback.

Figure 4.1 Instructional topics and sample course goal statements.

	Student-Centered Course Goals In this course, STUDENTS are expected to...	*Teacher-Centered Course Goals* In this course, TEACHERS are expected to...
Vocab	Study, analyze, and correctly use academic vocabulary from their reading course.	Help students enlarge their academic vocabulary, including words drawn from their reading course.
Sources	Read material in order to prepare to write and also learn official APA citation.	Provide one to two easy readings per paper for students to study and/or integrate into their text with appropriate forms of acknowledging sources.
Grammar	Improve their grammar and know their grammar trouble spots.	Use Dynamic Written Corrective Feedback (DWCF) and provide some direct grammar instruction as needed.
Timed writing	Experience and prepare for timed writing.	Assign students to write short, timed independent and/or integrated essays and teach timed-writing strategies.

Figure 4.1 (Continued)

The Process

To write goal statements, a course designer should first consider the purposes of the course and identify a handful of instructional topics. In Figure 4.1, these topics are identified in the left-most column and include things such as *writing, writing process, vocabulary, sources,* and so on. They refer to skills or content that will be covered in the class.

Instructional topics are usually straightforward, but even a basic class can have many of them, so it is a good idea for multiple stakeholders to brainstorm possible topics and then narrow that list to just a handful of the most important ideas. If a course is based on a textbook, the material in the text can be used as a guide for deciding on instructional topics, with the caveat that course goals should not be so dependent upon a textbook that a change in text would dissolve the curriculum. In addition, course designers should consult relevant literature and best practices for teaching a given course, because these resources can suggest topics and priorities that might not have been considered before. For a more complex course, such as an integrated reading/writing course, a culture course, or a content-based course, designers need to be especially selective about which course purposes to emphasize so as not to overwhelm the course with too many (and too disparate) goals.

Once a number of topics have been identified, single-sentence goal statements are crafted by indicating what teachers or students will do with regard to the topic. One goal for each topic is sufficient, though sometimes an especially expansive and important topic might receive two or even three goals. Each goal should begin with an action verb and then explain some type of quantity or frequency, such as writing at least 2,500 words over the course of a semester. At the goal level, it is not necessary to indicate exactly how student success will be measured. That is covered in the course outcomes. For now, simply indicating what teachers or students will do generally is sufficient.

Course goals are meant simply to be anchors upon which a rather flexible curriculum can be built. In our house metaphor, course goals can be thought of as the cement foundation for a building. The foundation provides support and general shape to the finished home and each room inside of it, but it does not necessarily dictate all the details of the finished product. Even after the foundation is poured, some walls can be rearranged, doors and windows can be moved, and building materials and paint colors can be adjusted, too. Thus,

---

Box 4.3   Weak Goal Statements

There are a number of things that can make goal statements ineffective. We list some of these here in hopes that curriculum designers will avoid them.

Overly general	Improve grammar.
Overly specific	Correctly punctuate the following structures: simple, compound, and complex sentences, adverbial and noun clauses, appositives and asides, quotations, and reported speech.
Jargon-filled	Reduce affective filter through CLT experiences in low-stakes language interactions on social media and hybrid instructional settings.
Multipronged (mixed in with outcomes)	Study the second 1,000 words on the general service list; determine which words students are already familiar with; begin using those words in both written and spoken communication activities; test students on 20 words at the end of each week.

goals should not be too complex and specific, nor should they be overly general or vague (see Box 4.3).

Course Outcomes

Courses, like the program, also have outcome statements. But unlike program outcomes, course outcomes are not procedural at all; they are specific, measurable statements of what students should be able to do by the end of the course. These outcomes are significant for determining whether students should pass a course. Just attending class is often insufficient for advancement, so course outcomes allow teachers to measure student performance against a standard. More on course outcomes, including how to write them, will be included in Chapter 7. In the meantime, see the additional explanation in Box 4.4 and the mission statement and associated course goals of a small writing program in the chapter appendix.

Box 4.4   Course Goals across a Curriculum

Goal statements are important because they provide continuity across courses taught by different teachers and across semesters, even if the courses are taught by the same teacher. They provide quick-access information about the course for teachers who are preparing to teach it, coordinators and administrators who need to see the whole program at a glance, and students who nervously anticipate all the work they will need to accomplish. Course goals (or their associated outcomes) are often included in the course syllabus for the benefit of students.

But creating cohesive course goals across an entire program does not happen by accident. In fact, it is surprisingly common for programs to have completely uncoordinated goals among and between courses. This happens when courses are created by different teachers or added on the basis of need, without much consideration for the wording of existing courses. At some point during the creation or revision of curricula, designers should take the time to edit all course goals in their language programs to conform to the three ideals illustrated in Figure 4.2: *Integration*, *Continuity*, and *Sequence*.

Integration

Course goals should be integrated across courses horizontally so that relevant content and skills discussed in one class are sufficiently recycled in another. A good example of this might be a subset of grammatical forms that students should learn in their grammar course but also practice with and recycle in their writing and speaking courses. The same might be true for a content course, in that a given theme could be recycled in the reading,

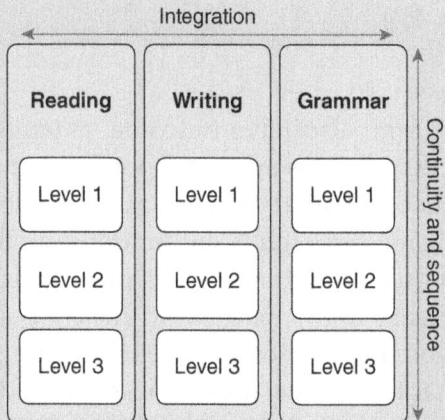

Figure 4.2 Graphic representation of integration, continuity, and sequence.

writing, and listening courses. Building integration into a curriculum is simply a matter of selecting relevant features to recycle in adjacent courses and then writing goals to reflect that integration.

Continuity

Courses within a skill or content area should demonstrate continuity by using consistent wording from level to level. Additionally, many instructional topics should be repeated among levels so that students (and teachers) don't perceive each course to be completely unrelated from the one before and after it in sequence. Not every instructional topic must be repeated; in fact, one feature of more advanced courses is that they include new and more complex instruction, so it is appropriate to have a few different instructional topics at the lower- and higher-level courses. However, continuity can still be practiced by keeping a set core of topics standard and using similar wording throughout the goal statements.

Sequence

Related to continuity is the feature of sequence, which dictates that course goals should be incremental so that they require more language proficiency as the course level increases, which naturally suggests that the goals feel more difficult. Sequencing can be as simple as designing more language input or expecting more output as course levels increase. It might also include higher expectations of performance or proficiency. Goal statements across the curriculum should reflect this sequencing. See the chapter appendix for a sample writing program's set of course goals. While there is no integration in this example (because all the courses are writing courses only), the continuity and sequencing should be apparent.

Class Objectives

Class objectives represent the governing documents for a single instructional unit. Usually, there are only between one and three of them per class. They are written at the top of a lesson plan and guide the day's instruction. They are statements that describe the content or skill to be mastered by the students in a class. Objectives are generally written as part of the lesson-planning process, so a teacher does not need to create every class objective before the first day of instruction. In fact, drafting objectives too far in advance can be problematic because student needs and interests may require teachers to be flexible about when and how they will accomplish class objectives.

Objectives Statements

Crafting class objectives is probably more familiar to most teachers than writing mission statements and course goals. Every class has at least one objective, so teachers generally get a lot of practice writing them. As with other governing documents, class objectives articulate the purpose of a given class, whether that be to introduce a particular language feature, practice it, review it, expand upon it, test it, or to do something different altogether. Every class objective should lead to completing some course goal, which in turn helps meet the mission of the program.

Class objectives are not intended to be measurable, unlike outcomes, which are expressly measurable (more on this later in this chapter and in Chapter 7). If students attend the class session, then it is typically assumed that they have accomplished the objective. Of course, teachers know that this may not be true and so some repetition of objectives is usually helpful. Also, a class might cover two or three objectives in a class session, or a single objective may take more than a single class to accomplish. So, there is flexibility in the crafting and teaching of objectives.

Sample Class Objectives

Class objectives can be written from a variety of perspectives, including those of the student or the teacher. In some cases, no actor is present in the objective. Since these are purpose statements for the class, they might also just be phrases or items in a list. Here are two full-sentence sample objectives written from the student perspective from an advanced writing course:

> *Students will practice using phrases that introduce a personal opinion.*
> *By the end of this lesson, students will have two strategies for transitioning between body paragraphs.*

The first objective here includes the content to be covered: *phrases that introduce a personal opinion* and the verb *practice*. These two features (topic and verb) are essentially all that are needed when creating an objective. The second objective focuses more on the content than on the verb.

The Process

Objective statements should be drafted after course goals have been articulated. For each course goal, identify instruction and tasks needed in order for students to reach that goal. These are then turned into objective statements, which can be mapped out on a class calendar. Some teachers will create very broad objectives, stated perhaps in a single word or two, and include these on the course calendar for students to see. This procedure simplifies lesson planning because teachers already have a general idea of what they will teach each day and can craft the class objectives as each class day approaches. See Figure 4.3 for an example of this approach.

An Objective vs. an Outcome

An objective and an outcome are essentially the same thing but are written with different purposes in mind. An objective is more general and informal than an outcome and reflects the purpose for holding a class. Outcomes, on the other

Course Calendar (what students see)		*Lesson Plan (what teachers see)*
Day	Topic	Objectives
Mon. 1/6	Course Introduction & Assignments	Introduce course syllabus, program statements, and books Discuss book report assignment Introduce article summaries assignment
Wed. 1/8	Article Summaries	Review article summaries assignment Practice writing article summaries as a class and in small groups
Fri. 1/10	Reading Skills	Introduce list of reading skills Practice three reading skill activities from the list

Figure 4.3 Sample calendar with associated class objectives.

hand, are very specific, measurable statements indicating how students will demonstrate that they have accomplished the objective. In this sense, objectives introduce a given subject or skill, while outcomes indicate how student proficiency will be measured in terms of that subject matter or skill.

Guiding Principles: Stability, Responsiveness, and Cohesion

When creating a curriculum from scratch, it is easy enough to develop a mission statement for the program, enumerate the various courses to be offered, draft their goals, and then assign teachers to begin making objectives for each class day. The whole process is one of creative invention within the contextual constraints identified earlier.

Things are very different, however, if an existing program is already in place and in operation when changes are intended to be made. Rewriting the mission statement in the middle of a semester or redesigning a course with limited time for teachers to adjust can be a major problem for teachers and students. Too much change at one time may confuse key stakeholders and make the curriculum unstable. However, too little change can also be problematic if a curriculum is unable to adjust to changes in student or teacher demographics, student needs and interests, or other legitimate constraints.

Adjusting a curriculum, then, is a tenuous exercise that requires foresight and skill. We suggest three guiding principles for developing a quality curriculum while balancing curricular change. These principles are *stability*, *responsiveness*, and *cohesion* (Evans et al., 2010).

Though all effective curricula must embrace some innovation, a ***stable*** curriculum implements change in a way that is orderly, systematic, and principled. For a curriculum to change in this manner and to remain viable, it must also be ***responsive*** to such factors as student needs, institutional and environmental changes, and current research. Without responsiveness, a stable curriculum soon stagnates. Finally, a sound curriculum is ***cohesive*** in that there is internal consistency and continuity between and across the various elements of the curriculum. These three principles can be applied to curriculum development and evaluation processes to ensure that the institution is functioning effectively.

The three interrelated principles of stability, responsiveness, and cohesion, when applied to a curriculum, serve two purposes. First, they guide curricular decisions. Without such principles, a curriculum could easily deteriorate into little more than a collection of well-intentioned ideas or activities.

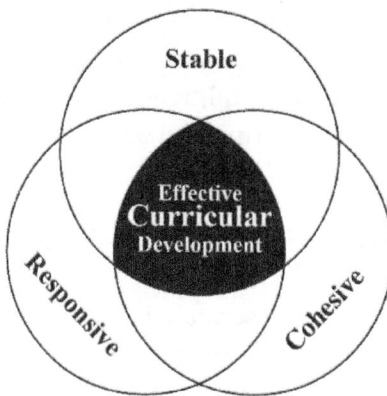

Figure 4.4 Effective curricular development is the intersection of a program that is stable, cohesive, and responsive.

Second, these principles establish the guidelines for curricular implementation and related research. In this regard, they help establish a much-needed institutional memory. Rather than just being moved by great ideas, or appealing new materials, a program's curriculum is grounded on a common base on which it can evolve to meet the changing needs of learners, stakeholders, and the environment, as illustrated in Figure 4.4.

Chapter Summary

In this chapter, we have discussed three essential governing documents in a language curriculum. Governing the whole program is a mission statement that should explain the purpose of the program to internal and external stakeholders and help administrators guide decision-making throughout the curriculum. Trickling down from the mission statement are course goals, several of which are listed for every course in the program. These goals indicate the essential content or skills to be covered in a given course. Collectively, the goals from all the courses in the program fulfill the mission statement. Above course goals are class objectives, which are individual purpose statements for each class. Objectives indicate generally what students will learn or be exposed to in each instructional unit; they are crafted to give structure to the class, and collectively, they fulfill each of the course objectives.

Activities

Activity 4.1

Identify the mission statement for your program or a program you are familiar with. Does it clearly articulate the purpose behind the program? Can you identify the *why*, *what*, *how*, *who*, and *where* of the curriculum? If you had liberty to revise it, how would you change this statement? If your program has no mission statement, then craft one.

Activity 4.2

Examine the websites of several language programs in North America. How accessible are the governing documents? Can you find the mission statement, a list of courses, and accompanying course goals?

Activity 4.3

Compare the mission statements of two or three language programs in North America. Which statement is easiest to read? Which is the most confusing? What features do you like or dislike in each?

Activity 4.4

Examine the course goals for a course you have recently taught or will be teaching soon. Are the goals comprehensive in that they cover all the expected skills and content of the course? Are there any goals that were never met during the course? Are the goals written from the teacher or student perspective?

Activity 4.5

Consider a course you are hoping to create in the near future (or a course you might someday create). Identify some of the key instruction topics and draft several course goals using the procedure outlined in this chapter.

Activity 4.6

Obtain goal statements for several courses in your program or a program you are familiar with (you may be able to use the same documents found in Activity 4.3). Ensure that you have goals from multiple skill levels and skill areas if possible. After looking over the documents, identify the degree to which the goals are integrated across skills and display continuity and sequence across levels. In what ways could these courses be more cohesive?

Activity 4.7

Examine some of your past lesson plans or sample lesson plans from another teacher. Read the class objectives if they are present and identify the verb and content in each. If there are no objectives, examine the lesson materials, and then create one or more objective statements that could be used next time the lesson is taught.

Activity 4.8

For an upcoming lesson you will teach, craft one or more thoughtful class objectives. Use the process described in this chapter.

Activity 4.9

Consider the amount of change that occurs in your language program or one you are familiar with. Which of the three curricular principles seems to be favored more in that program—stability, cohesion, or responsiveness?

Activity 4.10

A program director recently negotiated a contract with a business in Japan to offer English classes for their engineering executives. This language program had traditionally served college-age international students, many of whom are Asian. Because the populations seem so similar, the program director feels that the new student body will be easy to accommodate after adding the requisite "English for Engineers" classes. Based on the discussion in this chapter, what else might the director and others need to do in order to ensure stability, cohesion, and responsiveness in the language program?

References

Alegre, I., Berbegal-Mirabent, J., Guerrero, A., & Mas-Machuca, M. (2018). The real mission of the mission statement: A systematic review of the literature. *Journal of Management & Organization*, 24(4), 456–473. http://dx.doi.org/10.1017/jmo.2017.82

BYU English Language Center. (2022). *BYU English language center teacher handbook*. https://elc.byu.edu/teacher/teacher-handbook.php

Evans, N., Hartshorn, K. J., & Anderson, N. J. (2010). A research-based approach to materials development for reading. In N. Harwood (Ed.), *Materials in ELT: Theory & practice* (pp. 131–156). Oxford University Press.

5

Learner Analysis

Introduction

In the last two chapters, we discussed important components of curriculum design: the context of curriculum, and the governing documents—namely, mission statements, goals, and objectives. These two curricular domains articulate what the purpose and philosophy of a curriculum is, as well as information about what the curriculum will cover at all levels. An important third domain is that of the learners. A curriculum without learners is little more than a list of ideals and a mountain of documents. Although the learner domain could have been addressed in the contextual analysis chapter, we felt compelled to provide a fuller discussion of learners and to introduce this domain after outlining the governing documents as a matter of emphasis and practicality.

Since instruction must be targeted to meet institutional goals and objectives, an important element of curriculum design is to determine exactly what students need to learn (e.g., Hartshorn, 2018; Macalister & Nation, 2020). Ideally, curriculum designers are aware of these needs when they set goals and objectives, but often instructors must perform more tailored analyses of their students. In other words, instructors need to determine how much their particular group of learners, and even individual learners within a class, need to learn in order to achieve the objectives of the course. Thus, an important component of instruction is a needs analysis.

In addition to needs, students often have learning preferences and priorities that could conflict with or complement the foundational curriculum. An example of this is when students who want to develop some cultural literacy or vocational English attend a language school that is designed to provide academic English. Sometimes schools don't have the resources to address both the needs and the wants of their students. An effective needs and learner analysis will determine student needs and wants. Interpreting those analyses will lead developers and instructors to see where learners are deficient and will benefit from instruction.

Learners in the House Metaphor

Placing a needs analysis in the context of our house metaphor has limitations because when building a house, it's not always clear whose needs should be analyzed—those of the builders or those of the eventual homeowners. To keep things simple and tidy, we will think of the builders and the residents as the same people. It's easy to envision this for a home renovation, where the homeowners might spend time changing the layout of their home by removing a wall, tiling a floor, adding a new light fixture, or installing a new carpet. In this sense, the homeowners and the renovators both roughly represent the students in our house metaphor. It is their needs that we must understand. If we think about a new house development, imagine the future homeowners taking an active role in building the home. They might do much of the labor as directed by professional builders, such as the foreman, contractors, and subcontractors, each representing levels of administrators and/or teachers.

So, what does the building crew need? That depends entirely on what is being constructed or renovated. If the crew is working to shingle a roof, then the workers will have material needs (e.g., ladders, hammers, roofing supplies, etc.) and procedural needs (e.g., nailing lengths of tar paper, installing shingles in a specific pattern, properly installing flashing and vents, etc.). They may have other needs, such as time, money, a good tutorial or mentor to teach them how to complete the task, and perhaps motivation to keep working despite the weather. Interestingly, the homebuilders might already have a lot of these resources. Perhaps they have a collection of hammers, nails, and some extra roofing supplies from another job. If so, this is wonderful; taking an assessment of what the builders already have is part of the needs analysis. The discrepancy between what is needed to accomplish the job and what is already in the builder's possession could be described as lacks. Those lacks must be met for the project to be completed.

This metaphor can be superimposed on teaching. Student needs are entirely dependent upon the classes they are taking. Those needs are spelled out in goals, objectives, and outcome statements. In a literacy class, for example, students might be required to have productive knowledge of all the words in the New General Service List (Browne, 2014) or receptive knowledge of all the words in the Academic Vocabulary List (Gardner & Davies, 2014). They might further need to study a certain number of new words each week and pass various tests along the way to demonstrate that they are meeting these requirements. But if students enter the class with a good foundation of word knowledge, they may already know two-thirds of the required words. This does not change the fact that they need to know all 2,000 words; it merely means that students lack only one-third of the requirement. Teachers who are aware of this discrepancy can therefore adjust their instruction to target the remaining words or else adjust the needs or requirements of the class. See Box 5.1.

Box 5.1   Following the Metaphor to a Logical Conclusion

In our house metaphor, it should be noted that students can play a role as co-creators of the curriculum. From this perspective, it may be observed that a curriculum is ever changing and ever reinventing itself as students pass through it, even though the core of the curriculum—the governing documents—might remain constant. The metaphor also suggests that the end product of a curriculum is to have a complete house, but this is not totally accurate. As students help to construct the house, they gain or refine certain handiwork skills; that is, they become more proficient in construction. That proficiency will ideally transfer to novel situations. They might also develop endurance, patience, and increased self-awareness of their skills and abilities.

The same can be true of students completing a curriculum. The goal is not for them to have a set of documents and plans they can show others (unless they are in a curriculum development class). For language learners, one goal is to earn a certificate of completion from the program, whether that is a diploma or some other external validation. It is also for them to develop language proficiency that is elicited by hours of practice, study, class attendance, and test taking. These activities are built upon larger outcomes, objectives, goals, and the mission. The day-to-day activities are what build the curriculum for each student and simultaneously imbue students with language knowledge.

The end point of a curriculum for each student, therefore, is slightly different. All students will (ideally) leave a language program with both a final product and an internal skill set. Incidentally, both the product and the skill set are developed and built at the same time.

Learner Analysis

As stated earlier, in this chapter, we will systematically examine elements of learner analysis and show how an effective language curriculum is tailored to learner needs. A learner analysis has two parts: a deconstruction of learner assumptions and a needs analysis. The assumptions analysis must account for certain assumptions about the students in a program. These include assumptions about why students are studying in a particular program, what they should expect to get from the program, and what they want from it. The needs analysis requires a curriculum designer to invest time and effort in determining what learners need and want to know or do in order to accomplish specific learning tasks. To begin the learner analysis, we will first examine assumptions about learners and the purpose of assumptions in a program.

Learner Assumptions

A language program never exists in a vacuum. That is to say, the students who study in a language program exert a certain influence on that program, which comes from assumptions about those students. These include assumptions about the goals they might bring with them, their cultural, social, and economic backgrounds, and their expectations. Ideally, assumptions about language learners should be understood and articulated to some level by curriculum designers before students are even recruited and enrolled. For programs already in progress, a thoughtful investigation of learner assumptions will help dictate and narrow the direction of the remaining learner analysis. As a side note, this chapter deals with learner *assumptions* only. Collecting and analyzing the true demographics of students, such as language background and age, was covered in Chapter 3. Assumptions reflect institutional expectations of students. Demographics, on the other hand, reflect the reality of a student population; ideally, they overlap, but when they don't, either assumptions or the student body need to change.

To give an example of learner assumptions, consider the list here from an intensive English program that sought to prepare English language learners for university study. After extensive interaction with these students, administrators articulated their assumptions about language learners in the context of their own institutions.

1. The majority of our students want to go on to attend an English-medium university.
2. The majority of our students want to learn English to improve their standard of living.

3. The reasons for learning English are different and vary by student.
4. Students have different learning styles, abilities, and challenges.
5. Students learn English inside *and* outside of the English language program.
6. Students want to work while at the English language program.
7. Students come from a variety of educational involvements, backgrounds, and modes of education.
8. Students can do the assignments for their level.
9. Students need to be made aware of classroom and teacher expectations and the mission of the English language program.
10. Students have different levels of financial support.
11. Students experience culture shock.
12. Students in the same assigned classrooms have varying levels of proficiency.
13. Students are proficient in their own language.

Such a list could be further validated by additional administrators, teachers, and the learners themselves.

Notice in this list that each assumption can also be thought of as a reflection of the learners and a screening mechanism. For instance, the first assumption states that students hope to attend university classes in English. On one hand, the assumption is a guess or an informed opinion of the learners; perhaps program administrators noticed what the learners were yearning for, or maybe conducted a survey of students and found out their ambitions. On the other hand, the assumption is a screening mechanism, since it indicates the kind of students that should be admitted to the program: college-bound students who want to study in English. A language program without clear assumptions could, at its worst, become a catch-all educational program that admits any student for any reason. At its best, a program without clear assumptions might suffer from an identity crisis in which two administrators might have two very different sets of assumptions of their program, leading to a divided and unstable foundation. The solution is relatively simple: spend some time articulating the learner assumptions in your program. The following questions might prove useful in this kind of activity:

a. What kind of student is this program expected/geared to serve?
b. What regulations or laws govern the kinds of students that can be admitted?
c. What social or political conditions affect the kinds of students who enroll?

d. What level of English proficiency do students have?
e. What kind of formal schooling do students have?
f. What national, cultural, and linguistic backgrounds are students likely to bring with them?
g. What kinds of things limit students' studying time?
h. What groups or subgroups of students study in this program?

A list of assumptions like those here can be invaluable to an ESL program, particularly when it is time to revise or create a curriculum. The assumptions lay a kind of bedrock for other foundational elements of the curriculum design. To exemplify this, consider assumption 5. According to this assumption, students in this school likely have opportunities to use English outside of school, so a curriculum designer could make plans for students to take advantage of those opportunities as part of their education. Figure 5.1 illustrates how questions can lead to assumptions that can lead to curricular decisions:

Question	Learner assumption	Curricular decision
What kind of student is this program expected/geared to serve?	Students want to go on to attend an English-medium university.	Instruction should focus on preparing students for academic experiences.
What regulations or laws govern the kinds of students who can be admitted?	International students with F-1 visas must be enrolled in a full-time program.	Classes can meet any time during the day throughout the week.
What social or political conditions affect the kinds of students who enroll?	Most students are on a scholarship that limits their time in our program to 12 months.	Only the most advanced students (those who can prepare for university in a year) will be admitted.
What level of English proficiency do students have?	Students have high levels of English proficiency, particularly oral skills.	Instruction and materials should focus on accuracy above fluency.
What kind of formal schooling do students have?	Students have limited formal schooling or experience with higher education.	Teachers and advisors should provide a lot of support to help students meet the expectations of formal schooling.

Figure 5.1 Questions lead to assumptions and curricular decisions.

> **Box 5.2 The Benefit of Examining Assumptions**
>
> In one language school, students were placed into five different proficiency levels, and, because the program was connected to a university, it offered college language credit for the top three levels.
>
> Most of the language teachers in the program held the same assumption: that students knew how to study in an American academic setting. For some students, this indeed was the case; they were astute, hard-working, and well-adjusted. Over time, however, students with different backgrounds began to be admitted. Students who were far less prepared for college-style coursework became the majority. The change was so slow and subtle at first that teachers barely noticed it.
>
> Since the teachers' assumptions didn't keep up with the changing student body, many instructors were feeling a strong dissonance between their expectations of student behavior and actual student behavior. Some teachers began resenting their students, even those who were prepared for college courses. Some teachers even became angry or condescending toward students in class.
>
> At this point, the curriculum team performed a learner analysis. They articulated and examined their assumptions about students and came to realize that it was no longer appropriate to assume that students were college-ready. Instead, teachers needed to assume that students had little experience with an American college setting. The outcome of this shift in assumptions was twofold. First, teachers were encouraged to provide more "college preparation" training in their language courses. Second, teachers and administrators became more sensitive to their assumptions and more willing to adjust expectations based on the student body. Oftentimes, correcting inaccurate assumptions can be as useful for teachers as it is for students.

Just as it is important to understand and articulate initial assumptions about students, it is also important to revisit those assumptions regularly, as they are likely to change from time to time, which will necessitate a curricular change as well (see Box 5.2). For example, public universities in many border states in the United States enrolled high numbers of immigrant and resident ESL students throughout the 1990s and 2000s in their ESL programs. This population tends to have relatively high oral proficiency. Therefore, an assumption was that students in these programs could and would engage in classroom discussions about language. However, when the Chinese economy expanded in the late 2000s and the number of international students skyrocketed in these same schools, the expectation that students would talk willingly in class wasn't nearly as accurate. Doing business as usual by assuming all students would engage in classroom discussions was partially ineffective. The student body had changed, which meant that the assumptions had to change, which meant that the curriculum needed to change.

Needs Analysis

Among other curriculum professionals, Macalister and Nation (2020) have described the importance of examining student needs, lacks, and wants. An analysis of these three components represents a needs analysis. A needs analysis is a systematic approach used to determine what learners need to know or do in order to accomplish specific learning tasks. At its very simplest, it can be thought of as a comparison between what learners need to know or do and what they have yet to master. This is a scalable definition in that a needs analysis can be performed at any level of curriculum. For example, a program-level needs analysis should reveal the difference between what skills and abilities students need to possess at the end of the entire program (obtain a particular score on the TOEFL exam, for example) compared to their proficiencies at the beginning of the program. The same is true for a course-level learner analysis and a class-level analysis. To simplify the steps of a needs analysis, we will examine needs, lacks, and wants in that order.

Needs

The concept of *needs* can be difficult to determine in educational contexts. This is because the matter of what a student needs can refer to very general or developmental goals. For instance, students need to learn English, develop pragmatic awareness, or "pass" the TOEFL. Needs can also be very specific, task-based, and tied to an outcome, such as understanding the past-perfect tense in order to write an essay about life before returning to school or knowing how to form an adverbial clause with a relative pronoun. In our definition, we side with the specific perspective and define needs as any component of an end goal or task in a language curriculum. In this sense, broad language learning goals and tasks must be broken down into divisible components to identify learner needs. For example, if students are expected to read academic texts in English by the end of a reading course, then the components of that end task might include decoding words, recognizing academic vocabulary, identifying generic moves in academic writing, and interpreting charts or tables. Even more basic might be the needs associated with learning to read in the first place: letter recognition; sound-letter correspondence; blending; decoding and whole-word recognition; combining words into meaningful chunks; and understanding sentences, paragraphs, and passages.

Each of the aforementioned components represent needs that students have at a course level. Large-scale programmatic goals should also be analyzed by determining what learners will need in order to graduate from the program. And class-level lesson objectives should also be analyzed to determine what students need in order to accomplish those objectives by the end of the class. Curriculum designers and teachers have a responsibility to work together to identify the important components, or needs, of curricular end goals. Figure 5.2 illustrates one possible result of a needs analysis.

	Needs	Needs/Components
Writing Process	Students need to practice each step of the writing process and get different kinds of feedback to know what works for them.	Plan a paper using a variety of planning strategies
		Effectively invent, prewrite, draft, revise, and edit to create polished writing
		Publish at least one piece of writing by sending it to its intended audience
		Create a personal and ideal composing/revision process after experiencing teacher review, peer review, tutor review, and self-review
Vocabulary	Students need to study, analyze, and correctly use academic vocabulary from their reading class.	Review vocabulary from all sub-lists (1–10) of the Academic Word List (AWL) and become increasingly familiar with www.lextutor.ca/vp/eng/ & http://corpus.byu.edu/coca/ for analyzing vocab in context
		Identify AWL items in class readings
		Use at least 4% AWL words in genre-based writings and/or homework assignments
Sources	Students need to read material in order to prepare to write and also need to learn official APA citation.	Read, understand, and analyze (and sometimes find) text related to writing topics
		Analyze text organization, language use, and rhetorical moves in genre-based assignments
		Effectively and repeatedly summarize, paraphrase, quote, and cite from sources
		Effectively select, introduce, and integrate quotes to bolster an argument
		Use both in-text and reference page citation as well as APA format in at least one paper

Figure 5.2 Course goals with accompanying needs (components).

The purpose of examining needs is to determine all the goals and tasks that students will have to accomplish along with corresponding sub-components. This can be done without students around, since the objective process of identifying needed skills is under scrutiny, not student preferences, abilities, or backgrounds. Additionally, this first stage of a needs analysis does not have to be done all at once. While the ideal is to know every step for learning every skill, in practice, such omniscience is impossible. Language teachers and researchers routinely find new ways to teach a skill supported by new or different foundational steps. In short, the list of student needs can change or expand as new expectations and instructional approaches are developed. The point here is that the first stage of a needs analysis is to understand generally what students are expected to know or do by the end of a program (or course or class) and break that down into component elements in the best way possible. Once this is done, students enter the picture. Curriculum designers and teachers must determine how many of the subcomponents actually need to be taught and/or practiced. This is where an analysis of student lacks comes in (see Box 5.3).

Box 5.3 Generic, General, Intermediate, and Specific Needs

Students and teachers often bandy about the word *need* in almost a careless way. Students need time to complete their assignments, they need to work harder, they need more instruction, they need, need, need. We view these kinds of statements as generic needs. They are statements that are easy to say but hard to put into action because it's not always clear how these needs will be fulfilled. In some cases, it's not even clear if these are true needs or just statements of exasperation by students or teachers who want a quicker route to language proficiency. Unless they are deconstructed and worked into outcome statements, these needs often don't get acted upon.

General needs, on the other hand, are integral to the success of a curriculum. After all, every language program is built or designed to address educational needs. In many cases, the basic need is to learn or improve English. And to accomplish this purpose, language programs have courses that fulfill some intermediate needs. For instance, students may need literacy instruction, so reading and writing courses provide that. Within such classes, more specific needs are addressed, such as the need to identify and then form different types of thesis statements and topic sentences.

In a sense, generic needs are wishes, hopes, or ideals. General, intermediate, and specific needs, however, correspond to some extent with mission,

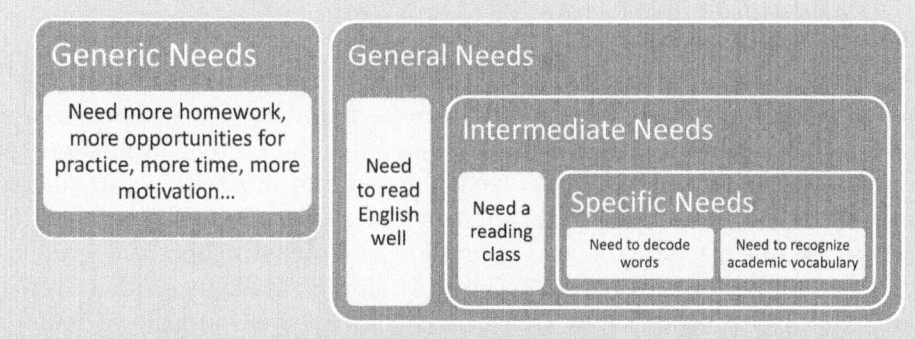

Figure 5.3 A breakdown of generic needs into intermediate and specific needs.

goal, and objective statements at the program, course, and class levels. This is because needs explicate all the steps students must take to accomplish each outcome. So, what do students need at the course level? To attend class, complete assignments, take notes, practice, etc. Figure 5.3 illustrates how needs can be segregated into different levels.

Lacks

A lack represents any unmet needs. If a student needs to recognize and use 10 given academic vocabulary words but is only able to use three of them on a consistent basis, then the student lacks full proficiency with seven words. The whole point of a curriculum is to efficiently and systematically fill lacks. This principle underscores the significance of having a clear set of language needs articulated for each learning task, as well as a reliable and valid measurement of student lacks and abilities.

Lacks can be presumed by teachers and curriculum designers, but they really should be ascertained by careful observation and assessment of students. A common lacks assessment is that of a diagnostic test at the beginning of a course where students indicate their ability (or lack of it) on a cross-section of topics or skills to be covered during the course. At the class level, students might fill out a pretest on a topic to be covered during the lesson as a form of lacks assessment. Teachers might also observe student performance and draw conclusions about what students do or do not understand. Other more formal assessments can also be used, such as proficiency tests or examinations, which offer opportunities for teachers to adjust their instruction based on student performance (a process called washback).

> **Box 5.4 Needs vs. Lacks**
>
> The images shown here illustrate the relationship between needs and lacks in two different scenarios. On the left, students might be very well prepared to meet the needs of a specific learning task, so their lacks could be relatively few. On the right, students might have almost no facility with a particular learning task, so their lacks might align almost completely with their needs. In this case, the teacher will need to provide a lot of instruction.
>
> Obviously, these images are deceptively simple. In reality, students can have multiple areas of needs and lacks, including areas outside of traditional instruction. For instance, students might have financial, emotional, physical, and psychological needs and lacks as well. There are also material needs, like textbooks, access to computers and printers, and teachers. For every language program, designers must decide what needs will be addressed through instruction and support services and what threshold of lacks is acceptable for incoming and continuing students.
>
>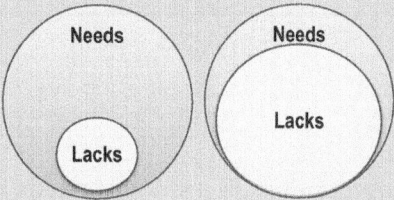
>
> **Figure 5.4** Needs and wants comparison.

It should be noted that a result from just a single test is less reliable and valid than results from triangulated assessments or observations. It is a good idea (when practical) to perform multiple forms of assessment at different times in order to increase the reliability and validity of the results, particularly as students begin to fill their gaps in knowledge or ability.

Wants

In addition to assessing needs and lacks, a learner analysis should ascertain what learners *want* to accomplish. Wants represent those skills or abilities that students feel are important but which may not be pertinent for achieving the end goals of a curriculum. Macalister and Nation (2020) note that sometimes student wants align with their needs and lacks. For instance, when a curriculum is built to teach occupational English, and students participate because they lack (and want) that language instruction, their needs, lacks, and wants align. However, sometimes student wants are at odds with their needs and lacks. Many language learners, for example, want extreme pronunciation instruction so that they can "sound like a native speaker." If a language program denies its students' wants by focusing on oral fluency or vocabulary instead of pronunciation, then the wants and needs are misaligned. Although wants may be considered tangential to a focused curriculum, designers can imperil their programs by ignoring student wants. After all, students are usually the customers in an educational program, so their desires are important to consider. However, not all student wants are equally valid or practical. So, when wants and needs conflict, curriculum designers might need to adjust curricular components to better meet student wants, or they may need to persuade students to better understand the purpose of the curriculum as it stands. Some combination of the two might be warranted. See Box 5.5.

Box 5.5 Wants in the House Metaphor

On the surface, all humans need more or less the same things in a home: shelter, safety, security, and privacy. When applied to curriculum, such a simplistic view may suggest that all language curricula can be boiled down to a handful of universal elements, which would include language instruction, some kind of oral or written interaction, and a set of tests or assessments. And this is certainly true; however, when viewed more critically, it is easy to imagine how one family's housing wants can differ radically from another's, and that a one-size-fits-all kind of house wouldn't work for all families. A big family, for instance, generally wants and needs a larger living space than does a single college student. A family with dogs might want a larger yard, and a family in a big city with good public transportation might not have a car and thus not need or want a garage. In addition to this, there are assumptions about what a house should be, and families from different cultures might have different expectations. In some cultures, it is a common assumption that multiple generations will all live together in one house, so the home environment is expected to be close-knit. In other cultures, the assumption may be that a home represents a person's wealth and prestige, so the bigger and more cavernous, the better. These assumptions influence decisions about how a house should be built. Likewise, student preferences and needs can and should influence decisions about how a curriculum is built.

Resources for Conducting a Learner Analysis

As mentioned, a learner analysis involves articulating assumptions about learners and identifying their needs, lacks, and wants. In some cases, this information can be very easy to collect by surveying, interviewing, or observing students. In other cases, the information will require expert knowledge or intuition about developing language proficiency. To make the process of learner analysis more efficient, we have listed some ways here to effectively collect data for a learner analysis.

Resources for Determining Learner Needs

To determine needs, a curriculum designer must start with a learning goal or task and break it down into component parts. Perhaps the quickest and easiest way to do this is to think through the learning procedure to identify the most important subskills. One word of caution is that different learners may have varying paths for learning a new skill, and some awareness of this should be reflected in the needs list. Curriculum designers could also ask recent students for their insights into the learning process. They may ask questions about what things the students learned first, how they organized their learning, or what subskills they think should have been taught. Other resources can include textbooks, webpages, colleagues, and professionals who have specialized insights into the learning process of certain language tasks.

Resources for Determining Learner Lacks

After creating a list of learning needs for a particular goal, it is possible to determine students' lacks against those needs. Placement procedures, proficiency exams, and diagnostic tests can all function to measure learners' lacks inasmuch as they are measured relative to their learning needs. For insights on creating effective assessments, see Chapter 8. Additional resources for language assessment are listed at the end of this chapter.

Some lacks can be measured very easily by having students take a pretest or try to accomplish a task at hand. Students will obviously need instruction and practice in areas or subskills where their scores dip down or they will become unable to accomplish the task. Bear in mind that the list of student needs may change, expand, or contract with further testing and as students become more proficient. Furthermore, all the goals or tasks in a program can change based upon the type and purpose of a language program. See Box 5.6 for assessment types for determining student lacks.

> **Box 5.6 Assessment Types for Determining Student Lacks**
>
> More formal assessments, such as a standardized assessment, can be used to identify student lacks. But these may only correspond to some needs, so additional, alternative, or more specialized assessment may also be necessary. Some of these assessment options are listed here:
>
> **Student self-assessment:** Students self-evaluate their own abilities and knowledge.
> *Advantages:* It is an easy assessment to write, deploy, and interpret.
> *Disadvantages:* Though self-assessment may be the best way to identify learner wants, it may be less reliable or valid for identifying learner lacks (though it may be important for understanding student perceptions).
>
> **Student reflection or think-aloud protocol:** Students reflect on the task procedures they used during or after a task, allowing teachers insight into students' abilities.
> *Advantages:* Teachers have access to student's thinking on a very specific task.
> *Disadvantages:* Potentially time-consuming for students and teachers; results can be difficult to interpret.
>
> **Teacher observation:** A teacher observes a student performing a language task.
> *Advantages:* Teachers have immediate access to students' real-time abilities on a very specific task and can seek clarification on student knowledge.
> *Disadvantages:* Potentially time-consuming for students and teachers; results can be difficult to interpret; only a limited range of tasks can be observed at a single time.
>
> **Proficiency assessment:** A student takes a pretest that measures his or her ability on a task.
> *Advantages:* Students are familiar with this type of assessment; it can be easy to deploy and interpret.
> *Disadvantages:* Only a limited range of tasks or knowledge can be assessed in this way. Results from these kinds of assessments, if aligned with the needs associated with learning goals, should function as a map of learners' deficiencies.

Resources for Collecting Learner Wants

Learner wants are usually very easy to ascertain through student self-reporting. Students can report their learning wants in prose, or they can respond to a rank item list crafted by a curriculum designer. In either event, it may be possible to collect these wants in advance, but usually teachers are the ones who solicit student wants at the beginning of or during a particular language course.

It can be difficult for curriculum designers to collect student wants early enough to incorporate them into a curriculum design, particularly if a student population is new or rapidly changing. Therefore, student wants may need to be addressed in creative ways by classroom teachers after a semester or quarter begins. Some curricula, on the other hand, are entirely built upon student wants as with a negotiated syllabus or curriculum (e.g., Christison & Murray, 2021). This may be the case with adult education or occupational language courses in which students have very strong reasons for mastering very specific kinds of language.

Using a Learner Analysis to Solve Programmatic Problems

A learner analysis is not a one-time event that curriculum designers perform at the inception of a new program and never again. In reality, teachers should constantly be engaged in learner analyses to ensure that their classes and the course meet student needs and accomplish their purpose while being sensitive to learner preferences. At the class level, this is straightforward, but at the programmatic level, it can be much more complex.

Programs that fail to perform higher-level needs analyses often have major curricular problems, but administrators don't always seem to know why. Curriculum designers who understand the principles of needs analysis can usually spot these problems early on. The authors of this book have seen an array of curricula with problems that stem from inefficient needs analyses. Here we highlight some of the more salient curricular problems with the hope that these examples can help curriculum designers avoid similar problems in their programs.

Two Populations

On several occasions, we have heard some variation of the following theme from a frustrated language program administrator: "About half of our students are diligent and dedicated, but the other half are just here to party. They don't do their homework, and they infuriate our teachers with their lackadaisical attitudes." Often the two types of learners are present in the same classes. The problem in the two-population scenario is that students with dissimilar needs, lacks, or wants are artificially placed in a class or program that addresses only one group's needs, lacks, or wants.

When trying to address this problem with administrators, we ask them why the two groups were placed in the same class to begin with, and usually the reply is that it was a historical placement procedure and only recently has one population increased enough to make the difference between the two groups obvious. This is significant because it suggests that curriculum administrators have not been sensitive to changing learner assumptions or performed a recent learner analysis and have failed to see the two different sets of wants associated with the two populations. The populations may also have different needs and lacks as well. We therefore try to get administrators to envision the two populations in separate classes and think about how those two classes might differ. We ask them to question what purpose the 'party' students have for attending their program. If they are required by law or some other policy to accomplish the same end goals or tasks as the other students, then we recommend that administrators alter the curriculum (including the use of a pull-out model, if necessary) to better account for student wants. If there is no language policy requirement, then we often advise administrators to take the 'party' students out of the mainstream curriculum and develop alternative classes that better meet their language goals. Or, we might suggest that administrators encourage the 'party' students to apply to a school more suited to their wants.

Unmotivated Students

We have also encountered administrators who observe that a subset of their students seems completely unmotivated in their studies. They may say something to this effect: "About half of the highest-level listening/speaking class has stopped showing up. They are all highly motivated in reading and writing and are planning to enter an MBA program in the near future, but their basic communication skills are inadequate, so they desperately need the speaking/listening curriculum."

Again, we recommend that administrators analyze their learners' needs, lacks, and wants, because the curriculum may not be meeting the learning goals of the unmotivated students, or it may be under- or overestimating their lacks. In many cases, simply listening to students by giving them a chance to voice their language goals or express what they want from a course or program can increase student motivation. Additionally, administrators should consider performing an updated needs analysis on the kinds of end goals students are meant to accomplish in a given period of time. Administrators could also conduct a lacks analysis and be very honest about what students are capable of within a particular timeframe.

Underachieving Students

The most frustrated administrators explain that their students are not achieving the course objectives. They may say, "We want them to learn twenty-five points on grammar, yet when we test them at the end of the semester, they are only getting about eight of the items correct." While there are a number of reasons that this may be the case, some can be traced back to mismatches among needs, lacks, and wants. For example, a curriculum may mandate that learners accomplish more than is developmentally possible in a certain time-frame, in which case the objectives of the class or program may need to be modified. On the other hand, the needs of specific end goals may be insufficiently detailed, resulting in ambiguous needs or inaccurate measurements of lacks. In this case, an updated needs analysis is in order, as well as a reevaluation of learning goals.

Evaluating the Learner Analysis

Throughout the learner analysis process, curriculum designers need to ensure that their analysis has a purpose and that it is accurate, reliable, and valid. The purpose dictates the focus and extent of the learner analysis. For instance, if an established curriculum is undergoing a change in student populations, the purpose of the analysis might be to better understand what lacks the new students bring with them. The learner analysis may, therefore, appropriately focus on students' lacks and wants rather than needs, since the learning goals may remain the same.

Once the purpose of the learner analysis is set, curriculum designers should ensure the accuracy, reliability, and validity of the results. Accuracy means that the results of the analysis represent reality, meaning the subskills identified in a needs analysis must be relevant subskills to the larger goal. For instance, if a learning goal for students is to master a set of Latin-based vocabulary words, then a relevant subskill may be to learn the roots and prefixes of those words. An irrelevant or inaccurate subskill may be to transform present tense verbs into past tense in a reading passage. While perhaps a noble goal, transforming verb tenses may be an irrelevant subskill of vocabulary learning. Thus, care should be taken to ensure that learning goals are broken into relevant subskills. Additionally, curriculum designers must ensure the accuracy of the learner analysis by not introducing errors into the results of ability assessments or interpreting these in fallacious ways. Errors can occur when transferring results from a paper-and-pencil exam to a computer. They can also be the by-product of an inaccurate answer key, a bookkeeping error, a faulty instrument or procedure, and so on. Errors in interpretation can occur when raters work too quickly, when data are poorly recorded, when evaluation criteria are unclear, and so on.

The learner analysis should also be reliable. This means that learner needs, lacks, and wants should be collected in a way that maintains their stability. In other words, if one curriculum designer identifies certain subskills in a needs analysis, then another designer should be able to come up with more or less the same list. If so, the needs analysis could be considered reliable. If two independent curriculum designers come up with separate lists of subskills for a language task and those lists have very different subskills, this indicates a problem. In this case, something must be done to improve the reliability of the lists—maybe combining the lists, eliminating subskills that are irrelevant or unnecessary, or revisiting data collection instruments and processes.

The same is true for lacks assessments: they should be crafted in such a way that if a student is assessed on one day, he or she should be able to provide more or less the same responses on any other day insomuch as learning has not taken place between the two assessments. If a student can't perform in similar ways on two different instances of the same test (assuming no learning has taken place), then the questions may be too vague or poorly worded. And of course, the same is true for a wants analysis.

Finally, the learner analysis should be valid, meaning that it identifies real learner assumptions and truly measures the needs, lacks, and wants of learners. An invalid analysis inadvertently measures things that are not part of the target construct. For instance, confusing lacks with wants would produce an invalid interpretation in a learner analysis: what students *lack* and what they *want* are not necessarily the same, so asking students to list what they want to learn and assuming that by addressing those items they will achieve the learning goals may be fallacious and invalid.

Chapter Summary

The basic notion of a learner analysis involves:

1. identifying learner assumptions,
2. determining what skills and subskills learners need in order to accomplish a specific learning task (needs),
3. determining what students lack in terms of those skills and subskills (lacks), and
4. determining what students want to learn (wants).

Once these four components are properly identified, a curriculum designer can begin the design phase of curriculum development.

Ultimately, a learner analysis is about truly understanding the learner. We explained this concept through the metaphor of a house: even though most houses are essentially the same from a distance, they all have slight modifications and adaptations depending on the needs and wants of the people who live there. This metaphor rings true with curriculum as well, in that all language programs are essentially the same from a distance, but they also require modification and adaptation based upon the needs, lacks, and wants of the learners.

Activities

Activity 5.1

Consider your current program or a program you are familiar with. Think about the student body and articulate five or six assumptions. It may be helpful to use the questions in this chapter.

Activity 5.2

Examine websites or other curricular materials from two different language programs. What assumptions are you able to articulate for each program? Are there similarities and differences between the two that you can identify? How do these differences manifest themselves in terms of different institutional cultures and practices?

Activity 5.3

Think about an existing program (or one you hope to create) and articulate learner assumptions and curricular decisions based on those assumptions. It may be helpful to create your own table, like the one shown in this chapter.

Activity 5.4

Examine the course goals for a course you have recently taught or will be teaching soon. What tasks are associated with those goals? How might you break one of those tasks into its subcomponents? Identify a number of student needs based on your analysis.

Activity 5.5

Consider a course you recently taught or observed. Identify some areas where most students lacked proficiency or knowledge. This task will require you to list some needs first and then compare these with student lacks.

Activity 5.6

Consider your own education as a language-teaching professional. What instructional content do you wish had been covered? To what extent do you think it would have been feasible for instructors to accommodate your wants?

Activity 5.7

If you are a language teacher, how do you go about learning students' preferences and wants? To what extent do you accommodate those wants?

Activity 5.8

Think about a curricular problem you have encountered either in your program or another program, and write a few lines explaining the problem. Then, consider how an analysis of students' needs, lacks, and wants might clarify the problem. Finally, consider some solutions that could help solve or at least minimize the problem.

References

Browne, C. (2014). The new general service list version 1.01: Getting better all the time. *Korea TESOL Journal, 11*(1), 35–50.

Christison, M., & Murray, D. E. (2021). *What English language teachers need to know volume III: Designing curriculum* (2nd ed.). Routledge.

Gardner, D., & Davies, M. (2014). A new academic vocabulary list. *Applied Linguistics, 35*(3), 305–327.

Hartshorn, K. J. (2018). Curriculum development. *The TESOL Encyclopedia of English Language Teaching*, 1–8.

Macalister, J., & Nation, I. P. (2020). *Language curriculum design*. Routledge.

Additional Readings and Resources for Language Assessment

Bachman, L. F., & Palmer, A. S. (1996). *Language testing in practice: Designing and developing useful language tests* (Vol. 1). Oxford University Press.

Brown, H. D. (2019). *Language assessment: Principles and classroom practices* (2nd ed.). Pearson Education.

Brown, J. D. (2005). *Testing in language programs: A comprehensive guide to English language assessment*. McGraw-Hill College.

Clapham, C., & Corson, D. (Eds.). (1997). *Language testing and assessment* (Vol. 7). Kluwer Academic Publishers.

Fulcher, G. (2013). *Practical language testing*. Routledge. http://dx.doi.org/10.4324/980203767399

Genesee, F., & Upshur, J. A. (1996). *Classroom-based evaluation in second language education*. Cambridge University Press.

Hill, C., & Parry, K. (2014). *From testing to assessment: English as an international language*. Routledge.

Hughes, A. (2002). *Testing for language teachers* (2nd ed.). Cambridge University Press. http://dx.doi.org/10.1017/CBO9780511732980

Weir, C. J. (2005). *Language testing and validation*. Palgrave Macmillan. http://dx.doi.org/10.1057/9780230514577

6

Contextual Synthesis

Introduction

A major premise in our approach to curriculum design is that most curriculum work is done in the preparation stages prior to any changes or new materials being introduced. This preparation was outlined in Chapters 3, 4, and 5 and includes determining the program's purpose, analyzing learners and teachers, and creating governing documents. Doing all this is critical, but so too is documenting it (Wang, 2006), and that is what this chapter addresses.

It is especially easy and common for faculty and administrators in a language program to plan or make decisions without keeping track of them. Some programs rely on the memory of staff members to document all their changes and reasons for changes. It is important to capture knowledge about changes and the program in general before those involved in important decisions leave the program or the institutional memory degrades (Hillman & Werner, 2017). A contextual synthesis allows for the capture and management of this important knowledge.

Curriculum designers should create a document that outlines their curricular decisions and encompasses all the governing documents. This contextual synthesis then becomes a living document that can be updated through successive periods of change and reshaping. In this chapter, we describe what a contextual synthesis is and how to create it. We also provide some examples to illustrate different approaches we have seen curriculum developers take when creating their own syntheses.

DOI: 10.4324/9781003306122-6

Contextual Synthesis

The contextual synthesis is an institutional document that reports on findings from both the contextual analysis and the learner analysis. It is a description of the context in which the teaching and learning are to occur. It is a document that can be used by administrators, curriculum planners, and new teachers to quickly understand and help guide the language program.

What Should be Included in a Contextual Synthesis?

The content of a contextual synthesis is entirely up to those in charge of the curriculum. As mentioned, the synthesis ought to be informed by the contextual and leaner analyses. For instance, it should include key information about the program or institution and how the setting may influence curriculum development and its implementation. The contextual synthesis should provide a broad picture of why the program exists, what is taught in the program, who the students are, how they are taught, and so on. It also should include the most prominent characteristics that define the program.

Ultimately, the contextual synthesis should include whatever details are the most important in defining a particular program or institution. Not all details will be of equal value in a particular context. Nor will the same details be equally important across contexts. Perhaps most important is the inclusion of program strengths and challenges. If an entirely new curriculum is being developed, some of the strengths or challenges may not be fully apparent. Yet, those preparing the contextual description should endeavor to be as complete and insightful as possible. In most cases, however, it is an existing curriculum that needs to be improved. In such cases, those conducting the analysis should look beyond the curriculum in its narrowest sense to see the broadest view of how the program is functioning within its context. Here are just a few questions that might be useful in deciding what to include in a contextual description:

1. What is the purpose of the program?
2. How well is the program fulfilling its purpose?
3. Who are the students? (e.g., backgrounds, needs, aspirations)
4. Who are the teachers? (e.g., qualifications, skills, needs)
5. Who are the administrators? (e.g., backgrounds, qualifications, needs)
6. What is the administrative structure within the program?
7. To whom is the program accountable?
8. Who provides support services?

9. Are there other stakeholders? If so, who are they, and what is their relationship to the class, course, or program?
10. Are there affiliate organizations? If so, who are they, and what are their roles?
11. What facilities and resources are available?
12. How is the program financed?
13. What are the program's greatest strengths and weaknesses?
14. What are the greatest challenges the program faces?

Those involved in compiling the synthesis should ensure that contributions come from a variety of perspectives. Once a draft has been generated, key stakeholders should work together to refine a final version that can remain in use until subsequent changes may be needed. As a living document, it should be revised as changes occur to and within the program.

There are no mandatory length requirements or limits for a contextual synthesis, although curriculum designers should be sensitive to the fact that a long report will probably go unread by busy teachers and administrators, so shorter is usually better. We have seen many effective syntheses that are just a couple of pages long and focused on the institutional structure of the program. That being said, we have also seen extensive syntheses that reached more than 50 pages because they included every governing document, exhaustive reports from thorough lacks analyses, and detailed organizational and historical information that documented how the programs operated and had developed. Different abridged, summarized, or excerpted versions might also be useful for different audiences, such as funding bodies or high-level administrators who need quick information. It makes the most sense to keep the contextual synthesis in an electronic format so that it can be easily added upon and modified through the years.

Uses for the Contextual Synthesis
The synthesis is a foundational tool used when designing, developing, and implementing new curricular components. First and foremost, designers look to the contextual analysis to see evidence of problems in the curriculum that need to be addressed. Information gleaned from the synthesis can also help explain the origin of a particularly complex curricular problem—something that might elude discovery if the curriculum were examined only in discrete chunks instead of holistically. The synthesis is especially useful for teachers to make informed teaching decisions when they can see the entire curriculum represented in a single document. It is also helpful for new teachers, as they try to wrap their minds around the program's core features, culture, and demographics. See Box 6.1 for contextual synthesis resources.

Box 6.1 Resources for a Contextual Synthesis

A contextual synthesis is informed by all the preparatory analysis described in the previous five chapters, plus any other relevant information that could be added and would be helpful for a given audience. We have provided a resource checklist here for easy reference that covers the basic analyses described in earlier chapters.

Some curriculum designers might choose to write the contextual synthesis by including statements that address everything on this checklist. That is certainly a feasible approach, and one that we have seen some language programs take. It should be noted, though, that some of the items on this list are redundant; for instance, the *why* question in the contextual analysis partially overlaps with the mission and program outcomes in the governing documents section. If different people are working on different parts of the synthesis, there should be some thoughtful coordination to avoid duplicate reporting.

In terms of presentation, we have seen some programs organize a contextual synthesis linearly according to this checklist. Other syntheses we have seen are an amalgamation of different reports; others are bullet-point lists; some are narrative descriptions; and still others contain extensive images, tables, and infographics. In other words, there is no set format for a contextual synthesis.

Critical Resources
- **Contextual Analysis**
    - **Why** — purpose of program
    - **What** — materials, process, or information to be taught
    - **Who** — students' demographics, abilities, interests, attitudes, ambitions, and motivations
        — teachers' demographics, training, skills, perspectives, personalities, assumptions, philosophies, and motivations
    - **How** — approach to language instruction
    - **Where** — geographic/physical location and facilities
        — social, cultural, economic, and political environment
    - **When** — time and duration of classes and courses
- **Learner Analysis**
    - **Assumptions** — perceptions of student goals, backgrounds, and expectations
    - **Needs** — skills, abilities, and knowledge students should gain in the program
    - **Wants** — student learning preferences
    - **Lacks** — gaps between student knowledge and their needs

> ◆ **Governing Documents**
>   o Mission and program outcomes
>   o Goals and course outcomes
>   o Objectives and class outcomes
>
> **Additional Resources**
> ◆ Pertinent Organizational and Historical Information
> ◆ Class offerings and Descriptions
> ◆ Program, Instructional, and Administrative Philosophies
> ◆ Relevant Faculty, Staff, and Stakeholder Information
> ◆ Vision for Future Direction and Changes

Sample Contextual Syntheses

Here we present significant portions of three contextual syntheses from three distinct language programs. The first two syntheses come from intensive English programs that are very similar to one another. Seeing them side-by-side illustrates how different even similar programs can be. The final synthesis reflects an intensive writing program housed in a large US research institution. Students placed into this program were required to complete it concurrently with other university classes; they had to pass all writing classes in order to remain a student at the university.

Contextual Synthesis Example A

Synthesis A comes from an intensive English program in the US. The program is associated with a local university but is otherwise self-supporting financially and largely independent of university decision-making. The school does not offer matriculated courses or college credit for students who attend. We have provided a running commentary in the margin that highlights some key points in the description that may be relevant for curricular change.

Contextual Description of a Pre-University IEP

> *Lab School*
>
> The English Language Center (ELC) is a non-profit, self-support intensive English program operating on a university campus. As a lab school, it has a dual educative purpose. First, it exists as an essential component of the Linguistics and English Language Department's MA degree

program in Teaching English as a Second Language (TESOL); graduate students use the ELC as a laboratory for teaching, administration, and research. Second, in order to provide graduate students with authentic experiences to refine their teaching skills, the ELC strives to provide the best English as a second language (ESL) instruction possible to its students. Since the ELC is a lab school, many of its teachers have limited teaching experience. At the same time, the program is well supported and influenced by university professors and informed by ongoing research.

> **Running Commentary**
>
> *Several very important details are provided at the outset. For example, this program is non-profit and self-supporting. We also learn that this program is a lab school and that many of the teachers have limited experience. Each of these are important factors that will affect the curriculum in different ways.*
>
> *Here we learn that the student body is diverse linguistically and culturally. We also learn that most students will need academic language skills in order to study at the university level.*

Students

The ELC teaches English to approximately 200–250 students each semester. Students range in age from 17 to over 50, with over half the population falling between the ages of 17 and 25. They come from more than 40 different nations and range widely in their proficiency (i.e., true beginners to advanced–high). Nearly three-quarters of the student body comes from six countries: Korea, Mexico, Taiwan, Japan, Peru, and Mongolia. Korea is the most represented country at the ELC, but Spanish is the most common native language among the students. Their language aspirations vary, but a large majority of the students hope to attend an English medium university as graduate or undergraduate students. Nearly a third of the students have already received a baccalaureate degree and hope to pursue a graduate degree. Most of the other students want to learn English in order to pursue other professional endeavors.

Faculty

The ELC faculty is composed of full- and part-time staff, ranging from a total of 30 to 40 individuals in a given semester. The primary purpose of the ELC is to provide meaningful teaching experiences for university graduate students who have completed prerequisite courses and their

Table 6.1 Faculty Composition

Faculty Category	Composition
Graduate Students (part-time)	40%
Non-Students (part-time)	45%
Program Supervisors (full-time)	14%
Faculty/Administrators (full-time)	1%

student teaching. Despite their quality training, many of these teachers have limited classroom experience. However, these less-experienced teachers are well supported by seasoned non-student faculty who teach classes part-time and mentor the graduate students. There are also six full-time administrators who teach classes and fulfill a variety of assignments as program supervisors and members of the ELC Executive Council. They also play a supportive role for the student teachers. These administrators are recent graduates with an MA degree in TESOL who have demonstrated outstanding skill in teaching and administration. However, they are only hired for three-year non-renewable positions. This is done to provide more graduates with administrative experience. In addition, some classes may also be taught by permanent full-time ELC administrators or faculty from the Linguistics and English Language Department. Although there are some fluctuations from semester to semester, Table 6.1 presents a general breakdown of the faculty composition by category. On average, student teachers are likely to teach only 3–4 semesters before graduating. Though some who graduate continue at the ELC part-time, turnover is fairly common, underscoring the need for effective teacher training and support.

> *It appears that while many of the teachers have limited experience, they seem well supported. However, extensive turnover could create unique challenges for teacher training and implementation of curricular components.*

Program Structure

The ELC teaches five proficiency levels, ranging from 1 to 5. Level 1 is for false beginners, and Level 5 is for students preparing for study at an English medium university.

Administration

The ELC is housed in the College of Humanities, specifically in the Linguistics and English Language Department, and is overseen by the respective Dean and Department Chair. In this regard, the ELC helps fulfill the overall academic mission of both the college and the department. The administration specific to the ELC consists of several levels. The ELC Coordinator works under the direction of the department chair and oversees all administrative functions of the Intensive English Program as well as ESL instruction and resources on campus for matriculated students. The next level consists of coordinators whose responsibilities are specific to the intensive English program for non-matriculated students, with responsibilities ranging from curriculum development and teaching, student life, testing, technology, evaluation, and research. The third level consists of six full-time administrators serving on three-year contracts. They serve as skill area coordinators and fulfill a wide variety of administrative assignments. In addition to teaching their own classes within their respective programs, they work closely with student teachers to help them be successful.

> Since the ELC works under two different deans in the College of Humanities and Continuing Education, there is the potential for challenges if these entities hold different views of the ELC and its mission.

While the ELC is a self-support program, Figure 6.1 shows how it is tied directly to the university through the College of Humanities, and the Linguistics and English Language Department with oversight from the College Dean and Department Chair. It also works closely with the Division of Continuing Education, which provides a variety of additional support services under the oversight of the Dean of Continuing Education. Each of the organizations in the ELC's superstructure has an important impact on how the ELC operates and may influence various future decisions about the ELC.

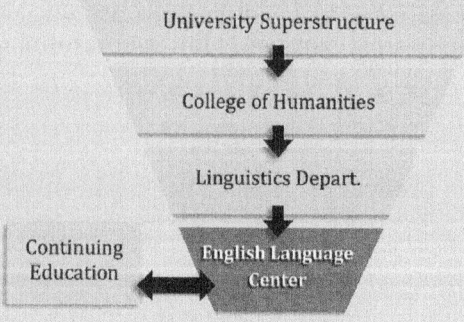

Figure 6.1 ELC Administrative Structure.

Support Staff

Support staff are in place to provide assistance to administrators, teachers, and students. This staff serves in the main office, the self-access study center (SASC), and the computer lab. The Executive Assistant supervises the part-time student secretaries in the main office, as well as manages the paid and volunteer tutors who work in the SASC. The part-time secretaries answer the phones, address questions from students, teachers, and visitors, make copies, check out resources to teachers and students, and complete a wide variety of the assignments to support the ELC programs. The tutors in the SASC meet with students by appointment to provide assistance with homework. The tutors provide feedback on writing assignments, meet with small groups of students for speaking practice, respond to grammar homework, and give input to students on their work. Assistant Computer Support Representatives (CSR) and Lab Attendants work in the computer lab. The Assistant CSRs provide support with computers and technology-related questions in the building. The lab attendants respond to student questions about computer assignments that students have received in class.

Resources

The ELC is housed in a university building that serves multiple purposes. The facilities of the building include a computer lab, a self-access study center (SASC), a teacher resource library, part-time teacher offices, full-time teacher offices, a main office with two copy machines, a staff/storage room, 20 classrooms, two small kitchens, and a gymnasium. There are approximately 85 student-accessible computers and 30 computers for faculty and staff use. Because the ELC is a self-supporting institution, its budget is directly related to student enrollment.

Program Strengths

The program has many strengths. All involved with the ELC enjoy the excellent facilities, including the classrooms, the computer labs, the exceptional teacher and student libraries and the many other resources such as the kitchens, gymnasium, the many LCD projectors etc. Though many of the faculty have limited teaching experience, they are energetic and eager to learn and to improve their skills. The administrative and support staff are excellent, and the program has very strong support from the university faculty. Finally, most students seem very happy with the teachers, the curriculum, and the ELC environment and resources.

Curricular Challenges

Despite the many strengths of the ELC, there are a number of challenges administrators would like to address:

1. Not effectively meeting needs of true beginners
2. Not always providing the right kind of English

3. Using only five levels may not reflect the time it takes to learn
4. There is a large proficiency gap between Levels 3 and 4
5. Not designed to accommodate students who repeat a level
6. The content focus in Level 5 has been too unwieldy
7. Level 5 students are not fully prepared for university-level study
8. No systematic approach to vocabulary teaching and learning

Contextual Synthesis Example B

The following contextual synthesis comes from an intensive English program, one that operates in a nearby city, as the program in example A. In fact, teachers in one program often hold simultaneous contracts in the other. In this IEP, students are matriculated and do receive college credit for passing some of the classes, which is general education credit and can count toward the completion of foreign language requirements.

Contextual Description of a University ESL Program

Contextual Information

Program Mission

The mission of the intensive English language program is to help non-native English-speaking students understand and successfully use academic English at an American university. To accomplish this goal, our faculty and coursework provide a broad range of excellent academic and social opportunities. These opportunities help students develop and show proficiency in the skills of reading, writing, grammar, and listening/speaking.

Historical Contexts

This ESL program resides in the College of General Education with basic math, basic English, and a few other skills-based, introductory, and career-exploration programs. The ESL program is self-funded and thus financially independent from the university;

Running Commentary

We learn that the program is designed for academic preparation and that it provides social opportunities as an important curricular component.

It becomes apparent that this synthesis is partially designed to respond to an advancement problem. In fact, the rest of the synthesis is made up of information from various contextual and learner analyses.

however, the university does provide some administrative control and oversight. Currently, the ESL Program consists of 5 levels:

Basic (low–beginning)
Level 1 (high–beginning)
Level 2 (low–intermediate)
Level 3 (high–intermediate)
Level 4 (advanced)

Teachers have been complaining for years that a significant portion of their students are consistently placed into classes that are academically too advanced for them. This problem seems to be more prevalent and severe among continuing as opposed to new students, as well as in classes with high numbers of non-traditional resident students and in Level 4 classes. Teachers of Level 4 often report that anywhere from one-third to two-thirds of their students are not prepared for the rigor of the advanced level, which is supposed to prepare students to successfully take undergraduate courses upon exiting our program. These teachers are then faced with the choice to either water down the curriculum to make it more accessible to the majority of their students or maintain the course rigor, resulting in students who are confused, frustrated, and unable to comprehend the material. Instructors who choose the latter complain that they are failing over half of their students, many of whom are legitimately trying to keep up but are simply not equipped with the academic skills to meet the Level 4 objectives. One proposed solution for

Although this synthesis includes information about placement and advancement mismatches now, future iterations of this synthesis will likely put this information in the historical context section, assuming that the advancement issues are resolved.

We learn here about curricular constraints related to the age, nationality, language learning experience, and future plans of students. The unique mixture of nontraditional international students is very different from the population of nearby language programs.

We learn here about the faculty of the language program. In some ways, the faculty makeup may be typical of other language programs. The education level, however, is rather diverse, since educational backgrounds span from a bachelor's degree to a Ph.D.

The kind of professional development teachers engage in is important because it can signal whether teachers are remaining active in their professional knowledge. In the case of this program, expectations for professional development appear to be minimal.

this problem was to develop an additional level of instruction, but a contextual and needs analysis was performed in advance of any development or implementation to determine if there really was a problem to begin with and to offer alternative/additional suggestions if any problems emerged. This synthesis offers some results from those analyses.

This synthesis indicates areas of weakness and possible solutions solicited from teachers. Although not comprehensive here (the actual analyses would be comprehensive), this document offers the most salient problems and suggestions. As these problems are addressed and resolved, they may or may not become notes in the historical context section of this synthesis.

Student Performance Analysis

The first analysis we performed confirmed teacher suspicions that many students were being advanced without sufficient language skills. Continuing students, in particular, were being advanced without merit. Table 6.2 shows that in almost every level, the majority of students scored below their current level in the end-of-semester proficiency exams. More detailed analyses showed extreme cases of social advancement, such as some students in Level 4 who actually earned Level 1 scores, indicating a total mismatch between proficiency and advancement.

Students

Age

On average, students in the ESL program are a year older than the typical matriculated student body. At 25, this puts the average student into the

Table 6.2 Students prepared to advance based on end-of-semester proficiency scores.

	New Students		Continuing Students	
	Scored below level	Scored into next level	Scored below level	Scored into next level
Basic Level	12%	88%	n/a	n/a
Level 1	52%	48%	73%	27%
Level 2	48%	52%	83%	17%
Level 3	60%	40%	88%	12%
Level 4	69%	31%	92%	8%
Average	48%	52%	84%	16%

"non-traditional" category, meaning that these students are likely more mature, have family and work obligations, and may have been away from formal schooling for some time. This is a mixed bag in that some of these attributes can both hinder and **facilitate** language learning. For instance, more mature students are better able to monitor and control their emotions, but they may also have more inhibitions against appearing foolish.

Nationality

Almost 40% of students come from Latin American countries, including Mexico, Chile, and Brazil, among others. Asian students make up another 28%, followed by Middle Eastern students (mostly from Saudi Arabia). The large percentage of Spanish- and Arabic-speaking students presents something of a challenge in terms of linguistic diversity. Many students associate with peers who speak the same native language, and classes may be dominated by one language group. Teachers therefore need to be sensitive to these demographics and seek to provide diversity in group work or otherwise encourage English language use in classes. Most of our students (90%) are international; just 10% are long-term immigrant students.

English Language Study Experience

ESL students in our program also tend to come with some experience learning English as a foreign language in their home countries, more than 4 years on average. Students study ESL in our program for an average of just over 2 semesters out of 5 possible. Considering that many students are placed at level 2 or above, this suggests that when students start the ESL program, they remain in it, although many students appear to transfer here from other programs. One reason that ESL students are likely drawn to our program is the college credit and matriculation arrangement offered through the university. In addition, students can study here without meeting a TOEFL requirement, and once in can potentially transfer to other universities without a TOEFL score.

Future Plans

The majority of students plan to continue studying in college after completing their English studies, so our program focuses primarily on teaching academic English rather than vocational English. The most common major among students is engineering, followed closely by business, information technology, and nursing. Students reported *speaking* as their most preferred language skill. It was more popular than all the other skills put together. Overall, our ESL students are very concerned about their speaking instruction. This came up in the staff focus group as well, wherein former students lamented that their speaking instruction did not prepare them adequately for study or employment after the ESL program.

Faculty

Size and Makeup

About 35 teachers work in our program at any given time. These include eight full-time faculty members (three of whom are tenured faculty), and about 27 part-time adjunct instructors. The full-time faculty coordinate the four skills (Reading, Writing, Listening/speaking, Grammar) and also teach 15 credits per semester (three classes), unless they receive a course release for special assignments. The adjunct instructors generally teach one or two classes each semester and thus take on the bulk of the teaching load in the ESL program. However, they have no benefits through the university, such as health care or pension accounts. They share a common work room instead of having dedicated offices. Half of the adjunct instructors also teach at other ESL programs in the area.

Education and Experience

The average age of teachers in our program is 40 years, suggesting a fairly mature group of teachers with significant life experience to draw upon. Most instructors (70%) hold a master's degree in TESOL as their highest degree, though some instructors hold only a bachelor's degree and three instructors hold a Ph.D. Teachers report having taught ESL for an average of 7.5 years, 4 of which have been in our program. Nearly all of our ESL faculty are native English speakers.

Professional Development

All teachers report at least some measure of professional development to improve their teaching. The most common form is on-the-job learning, which includes learning from teaching classes and self-reflection. In other words, the most common approach to improving professionally was nothing more sophisticated than working and thinking about work. The next most common form of professional development reported was formal teacher training through graduate coursework. Almost no teachers attend professional conferences or publish research in academic venues, since these activities are neither required nor supported financially by our program.

Programmatic Problems

Teachers have expressed a number of frustrations with our ESL program. The largest category relates to relaxed administrative support, especially in enforcing policies of attendance and cheating. This may be a sign that attendance and cheating policies are currently unenforceable or do not meet the needs of the students. Teachers have also commented on poor placement and advancement conditions, some stating that students were incorrectly placed, that there is too much variety in student skill level within a single class, and that students are advanced without appropriate skill. Also, teachers have expressed frustration with textbooks and the overall curriculum in that the textbooks do not align with student needs or curricular expectations. This may be due to poor textbook selection, but it may also be because the class objectives are too vague and thus make it difficult to know what parts of the textbook should be emphasized, used, or abandoned.

Suggestions for our ESL Program

Teachers have made several suggestions for improving the ESL program. The most frequent comment is to provide more professional development. Teachers want training, guidance, and encouragement on their work as language teaching professionals. Teachers have also recommended better academic standards, including more rigorous and explicit objectives and better assessments. They have additionally suggested better communication among instructors and better textbooks.

Box 6.2   The Cookie-Cutter Curriculum

In order to reduce costs and increase profits, large home building companies will often build houses using standard designs and construction plans in large-scale developments. This can lead to neighborhoods where all of the houses have similar or even identical floorplans, resulting in what some have termed *cookie-cutter* house designs.

Even in incidences of identical construction, can two houses (even cookie-cutter houses) really be exactly the same? In principle, perhaps, but in practice, we say no. There are myriad forces that act on even identical houses to make them different. These forces include the type of ground the houses are built on; variations in the underground water table; wind, sun, and shade patterns; and proximity to other homes. In addition, the humans who occupy these homes add their own personalities through both interior and exterior designs, as well as the sounds, smells, and sights of daily living. The number of occupants (including pets and couch surfers) affects the personality and ultimately the context of seemingly identical homes.

Likewise, there are no cookie-cutter curricula. Two programs with identical purposes will still have countless contextual differences. These include differences in mission statements, course offerings, student demographics, teacher qualifications, curricular oversight, budgets, tuition, programmatic culture, and so on.

Organizational behavior theorists recognize that adjusting to a new work environment can be very difficult for numerous reasons (see Brown & Lent, 2005). We have found the same to be true for teachers who accept a position in a different language program. Even though the essential job might be identical in both programs, the purpose and culture are often very different. This provides the first justification for articulating one's context: it allows curriculum designers to know just what they are dealing with. An added benefit of such a document is that it can help new teachers understand their jobs more quickly.

See Box 6.2 for an analysis of whether any two curricula are actually the same.

Contextual Synthesis Example C

The last contextual synthesis is shorter, looks very different from the previous two, and comes from a university writing program where ESL classes are taught. This synthesis focuses more on the historical context of the program after major curricular changes were implemented. It also offers some generic student needs that help illustrate the unique nature of the program.

ESL Writing Curriculum

Context: The ESL writing program moved from the English Department to the Linguistics Department in the 1980s. Meanwhile, the developmental writing course was outsourced from the English department to a third-party community college in 1993. Finally, the First Year Composition program (FYC) was separated from the English Department in 2004. Thus, under the most recent system, a student designated as a freshman ESL writer began in the Linguistics department (taking one or more courses in the series), then moved to Developmental Writing at a Community College, and then to the FYC program in a confusing, uncoordinated, and labyrinthine workflow shown in Figure 6.2.

Until 2010, the ESL program in the Linguistics Department was *coordinated* by long-term lecturers without tenure, though the official *director* had been a separate position held by a linguistics professor with tenure. But this

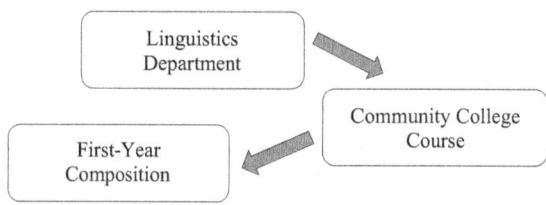

Figure 6.2 Early ESL writing structure.

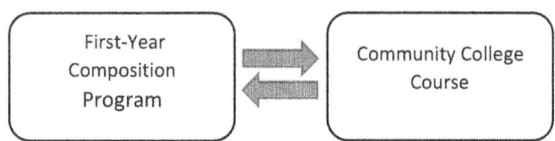

Figure 6.3 Revised ESL writing structure.

was by appointment and did not necessarily reflect the interests or expertise of the faculty member.

In 2013, however, much of this changed. The FYC program assumed responsibility for the ESL classes formerly housed in the Linguistics department so that ESL freshmen would begin by taking ESL courses as supervised in the FYC program, move to the community college for one course, and then return for their final FYC experience, as in Figure 6.3. With this move came better oversight of the ESL program, as it is now directed by a tenured faculty member with practical experience with teaching ESL teachers and a supportive research agenda. The ESL program is also partially administered with the assistance of graduate students, lecturers, and a dedicated support staff. The ESL program is funded by the Provost's office, with funds approved by the office of the Vice Provost of Undergraduate Education, whose commitment to ESL needs on campus is strong.

In fall 2013, a total of 655 international and Generation 1.5 (resident US-educated) ESL students were placed into one of the ESL classes in the FYC program. It is anticipated that this number will grow incrementally as the university actively enrolls greater numbers of international students. This emphasis on admitting more international students is part of a university-sponsored initiative that is projected to increase overall student enrollment at the university by 5000 new students.

Our three ESL courses comprise a developmental writing sequence for undergraduate students who require language instruction. Students may be placed in one of three ESL courses in this sequence (ESL 1, 2, or 3). After completing Level 3, they move on to a developmental writing course administered on our campus by a local community college. This is the final developmental course prior to their FYC class.

Learner Assumptions: Students in this program are placed here by scores on an entrance examination and are under extreme pressure to complete the course within a small number of semesters. Together, this situation makes for students who are somewhat resistant to these classes and are eager to move on as quickly as possible. They are also concurrently enrolled as full-time matriculated undergraduates, and thus their academic focus is split among other major and general courses.

There are at least two major student populations: resident and international ESL students. Resident students generally have a high familiarity with American culture and are "ear learners," meaning that they tend to learn language more by hearing it than studying the written form. They may even sound like native English speakers and yet write like ESL students. International students generally have little knowledge of American culture but have studied English as a foreign language for years in their home countries. They are usually "eye learners," meaning that they are more comfortable learning through textbook and worksheet study than through talking or conversation. They may have an intense understanding of grammar and yet struggle to produce error-free prose.

Student Needs: At all levels, students need to develop skills of writing, revision, citation, reading, vocabulary, sentence structure, and grammar. Lower-level students have a greater need for vocabulary, sentence structure, and grammar. Higher-level students have a greater need for audience awareness, genre awareness, and persuasion.

Student Wants: Teachers in all classes should focus on determining student wants and, to the degree possible, selecting materials and activities that address these wants.

Mission Statement: The ESL 1–3 Series educates L2 and Generation 1.5 ESL learners in areas of grammar, vocabulary, reading, and composition in order to prepare them for university-level writing in their discipline-specific courses, as well as the first-year and second-year writing classes. This ESL series meets students at their language level by providing classes that are targeted to distinct language levels, which progress from a strong focus on grammar to high-level composition tasks. In all classes, the curriculum provides developmental English instruction about (and requires practice of) cultural, linguistic, and rhetorical competencies to enable multilingual writers to succeed in a top-tier, US research institution.

Planning a Contextual Synthesis

Creating the synthesis, especially if it involves updating any of the governing documents, is a big task that requires planning and might require the assistance of several people involved in curricular design or revision. We advise dividing the tasks of the contextual synthesis among members of a curriculum committee and then setting deadlines to ensure that those tasks are completed and reported on.

In Figure 6.4, we illustrate an example of a planning schedule that was used to organize the various analyses in a curricular redesign. The program

ESL Program Task Schedule

Task	Description	Responsible	Due Date
Historical Context	• Schedule meetings with faculty and admin • Collect historical info • Historical context write-up	John John John	Jan 10 Feb 10 March 10
Program Data	• Compile program data • Analyze program data • Write-up program data	John Deb Deb	Jan 20 Feb 10 Feb 28
Student Surveys	• Send out surveys to students • Qualitative survey analysis • Quantitative survey analysis • Analysis Write-up	John Deb Robert Robert	Jan 10 Feb 17 Feb 17 March 17
Teacher Surveys	• Send out surveys to teachers • Qualitative survey analysis • Quantitative survey analysis • Analysis Write-up	John Deb Robert Robert	Jan 17 March 24 March 31 April 20
Focus Groups	• Schedule focus groups • Teacher analysis • *Teacher write-up* • Admin analysis • *Admin write-up* • Student analysis • *Student write-up*	John Robert Robert Deb Deb Deb Deb	March 1 March 24 March 31 March 24 March 31 April 7 April 14
Governing Docs Analysis	• Writing goals & outcomes • Reading goals & outcomes • Listening/Speaking goals & outcomes • Grammar goals & outcomes	Robert Greg Deb & Robert Chad & Robert	April 7 April 7 April 14 April 21
Final Report and Contextual Synthesis	• Write up of report	Robert	May 27

Figure 6.4 Planning schedule for a curriculum redesign.

served more than 200 students and offered ESL skill-based classes at five different levels, from true-beginning to high-intermediate. The curriculum analysis took one full semester (about 15 weeks) and the work of several teachers who served on the curriculum committee.

A planning document like this ensures that all the major tasks are completed that inform the contextual synthesis. Other tasks are not included on the table but might be needed or helpful, such as a revision of the mission statement, examination of class objectives and outcomes, and vision documents indicating where the program is headed. Small curricular revisions might require less information and analysis and may only require the efforts of one or two people and very little planning at all.

The planning document we have presented outlines major components in a succinct manner, but there is always room for added detail, such as an explanation of what each analysis consists of, a full timeline for each project, and a complete list of individuals involved. The focus group feature, for instance, required the coordination of many details among faculty, staff, administrators, and students. Each focus group consisted of several hour-long meetings with 4–6 teachers, students, and administrators (separate meetings for each group). Each meeting required planning, coordinating schedules, and determining focus questions; much of this was handled by the curriculum developers in concert with the program's lead administrative assistant. In each meeting, we needed a discussion leader and note taker, who also created an audio recording of each session. The session leaders had to remain objective since they would ask about the program's strengths and weaknesses and probe into other areas that were not covered by teacher or student surveys. Afterward, the session leader needed to synthesize the session by using notes, the recording, and personal impressions and insights. All told, the focus group sessions took about 6 weeks from start to finish.

Of course, not all curricular syntheses require so large an investment in time and resources. Sometimes, the synthesis planning procedure can be rather small, informal, and/or routine. In one adult education program we are aware of, a single, experienced teacher was responsible for all aspects of a language program that consisted, on average, of 3–6 mixed-skill classes. The program lasted only ten weeks and then was essentially dissolved until the next year. In a sense, each iteration of the program required a fresh contextual analysis based on new student and teacher demographics, but these were easily and quickly analyzed by a single individual and then documented in personal notes as a synthesis. And while the student and teacher demographics changed yearly, many features of the curriculum remained the same, so the task was not especially daunting or time consuming.

Other similarly simple and easy curricular changes take place any time a teacher edits his or her syllabus for a new class. The syllabus in many ways reflects updated assumptions or observations about curricular contexts and includes many governing documents for the class. Typically, a teacher makes changes alone or perhaps in consultation with a colleague or supervisor; thus, the analysis planning itself can be very informal for small, localized changes.

Addressing Challenges Identified in the Contextual Synthesis

In the end, a contextual synthesis does more than just describe a curriculum, though that is a major aim. The most important outcome of a synthesis is an identification of problems that need to be addressed. Generally, curricular analyses and revisions are initiated because some curricular problems are already known to exist. The various analyses and culminating synthesis demonstrate, illustrate, contextualize, and/or quantify complex curricular problems. That is why there is so much wisdom in taking the time and energy to deeply understand a problem before attempting to solve it.

The curricular analyses might uncover more than just one single problem or challenge, and examining all the challenges in the broader context of a program is an appropriate place to begin looking for the origin of problems as well as possible ways to address those problems. Sometimes, a particularly obvious challenge may prompt the need for change, and yet, the most obvious challenges may not always be the most important challenges to address. Therefore, it is important to carefully evaluate all of the challenges a program faces and then to prioritize them.

For instance, if teachers in a program appear to be unprepared for their classes and student enrollment is consistently reducing each semester, the latter problem seems bigger. After all, without students, it does not matter how prepared the teachers are. However, addressing the teacher issue first might help solve the enrollment problem. Even if all the challenges are equally important, limited time and resources might prevent curriculum developers from addressing all of the problems at the same time.

Not all challenges within a particular program are likely to have a simple curricular solution. For example, problems associated with a lack of administrative support for particular aspects of a program might not be something that could be resolved at the curricular level. Nevertheless, such challenges should be included in the contextual description because they could impact curriculum development in significant ways. However, when a contextual synthesis is informed by contextual and learner analyses, it includes a great deal of information vital to the context of the curriculum and helps the reader to consider possible ways to improve the curriculum.

Chapter Summary

This chapter represents the culmination of the first five chapters of this book. All the contextual and learner analyses, as well as the creation of a mission statement and other governing documents, come to a head in the contextual synthesis. Such a synthesis describes the most salient and unique components of a curriculum for the benefit of current and future teachers as well as governing bodies, administrators, and possibly other stakeholders. In addition, the contextual synthesis lists curricular challenges or problems that need to be addressed. These challenges should be fully contextualized, given their prominence on the contextual synthesis so that curriculum developers can begin designing solutions.

A contextual synthesis does not have a length requirement or limit. It can be formatted in any way that seems reasonable and should include information pertinent to the program for which it is written. The very least requirement is that it should be informed by some kind of contextual and learner analysis. For large-scale, complex programs, the analysis and synthesis process may need to be planned pragmatically and assigned to specific individuals to keep things moving. Once challenges are identified through the analysis process, they need to be prioritized so that the most important challenges are addressed first.

Activities

Activity 6.1

Consider your current program or a program you are familiar with. Begin sketching out a contextual synthesis based on what you know about the program. It may be helpful to use the questions in the section titled "What Should Be Included in a Contextual Synthesis"?

Activity 6.2

Compare and contrast the three example contextual syntheses in this chapter. How are the syntheses alike and different? What features do you like or dislike? What information is the most helpful in understanding the program? What additional information would you prefer in each synthesis to help you understand the nuances of each program?

Activity 6.3

Compare one of the sample syntheses to your current program or one you are familiar with. What are some of the most obvious ways in which the sample institution may be similar to, as well as different from, your program?

Activity 6.4

Find the online web presence of two language programs you are familiar with. Read through their websites to get a sense of the critical features that make the program unique and that may belong in a contextual synthesis.

Activity 6.5

Consider the eight challenges included at the end of the contextual synthesis example A. Do each of these challenges seem equally important, or do some challenges seem more important than others? How might these be prioritized? One approach that might provide insight is to return to some of the critical questions discussed in the What Should Be Included in a Contextual Synthesis? section. For example, why is the teaching and learning needed, who are the students, what is being taught, and how is it being taught? There may be insights from such critical questions that make it easier to prioritize efforts to create curricular solutions to programmatic challenges.

Activity 6.6

Given what you know about your current program or one you have recently worked in, list several problems or challenges you think should be addressed, and then prioritize them from most urgent to least.

Activity 6.7

If you have access to your program's contextual and learner analyses, draft a one-page contextual synthesis that includes both program strengths and weaknesses. For advanced readers, write a full contextual synthesis for your program. Suggestions: It may be helpful to use a piece of paper with a line drawn down the middle. Use the left column to list the most salient characteristics of your program that you believe should be included in the synthesis. For inspiration, return to the section titled, "What should be included in a contextual synthesis?" and the sample contextual descriptions included in this chapter. Then, use the space in the right column to prioritize your list according to importance. Be sure to include the strengths and challenges of your program. Where possible, have colleagues or other stakeholders review your work and offer suggestions and alternative perspectives. Make appropriate refinements to your description.

Chapter 6 Appendix

University Preparation ESL Writing Curriculum
Mission Statement and Course Goals
Mission Statement: The University Preparation Series educates L2 and Generation 1.5 ESL learners in areas of grammar, vocabulary, reading, and

Course Goals: Teachers will...				
	Writing 1	**Writing 2**	**Writing 3**	**Writing 4**
Writing	1. Provide students with instruction, activities, and exercise to help them compose academic paragraphs in at least the following genres: a. Response/reaction statement b. Academic or business email or letter c. Report of primary research	1. Provide students with instruction, activities, and exercise to help them develop the skills necessary to write academic texts in at least the following genres: a. Opinion-based essay b. Compare/contrast essay c. Analysis	1. Provide students with instruction, activities, and exercise to help them develop the skills necessary to write persuasive academic papers in at least the following genres: a. Argumentative essay b. Blog post c. Critical response (agree/disagree) essay	1. Provide students with instruction, activities, and exercise to help them develop the skills necessary to write persuasive academic papers
Revision	2. Help students develop revision strategies and manage their revision tasks through peer-review and teacher feedback	2. Help students develop revisions strategies and manage their revision tasks through peer-review, teacher feedback, and tutor feedback	2. Help students develop revisions strategies and manage their revision tasks through self-reflection, peer-review, teacher feedback, and tutor feedback	2. Introduce students to tone, style, and rhetorical conventions in academic writing
Citation	3. Introduce students to appropriate forms of acknowledging sources	3. Introduce students to appropriate forms of acknowledging sources	3. Provide students with strategies and skills for textual research	3. Help students develop revisions strategies and manage their revision tasks through self-reflection, peer-review, teacher feedback, and tutor feedback

Reading	4. Provide students with strategies and skills for reading and comprehending short academic texts	4. Provide students with strategies and skills for critically reading and comprehending short texts in varying genres	4. Provide students with strategies and skills for textual research
Vocabulary	5. Help students enlarge their vocabulary	5. Help students enlarge their academic vocabulary through use of the Academic Word List (AWL)	5. Introduce students to appropriate forms of acknowledging and documenting sources
Sentences	6. Provide students with practice in revising sentences for clarity and grammatical precision	6. Provide students with practice in revising sentences for clarity and grammatical precision	6. Provide students with strategies and skills for reading and comprehending academic source materials
Grammar	7. Help students improve on areas of English grammar that reflect their needs and their assignment requirements through guided instruction and student-centered language learning	7. Help students improve on areas of English grammar that reflect their needs through guided instruction and student-centered language learning	7. Provide students with practice in revising sentences for clarity and grammatical precision
			7. Help students enlarge their academic vocabulary through student-guided vocabulary learning

Figure 6.5 An illustration of the goals for each level of the University Preparation Series courses.

composition in order to prepare them for university-level writing in their discipline-specific courses as well as the first-year and second-year writing classes. This developmental series meets students at their language level by providing classes that are targeted to distinct language levels, which progress from a strong focus on grammar to high-level composition tasks. In all classes, the curriculum provides developmental English instruction about, and requires practice of, cultural, linguistic, and rhetorical competencies to enable multilingual writers to succeed in a top-tier, US research institution. See Figure 6.5 for the Course Goals.

References

Brown, S. D., & Lent, R. W. (Eds.). (2005). *Career development and counseling: Putting theory and research to work*. John Wiley & Sons.

Hillman, D. R., & Werner, T. K. (2017). Capturing generation-based institutional knowledge utilizing design thinking. *Performance Improvement, 56*(6), 28–36. http://dx.doi.org/10.1002/pfi.21704

Wang, F. (2006). Applying case-based reasoning in knowledge management to support organizational performance. *Performance Improvement Quarterly, 19*(2), 173–188. http://dx.doi.org/10.1111/j.1937-8327.2006.tb00371.x

7

Learning Outcomes

Design, Develop, and Implement

Introduction

The next three chapters discuss three essential components of any curriculum: learning outcomes, assessment and feedback, and learning experiences. Curriculum designers need to carefully and thoroughly work through the design, development, and implementation phases for each of these components. They also need to consider the different curricular levels of program, course, and class in order to keep the program cohesive.

Of these many considerations (curricular components, design phases, curricular levels), some can be worked on concurrently, but others need to form the foundation for the rest of the curriculum. For example, at both the program and course levels, it is essential to have clear design specifications that articulate what the learning outcomes include and how they will be structured. These design specifications are like test expectations in that they form a frame for the program and its learning outcomes just as test specifications outline an assessment. Without a clear vision for the design of learning outcomes, developing the learning outcomes would become untidy and muddled. It seems clear that there should be an order—design, develop, and implement at the program, then course, then class level—but this initial order can and should be interrupted by new insights gained from observation, experience, or other feedback.

In Intensive English Programs, the class level is often designed by teachers and informed by program and course curricular decisions; therefore, it will not be focused upon in this chapter. Nevertheless, the principles used to create or modify curriculum at the program and course levels can be applied to classroom instruction. See Boxes 7.1 and 7.2.

Box 7.1 Principled Curriculum Approach

Previous chapters focused extensively on analyzing a curriculum, which forms the outer ring of the ADDIE model of curricular development shown in Figure 7.1. A careful analysis is essential to curricular development or change.

The next three chapters focus on the design, development, and implementation stages in the innermost circle of the ADDIE model. Rather than organize our chapters by design phase, we have chosen to organize them by curricular component. Thus, this chapter relates to the design, development, and implementation of the most basic curricular component—learning outcomes.

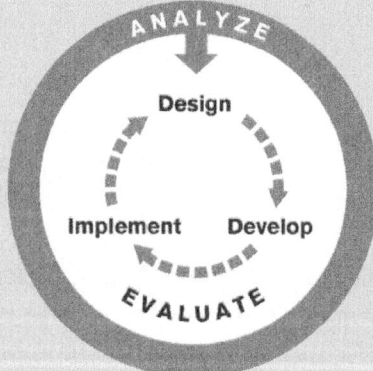

Figure 7.1 Graphic representation of the five steps of the ADDIE model.

Box 7.2 Contextualizing Learning Outcomes

In Chapter 2, this graphic was used to illustrate the place of governing documents in a curriculum in an IEP. Each curricular level has a governing document that is used to develop the learning outcomes. Thus, there are program outcomes, course outcomes, and class outcomes, as shown in Figure 7.2.

In an IEP, the audience for these outcomes is students and teachers and should be comprehensible to both. There may be less programmatic oversight of learning outcomes at the course and class levels, because individual teachers often decide how to translate course goals and class objectives into actual instruction. However, in some programs, the course outcomes are tightly controlled.

	Program Level	*Course Level*	*Class Level*
Governance	Mission	Goals	Objectives
Learning Outcomes	Program Outcomes	Course Outcomes	Class Outcomes
Assessments & Feedback			
Learning Experiences			

Figure 7.2 The program outcomes, course outcomes, and class outcomes in context of missions, goals, and objectives.

The House Metaphor

Learning outcomes fit into the house metaphor with a little effort. It may be convenient to think of them as a list of tasks that laborers should accomplish. But a better way to look at outcomes in the house metaphor is to think of them as a list of tasks that laborers will have accomplished once the house is done. The emphasis, then, is not the doing of the tasks (that comes later, in Chapter 9); rather, the focus is on the finished product and, more precisely, looking through a visionary lens to see the finished product. For homeowners with no experience running electrical wire, an appropriate home-building outcome may go something like this: "By the end of this process, new homeowners will know how to install electrical wire in a home and will have successfully wired their own home." For neophyte laborers, the outcome would be similarly worded. For experienced craftsmen who already know how to accomplish the task at hand, the outcome may simply be a statement of what will be accomplished: "By the end of this process, skilled electricians will have successfully wired yet another home."

From Contextual Synthesis to Learning Outcomes

Prior to this chapter, the steps used to carefully gather and synthesize curriculum data into a contextual synthesis were described. It is essential that the output from that synthesis be influential in shaping the design, development, and implementation of not only the learning outcomes but also the assessment and feedback and learning experience components as well (Christison & Murray, 2021). Therefore, all members of the development team should have access to the synthesis. In some cases, documents such as the samples given in the previous chapter may be useful, and in other cases, an executive summary may be sufficient.

Learning Outcomes for Virtual, Hybrid, and Distant Learning

The contextual synthesis may have suggested unique needs, lacks, and wants in non-traditional contexts. As curriculum developers carefully use these analyses, the concepts, guiding principles, and processes outlined in this chapter will be equally applicable to these contexts. Learning outcomes focus on what students are able to do and not on the teacher delivery of experiences and assessments. However, the articulated learning outcomes will impact the types of learning experiences and assessments that occur in virtual, hybrid, and distant learning.

Learning Outcomes

Throughout the literature on curriculum design, it becomes apparent that several terms related to outcomes are either used synonymously or have slight nuances that differentiate meaning. *Objective, goal, aim, desired result,* and *outcome* are all terms that focus on the end result of some action. Additionally, related terms include *experiential objectives, learning outcomes,* or *institutional aims*. We have chosen to use *outcomes* in our curricular design for a few different reasons.

First, *outcome* is generally used to label the result of some action. For example, people vote for political candidates to fulfill certain government responsibilities. When people talk about the results of the election, they are more likely to use the term *outcome*: "What was the outcome of this year's election?" The prolific use of *outcome* as a word that means *effect* makes it easier for us to talk about the intended result of instruction.

Second, in many contexts, the terms *objective, goal,* or *aim* place emphasis on the actions needed to reach a desired result or outcome. Generally, teachers provide instruction that is intended to result in a change in the learner. The result of this change is the outcome.

Third, in non-language contexts, *outcome* is often used to describe actions or skills that the program or course expects learners to be able to do, while the term *objective* is often used to describe the content to be delivered to students. Language, by its very nature, is much better described as skill proficiency rather than knowledge learned, analyzed, or evaluated.

Guiding Principles

An outcome should be an answer to the following question: What should students be able to do as a result of the intended intervention? In our case, the intervention is language teaching. The following guiding principles should influence the design and development of the learning outcomes:

1. **Outcomes are based on the program mission statement.** The outcomes at both a program and a course level are not divorced from the mission statement. In many ways, the program outcome is a result of the program accomplishing its intended purpose or mission. Some segments of mission statements may be worded so that they can be used as program outcomes. Course outcomes should be connected to program outcomes, and class outcomes should be attached to course outcomes. This relationship ensures that learning outcomes at each curricular level are tied to the mission statement.
2. **Outcomes are based on the information obtained in the contextual synthesis.** In the previous chapters regarding analysis, curriculum designers looked at the context and the learners to identify student and program needs. Outcomes should work within the articulated contextual synthesis and operationalize the learner gaps to maximize learning. The assumptions and perceptions articulated in the synthesis can also be guiding factors that shape the writing of effective learning outcomes.
3. **Outcomes are feasible.** While it is easy to draft an all-encompassing learning outcome that describes significant increases in language learned, it is essential that the outcome be realistic and attainable. There are three primary constraints that affect the feasibility of a learning outcome: time, resources, and the actual nature of language learning. Regardless of whether developers are renovating an existing program or crafting a new one, they probably have a good idea of these constraints. Depending on individual situations, developers will most likely have to construct their learning outcomes with these in mind. In other situations, learning outcomes may influence the structure and resource allocation of a program.
4. **Outcomes are measurable.** Each outcome should be measurable through appropriate and valid assessments (Graves, 2000; Christison & Murray, 2021). These assessments may be quantitative or qualitative in nature. They may be objective or subjective. Some

outcomes may be directly assessable and others indirectly assessable. Regardless of the type of assessment, the outcome should be measurable in order to evaluate the effectiveness of the program as a whole or as an individual part of the program.

5. **Outcomes are clear and complete.** Outcomes should cover the full range of expected language proficiency and should be clear to teachers, students, and other stakeholders. As a discrete statement, a learning outcome should include all the pertinent information that clearly articulates the intended student performance.

As long as the outcomes meet the aforementioned criteria, they can take on any structure. It is also important to recognize that learning outcomes that meet these criteria should facilitate the selection or creation of learning experiences (Tyler, 2013). Generally, *students* are the subject followed by the modal *can* or *be able to* and an action verb related to language production or reception (Graves, 2000). Often, outcomes may also include qualifying or clarifying language that explains the degree to which students can perform and the context in which the language occurs.

Designing Program Learning Outcomes

With a general sense of *what* learning outcomes are, and an acknowledgement that a programmatic analysis should inform development of those outcomes, consider the following step-by-step process of creating learning outcomes. The present section deals with *designing* program learning outcomes, which will be followed by developing and then implementing those outcomes, all at the program level. Subsequent sections in this chapter will deal with designing, developing, and implementing outcomes at the course and then class level. See Box 7.3.

Box 7.3   Why Design Outcomes Before Developing Them?

We make an important distinction in this book between designing a curriculum and developing one. The purpose of designing before developing is to ensure a quality standard and allow for collaboration. For example, if the curriculum has thoughtful and stable design specifications, then multiple developers can work on fleshing out the curriculum, and they can do it with a certain quality of work in mind. Additionally, a careful design means that future curriculum developers can look back at the original design

> specifications and make changes systematically and strategically rather than haphazardly or capriciously.
>
> So what exactly does a curriculum design look like? It's usually a collection of informal tables and notes about what various curricular components should look like and include. In some cases, designs are discussed orally in design meetings, so the rushed notes or minutes from those meetings serve as the official design documents. In the following sections, we offer some straightforward examples of design specifications.

Designing learning outcomes involves combining the guiding principles listed earlier with the desired outcomes for the program and adding additional specifications by which the finished learning outcomes can be evaluated. These specifications may include a standard length, a common tense, or other details that are important to a program.

At the program level, we've already taken a giant step toward writing learning outcomes. The mission statement most likely includes text that gives purpose to a program. Now, take that purpose and adapt it into a statement that reflects the outcome of implementing the program in terms of student performance. In many situations, the mission statement may already be stated in terms of a learning outcome. Consider the following mission statement: *Our mission is to prepare non-native English language learners for university coursework.*

Let's look at the guiding principles:

1. If the mission statement and program learning outcome are one and the same, then it is safe to say that the learning outcome is based on the program's mission statement.
2. Assuming that the contextual analysis indicated that this is the need of the students, this criterion is met as well.
3. It is feasible to successfully prepare students for university coursework.
4. It is something that can be measured.
5. The mission statement, or program learning outcome, is very clear and complete.

The simplicity of using the mission statement as the overarching program learning outcome is appealing, refreshing, and lean. However, like many other programs, this outcome might not work for every participant who comes through a program. In an IEP, students of varying proficiency start a program and leave it at different points depending on their circumstances. Some students decide to transfer to another program, while others decide to return home. For these, and perhaps other reasons, one single program-level outcome is usually insufficient. Instead, an IEP generally needs program-level outcomes for each level of instruction, each skill area within that level, and perhaps even different outcomes for different types of learners. Thus, programmatic learning outcomes need to be created for every course.

Referring to the contextual synthesis is essential. What is the proficiency of the students entering the program? What proficiency do they need to be completely prepared for university coursework? Whether a curriculum designer is starting from scratch or already has existing data, looking at predefined proficiency levels, such as the ACTFL, ILR (Interagency Language Roundtable), or CEFR (Common European Framework of Reference) scales, can be essential in determining program learning outcomes. A given program may already have some sort of proficiency scale that works well.

It is essential to look back at the contextual synthesis for other important data. In addition to answering the questions about proficiency, there may be other information that will prove helpful. For example, if students enter and exit the program at varying proficiency levels, it would be helpful to know the minimum time students are required to be a part of a program. In many programs, this may be one semester. In other programs, it may be two semesters, or the program may be structured such that students are required to continue until they reach the highest proficiency offered by the school. If students generally only stay in the program for a single semester, an important question to be answered is: What proficiency should students reach after completing a semester of instruction based on their entry level?

To illustrate the somewhat complex design process for a full set of programmatic outcomes, let's imagine that the contextual analysis provides the following information:

- The mission statement is to prepare non-native English language learners for university coursework.
- The program contains six levels of instruction and teaches three ESL classes at each level, which students are required to take concurrently: Listening/Speaking, Reading, and Writing.
- The program uses the ACTFL scale as a proficiency measure for placing and grouping students with similar proficiencies.

Level	Entry Proficiency	Exit Proficiency
1	Novice Low & Novice Mid	Novice High
2	Novice High	Intermediate Low
3	Intermediate Low	Intermediate High
4	Intermediate High	Advanced Low
5	Advanced Low	Advanced Mid
6	Advanced Mid	Advanced High

Figure 7.3 Level learning outcomes based on our design specifications and using the prototype as a template.

- ESL students entering the program range from Novice Low to Advanced Mid.
- ESL students complete at least one semester of the program.

Based on this information, a basic structure of the program can be designed that will help developers write more specific program learning outcomes for each level.

The mission statement or program learning outcome does not state that all students in the program will reach an Advanced High proficiency. It does say that the program prepares students for university coursework. If students enter with Novice High proficiency (level 2) and leave with Intermediate Low proficiency (level 3), those students are more prepared than they were at the beginning of the level, but are still not ready for university coursework (see Figure 7.3).

With this context in mind, there is a clear need to add program learning outcomes that correspond with the various levels of proficiency. Based on the contextual synthesis, curriculum designers create guidelines or design specifications that will inform the development of the program learning outcomes. Creating these design specifications is the primary goal of the design process. The actual outcomes are not created until the development process, which is described in the following section. Furthermore, design specifications should be unique to each program. While some sample design specifications are offered in Figure 7.4, these are only a handful of possible specifications.

The specifications are clearly informed by the principles of effective outcomes. Designers (or developers, for that matter) may need to create additional specifications moving forward. It's important to remember the iterative process of curriculum development and to be willing to go back and make changes, additions, or deletions to the specifications. See Box 7.4.

Guiding Principles	Design Specifications	Rational
Outcomes should be based on the program mission statement.	Outcomes should focus on academic English	The mission statement indicates that the program prepares non-native English language learners for university coursework.
Outcomes should be based on information obtained during the contextual synthesis.	Outcomes should be based on ACTFL proficiency levels	The contextual synthesis indicates that students, teachers, and administrators are most familiar with ACTFL guidelines as opposed to other frameworks.
	Outcomes should include information about functions students can perform, text types, fluency, and comprehensibility	These domains are closely related to the domains used by ACTFL in determining proficiency and provide a framework for future curriculum development.
	Outcomes should account for students who enter and exit at different places in the program	The contextual synthesis describes the learners as being at various proficiency levels. It also indicates that most students leave the program prior to having Advanced High proficiency.
	Outcomes should be general enough to describe overall proficiency	The contextual synthesis also indicated that students who are less proficient in only one skill area may have sufficient proficiency to move to a different level of instruction upon completion of a semester of coursework. Therefore, the outcomes will be most helpful if they are written generally.

Figure 7.4 Program Learning Outcome Design Specifications.

Guiding Principles	Design Specifications	Rational
Outcomes are feasible.	Outcomes should represent what can be accomplished in one semester	Setting higher expectations of what can be accomplished during an academic period of time will most likely result in outcomes that are difficult or impossible to achieve.
Outcomes are measurable.	Outcomes should mostly be stated in terms of what students can do	When stated with student ability and proficiency in mind, the outcomes can inform assessment designs that are focused on student proficiency and learning activities that help students increase or enhance the language ability and proficiency.
	Outcomes should include statements that show student limitations or inabilities	Articulating what students are unable to do can help identify proficiency ceilings and floors.
Outcomes are clear and complete.	Outcomes should be needed for each level in the program	Students, teachers, and administrators need to understand the proficiency expectations for those entering and exiting the program at any level of proficiency.
	Outcomes should be written for all Skill Areas at each level—Listening, Speaking, Reading, Writing	The contextual synthesis affirmed the assumption that overall proficiency is best measured by looking at all skill areas. In order to be complete, all skill areas need to be addressed.
	Outcomes should address grammar, pronunciation and vocabulary in terms of the various skill areas	The four major skill areas are supported by these subskills, which should be addressed in the learning outcomes.

Figure 7.4 (Continued)

> **Box 7.4 Creating a Prototype**
>
> Before developing program learning outcomes, there is one other activity that teeters on the edge between design and development: *prototyping*.
>
> While a complete fleshing-out of the entire set of program learning outcomes would be best suited to the development process, creating an example prototype or template of the learning outcomes for each level can be helpful so that those involved have a clear vision regarding the targeted end product.
>
> The prototype should be simple, and those creating it should not feel obligated to have a finished product or spend exorbitant amounts of time wordsmithing. Figure 7.5 illustrates one prototype that could serve as a template for objective documents at all levels of the program.
>
> *Level 1: Novice Low/Mid → Novice High*
>
> *Students can perform the following functions while meeting the*
>
> **Listening**
>
> **Function:** Students can understand main ideas and major details of direct, simple and predictably organized speech. They demonstrate understanding of short, discrete factual statements, instructions, questions, and descriptions through appropriate responses.
>
> **Text:** Students comprehend short conversations consisting of simple sentences with clear turn-taking about all survival needs and limited social demands with some repetition and non-verbal support.
>
> **Fluency:** Students can listen to discourse appropriate speed at 70% comprehension
>
> **Speaking**
>
> **Function:** Students can participate in conversations and make presentations on some familiar topics. They almost exclusively...
>
> **Figure 7.5** A sample prototype that could be a template for objective documents at all levels of the program.

Developing Program Learning Outcomes

With clear design specifications and an example prototype, curriculum writers can now begin to construct the actual full learning outcomes for this IEP. Essentially, development is the construction arm of the design process. Developers create what was designed. Their successful and effective development is a foundation for the other two curricular components to be discussed in the next two chapters: feedback and assessment and learning experiences.

While there are different ways to approach the development process, some key principles should be remembered and followed to ensure successful development.

1. **Development is an iterative process.** Developing any artifact for use in the curriculum should be taken seriously and revised often. Constant modification based on effective evaluation ensures that the curriculum is well-planned, intentional, and better accepted by stakeholders.
2. **Development should be collaborative.** One person developing and evaluating the curriculum often results in a product that lacks insights from stakeholders. Evaluations of the product are more likely to be biased when conducted by the sole developer. Collaborative work brings various stakeholders together who can contribute in different ways; however, small groups may produce more than large groups. A lean team of developers can accomplish more goals in less time than a large team with several developers.
3. **Completeness and clarity are more important than polished work.** The entire curriculum design experience is interconnected. The content should certainly be complete and accurate, but polishing is often best left until after the product has been implemented and evaluated. Implementation of a development draft can be just as effective as the implementation of polished development versions.

The Iterative Development Process

Any inventor or engineer can attest to the iterative nature of their product development. This is no different in terms of curriculum development. The various iterations should result from evaluations of the developed product—in this case, it is our level learning outcomes. Even though multiple iterations of the development-trial-evaluation cycle could go on forever, focused and planned evaluation can maximize the time spent going through these iterations. This is not the same thing as trial and error.

Pre-implementation iterations are characterized by frequent, informal evaluations on the part of the developers. During the development process, stakeholders should be able to weigh in on prototypes so that developers can adapt the product in such a way that reflects the values of the stakeholders and the previously articulated design of the learning outcomes.

Piloting a prototype and collecting feedback is another step in the process that can yield revised iterations. Stakeholders and developers cannot predict all of the potential issues by simply looking at the prototype—it needs to be piloted. The prototype provides additional insight that can only come from a soft implementation of the product.

Collaborative Development

Consider the following cases as potential ways to approach the development phase, keeping in mind that these examples may not work in every situation.

The Collaborative Solo Worker

Sarah is a faculty member in an intensive English program. The program employs about 30 faculty members to teach 150 enrolled ESL students. She was recently part of a committee of five individuals who analyzed the current curriculum and subsequently created design specifications for program learning outcomes at each level of instruction. The chair of the committee asked Sarah to use the design specifications to develop learning outcomes for an intermediate level in their program. Other members of the committee were given the same task for other levels. Despite Sarah's other responsibilities, she manages to find 30 minutes each day to work on this project. Each week, she emails a draft of her learning outcomes to one of the colleagues on the committee. She receives feedback and continues to work. In turn, she also gives feedback to her peers who are doing the same task but for different levels.

The Collaborative Pair

Lidia is also a faculty member in an intensive English program similar to Sarah's. After contributing to the design specifications for their program learning outcomes, Lidia is assigned to work with Triston to write outcomes for a novice level in their program. They meet together weekly for about four hours and work on the outcomes together. After the outcomes have been completed, they are reviewed by another small group, and Lidia and Triston likewise review the work of their peers.

The Collaborative Working Meeting

Five faculty members, three administrators, and four interns in an intensive English program are revising the learning outcomes for each of the six levels in their program. They meet twice each week in a large conference room. One of the administrators is the curriculum coordinator. She leads these meetings and gives directions. The group is divided into pairs, and each pair is given a task that moves the entire group toward unified goals. During the first two weeks, the curriculum coordinator has each pair work on learning outcomes for a specific proficiency level. During the following two weeks, everyone is given a copy of the drafted revisions and put into four groups of three. Each group is assigned a skill area and is tasked with revising to improve conformity and cohesion among the various levels. For example, the reading skill area group first looks at the reading outcomes for the first two levels. They look for discrepancies or inconsistencies between the two levels. Are the outcomes for the lower of the two levels more difficult than those listed in the higher level? Is the difference between these levels, as indicated by the learning outcomes, too great?

These are just three ways developers might manage individuals in the development of the designed learning outcomes. Each has advantages and disadvantages. The solo worker has the potential to be more productive, but the end product may benefit from more consistent input from more stakeholders. Working in pairs helps add diversity of thought. The developed product will be stronger through the collaborative process, but the process may take longer. The working meeting is also an interesting concept. It involves several stakeholders contributing in meaningful ways and allows them to become more familiar with the emerging curriculum. It also results in broader successful adoption of the new materials. The power of a working meeting comes from the focused, scheduled, and organized time that people are brought together to work toward a common goal. But, much like the collaborative pair, there is the potential for wasted time through off-task communication or even on-task disagreements.

Completeness and Clarity in Development

Before continuing, it is important to note that curriculum design and curriculum revisions never result in perfect products. Rather than seek perfection, curriculum developers should seek to perfect. At some point, developers need to implement the curriculum and let it try to fly even if the feathers are new. From there, developers can continually monitor and revise the curriculum.

Having said that, the developed artifact should have a sense of completeness. The written learning outcomes should reflect what is in the design specifications. A complete product accounts for every design specification. In some cases, this might mean that the design needs to be revisited to remove impractical or impossible expectations. Perhaps a few minor tweaks to the design might lead to better development. Additionally, the learning outcomes should be written clearly to ensure that there is no ambiguity in conveying the intended learning outcome.

Box 7.5 is an example of level learning outcomes based on our design specifications and using the prototype as a template.

> **Box 7.5 Draft of Level Learning Outcomes**
>
> **Level 1: Novice Low/Mid → Novice High**
>
> *Students can perform the following functions while meeting the outlined text and fluency/comprehensibility expectations.*
>
> **Listening**
>
> **Function:** Students are able to understand direct, simple, and predictably organized speech. They sometimes demonstrate understanding of short, discrete personal statements, classroom instructions, basic questions, and lists of characteristics through appropriate responses.
>
> **Text:** Students comprehend short conversations consisting of simple sentences with clear turn-taking about most survival needs with repetition and nonverbal support. Speech samples will be highly modified in rate and clarity and will consist primarily of high-frequency words and phrases. Speech samples generally consist of no more than two speakers and are primarily a series of direct statements or self-centric descriptions.
>
> **Fluency:** Students can listen to discourse-appropriate speech at 70% comprehension.
>
> **Speaking**
>
> **Function:** Students can meet very limited practical speaking needs. They almost exclusively speak in present tense and typically use recombinations of learned vocabulary and structures. They can handle short interactions in everyday situations by asking and answering a few simple questions. Students express personal meaning by combining and recombining what they have learned or memorized.
>
> **Text:** Students speak in short and discrete sentences that use basic syntax.
>
> **Comprehensibility:** Students can generally be understood by sympathetic listeners who are accustomed to dealing with non-natives, but this usually requires repetition or rephrasing. Students' speech is filled with hesitancy and inaccuracies as they search for appropriate linguistic forms and vocabulary. Students' pronunciation, vocabulary, and syntax are strongly influenced by their first language.
>
> **Reading**
>
> **Function:** Students understand short, non-complex texts that convey basic contextualized information. They can understand key words and cognates, as well as formulaic phrases. They can understand texts that include learned vocabulary and phrases. Students use titles and headings to preview texts. They use scanning to quickly locate known words.

> **Text:** Students comprehend straightforward, non-complex, predictable language as found on schedules, roadmaps, and street signs. Texts are usually engineered specifically for readers at this proficiency level, but often resemble authentic language as found in informational and social texts. The text is primarily made up of single words, phrases, and sentences. These texts primarily contain learned vocabulary.
> **Fluency:** Students can read 200 words per minute or above with 70% comprehension.
>
> **Writing**
>
> **Function:** Students are able to meet very limited, basic, practical writing needs using lists and short messages. They typically write learned vocabulary and structures. They rely mainly on practiced material. They write primarily about personal topics and common elements of daily life.
> **Text:** Students recombine learned vocabulary and structures to create simple sentences on very familiar topics, but are not able to sustain sentence-level writing.
> **Comprehensibility:** Students can be understood by native speakers who are accustomed to the writing of non-natives, but gaps in comprehension may occur.

Implementing Program Learning Outcomes

The next step in our Principled Curriculum Approach is that of implementation. On the one hand, implementation may simply mean getting the word out about the finished outcomes. This might include posting them on a program website or circulating them among a program's faculty members. It might also mean referring to them in decision-making meetings where new curricular proposals are introduced that might affect the existing curriculum. All of this is a simple approach to implementation. A fuller approach recognizes that implementing program learning outcomes is something of a misnomer. Doing so requires designing a method, scope, and sequence by which these outcomes can be achieved. The implementation of such a plan requires the design, development, and implementation of course and class learning outcomes first. In other words, it is not possible to implement program-learning outcomes in a vacuum. They are achieved only as students attend class and complete class learning outcomes, which collectively fulfill course outcomes.

Consider the previously designed levels and the program learning outcomes that have just been created. How will these outcomes be achieved at

Level	Courses				
1	Listening	Speaking	Reading	Writing	Vocabulary
2	Grammar	Listening/Speaking	Reading	Writing	
3	Grammar	Listening/Speaking	Reading	Writing	
4	Grammar	Listening/Speaking	Reading	Writing	
5	Grammar	Listening/Speaking	Reading	Academic Writing	
6	Grammar	Content Based	Content Based	Academic Writing	University Skills

Figure 7.6 Courses needed to meet program learning outcomes.

each level? What courses are necessary to facilitate the proposed language proficiency growth from one level to another? What other considerations should be addressed that will aid in meeting the level learning outcomes? It is also important to consider legal implications. For example, students with ESL I-20s must complete a specified number of hours in class each week.

Continuing with our previous example, look at Figure 7.6—the level 1 learning outcomes. After careful consideration, the curriculum team may decide that there should be five courses offered. Each course will be charged with helping students meet aspects of the level learning outcomes. Every course would focus on a skill area (listening, speaking, reading, and writing). A fifth course could focus on vocabulary to help novice students progress. For level 2, the team may decide to collapse listening and speaking into one course and to add a course for explicit grammar instruction. For Level 6 students, the team may decide that the outcomes are best reached through content-based courses. In the end, course offerings may look similar to those in Figure 7.6.

Designing Course Learning Outcomes

The next step in implementing the program learning outcomes is to design, develop, and implement *course* learning outcomes. As mentioned earlier, the program outcomes cannot be fully realized until the course outcomes are realized. Likewise, course learning outcomes are incomplete without class learning outcomes. Incidentally, all learning outcomes can only be implemented when they are used in tandem with assessment and learning experiences, which will be discussed in future chapters.

At this point, we've already introduced guiding principles for designing learning outcomes that can be used at all curricular levels—program, course, and class. Tunneling through the curricular levels, their wording should be slightly adapted. For example, instead of the course outcomes being based on the program mission statement, they should be based on the program learning outcomes. If these outcomes have been carefully crafted, course learning outcomes can be specific while maintaining a focus on the program mission.

Types of Learning Outcomes

There are myriad ways to classify different learning outcomes. Some designers divide learning outcomes into two categories: general instructional objectives (GIOs) and specific learning outcomes (SLOs). We will do the same, but to stay consistent, we will refer to GIOs as general learning outcomes (GLOs).

GLOs are the core outcomes that students need to achieve. They generally begin with a verb that indicates the type of expected performance. GLOs are succinct, general, and singular. One GLO should refer to only one outcome. Each GLO should be supported by SLOs. SLOs are connected to a GLO in that they state what students should be able to do or how they should perform certain tasks. They must be relevant to the nature of the GLO, and they should be useful to designers, teachers, and students. It is essential to remember that SLOs are representative in nature with regard to their relationship to a GLO. A list of SLOs is not exhaustive; rather, it is a representative sample that illustrates specific learning outcomes that contribute to general ones.

Figure 7.7 outlines design specifications for course learning outcomes in an IEP. Because the design process is iterative in nature, as individuals begin to work with the design specifications, they may need to adjust the design. Additionally, creating a prototype to guide and direct the development of course outcomes can prove beneficial.

Guiding Principles	Design Specifications	Rationale
Outcomes should be based on program learning outcomes.	Course GLOs should focus on performance as indicated in the program learning outcomes. Course SLOs should be based on discrete tasks that, when correctly performed, provide evidence of meeting the GLO.	Program outcomes are based on the mission statement and contextual synthesis. Aligning course outcomes to the performance standards of the program learning outcomes will help students be successful in meeting program outcomes.

Figure 7.7 Course learning outcome design specifications.

Guiding Principles	Design Specifications	Rationale
Outcomes should be based on information obtained during the contextual synthesis.	Course outcomes should focus on academic language tasks.	The contextual synthesis indicates that academic English is the target for instruction.
	Course outcomes should be easily understandable by novice teachers and provide enough detail to inform instruction.	One purpose of the program is to provide graduate students opportunities to gain experience. Many of them are new or novice teachers.
Outcomes are feasible.	Course outcomes should represent what can be accomplished in a given semester.	Setting higher expectations of what can be accomplished during an academic period of time will most likely result in outcomes that are difficult or impossible to achieve.
Outcomes are measurable.	Course outcomes should be stated in terms of what students can do.	When stated with student ability and proficiency in mind, the outcomes can lead to assessments that are focused on student proficiency and learning activities that help students increase or enhance the language ability and proficiency.
Outcomes are clear and complete.	Course outcomes are needed for each course of each level in the program.	Students, teachers, and administrators need to understand the proficiency expectations for the classes they teach as well as those for the other classes in that level.
	Course outcomes should not only be confined to one skill area.	No one skill is learned alone. Effective
	Course outcomes should address grammar, pronunciation and vocabulary in terms of the various skill areas.	The four major skill areas are supported by these subskills, which should be addressed in the learning outcomes.

Figure 7.7 (Continued)

Developing and Implementing Course Learning Outcomes

The development of the course outcomes follows a similar process to that of developing program level outcomes. The three key principles to remember in developing learning outcomes are as follows:

1. Development is an iterative process.
2. Development should be collaborative.
3. Completeness and clarity are more important than polished work.

In developing course outcomes, consider the makeup of the development team. Success is often attained when the team working on the course includes instructors who have experience teaching that course. However, in some circumstances, you may have only one developer or a pair of developers.

Implementing course learning outcomes is similar to implementing program outcomes in that they are connected to the implementation of class outcomes. In an IEP, teachers are generally relied on for the design, development, and implementation of the class outcomes, which in turn is the implementation of the program and course outcomes. As such, the implementation of course outcomes may simply mean informing teachers of the course outcomes and instructing them to include the GLOs on their syllabi. See Box 7.6.

Box 7.6   Prototype from Design Specifications for Course Outcomes

The GLOs are numbered and followed by the SLOs that are lettered. The GLOs serve as an overall expectation of student outcomes. The SLOs are a representative list of outcomes that lead to meeting the corresponding GLO. After constructing a prototype, designers should review it against the design specifications. What is missing? What should be removed? Asking these questions early can make the development of the course outcomes easier.

Level 1—Reading

Course Description

This course helps students develop emerging reading abilities by increasing fluency and comprehension. Students in this course also begin to use appropriate reading strategies to enhance fluency and comprehension. This course also helps students increase their vocabulary and pronounce words correctly.

Course Emphasis

Reading—70%; Pronunciation—15%; Vocabulary—15%

Course Learning Outcomes

Students who successfully complete this course will be able to do the following:

1. Read level-appropriate material (both narrative and expository texts) at 200 words per minute and 70% comprehension.
2. Understand level-appropriate text (i.e., very short passages, simple maps, receipts, etc.).
    a. Recognize letters, numbers, symbols, and other characters.
    b. Identify key words, cognates, and practiced vocabulary.
    c. Understand basic main ideas with context clues and multiple rereadings.
    d. Identify and describe main parts of a narrative (setting, characters, events, etc.).
    e. Make predictions about a story based on details from the story.
3. Implement basic reading strategies.
    a. Use context clues and background knowledge to derive meaning.
    b. Preview text prior to reading.
    c. Identify key words, important images, and organizational structure.
4. Acquire new vocabulary words.
    a. Understand learned vocabulary in context.
    b. Understand meaning of new, high-frequency words with teacher support.
    c. Understand the high-frequency words on Reading Horizon's Most Common Words lists 1–13.
5. Read with some comprehensible pronunciation.
    a. Accurately predict the pronunciation of unfamiliar, high-frequency words.
    b. Correctly pronounce high-frequency general vocabulary words in isolation.
    c. Produce two- and three-word chunks with appropriate co-articulation and blending.

Developing and Implementing Class Learning Outcomes

Briefly turning to class learning outcomes, hopefully it is apparent what each phase of design, development, and implementation looks like in terms of learning outcomes. Remember that a class refers to a single, time-bound instructional period.

The nature of a class makes teachers the heart of the design process for learning outcomes. A teacher may work alone to articulate learning outcomes for the class, or many teachers teaching sections of the same class may collaborate. Regardless of the participants, working with class learning outcomes requires constant referrals to course outcomes. In fact, class learning outcomes might be the same as the course GLOs or SLOs.

Based on the prototype for course learning outcomes, a level 1 reading teacher may decide to have a 10-minute activity based on the first learning outcome: *Upon successful completion of the course, students will be able to read level-appropriate material (both narrative and expository texts) at 200 words per minute and 70% comprehension*. The teacher could use this program outcome to set her class outcome for the 10-minute period: *Students will increase their reading rate by participating in a reading fluency activity*. In this example, the learning outcome is intertwined with a need for appropriate assessment tools and learning experiences that measure student ability and help students reach the outcome. See Box 7.7.

Box 7.7   A Refresher on Class-Level Learning Outcomes

Class learning outcomes are a vital component of any lesson plan. Usually, there are between one and three outcomes for any 60-minute class. Here is a short reminder about crafting effective outcomes.

Outcomes should be

- Based on the course goals or mission statement
- Feasible for learners to accomplish
- Concrete and measurable
- Clear and complete

Outcomes should have a rather stable syntactic structure: *Subject + "will" or "will be able to" + Verb + skill statement*

Some outcome statements reflect what teachers want to do in class but are otherwise weak statements of student performance. Examine Figure 7.8 for examples of weak class objective statements. Reasons for their weaknesses are listed in the column on the right.

Strong Class Objective Statements

Students will locate three books that match their interest levels by navigating the Lexile.com website

Students will be able to interpret dates and prices in a cruise ship brochure

Students will correctly match 12 vocabulary words to appropriate dictionary definitions

Students will raise their reading speed by 10 WPM during a rate build-up activity

Weak Class Objective Statements	Explanation
Students will understand the meaning of the word "anti-trust"	← Hard to measure student "understanding" without criteria
I will have students read their books in class	← Should be student-focused; "read their books in class" is not especially concrete
Study vocab	← No subject; not concrete or measurable
Increase our understanding of the importance of reading for pleasure	← Should be student-focused; hard to measure "increase" and "understanding" w/o criteria
Know why reading is hard sometimes	← No subject; not clear or complete; hard to measure without criteria
Students will be able to recite MLK Jr.'s "I Have a Dream" speech from memory	← May not be feasible in a single, short class

Figure 7.8 Examples of weak class objective statements.

Overall Implementation

While some developers insist that the curriculum development process is always going to be messy, hopefully this is not what is conveyed here. What is usually referred to as messiness is the misperception of the interconnectedness of the design process. Learning outcomes are designed, developed, and implemented concurrently with the design, development, and implementation of the assessment and learning activities. The three curricular components work together to maintain a stable, responsive, and cohesive curriculum. Likewise, the curriculum design of the three curricular levels—program, course, and class—is an interconnected process. In the case of learning outcomes, curriculum designers may have to shift between the program, course, and class levels. For example, while working on the course-level outcomes, the designers may return to evaluate the program's structure. Such recursion and shuffling from curricular activity to curricular component to level is normal and representative of a healthy curricular balancing act.

Chapter Summary

In this chapter, we have addressed the broad topic of learning outcomes. Outcomes are critical curricular components, since they ultimately outline what students will do in the program on a day-to-day basis. In our view, simply drafting outcome statements at the program, course, and class levels is insufficient for an effective curriculum. Rather, outcomes should be designed with a stable set of specifications in mind for the benefit of continuity and quality assurance. With these specifications in mind, developers can then draft the outcomes, and then the outcomes can be implemented. The implementation process may include posting the programmatic outcomes on a website and referring to them in decision-making meetings, but this alone is only part of it. Program-level outcomes are implemented through the creation of course learning outcomes that are posted in syllabi but then are themselves implemented through class learning outcomes. Thus, the day-to-day work of students really does fulfill the entire curriculum from class to course to program.

As was illustrated in the house metaphor at the beginning of this chapter, outcomes are not a description of activities that students will perform; rather, they are statements of what students will be able to do (or will have done) by the end of a program, course, or class. In this sense, they are visionary statements that describe the end goal of student performance. How that performance will be assessed and what activities will be used to generate that success will be discussed in the following two chapters.

Activities

Activity 7.1

Consider the mission statement and outcomes for a program you are familiar with. Based on the outcomes, identify the underlying design specifications that informed the creation of the outcomes. If there are no programmatic outcomes, then create some design specifications that could guide the creation of these outcomes.

Activity 7.2

Imagine you have been tasked with designing program outcomes for the following specialized mission statement: "Our US-based Intensive English Program provides pre-matriculated international MBA students with speech, pronunciation, and presentation instruction intended to supplement their business education and allow them to succeed in oral tasks as business professionals." Assuming that this program accepts students at two proficiency levels (intermediate high and advanced low), develop a simple learning outcomes prototype.

Activity 7.3

Working with the mission statement in Activity 7.2, develop a table illustrating the kinds of courses that could be offered at both the intermediate and advanced levels of oral language instruction. Include programmatic outcomes for each class based on the prototype developed in Activity 7.2.

Activity 7.4

Envision a specific language course you might like to teach in the future (or one you are designing right now). Following the discussion on design specifications for course learning outcomes, create your own table of design specifications based on the guiding principles for the course learning outcomes.

Activity 7.5

After completing the design specification task in Activity 7.4, complete the course outcomes design process by writing a prototype table of course learning outcomes for your hypothetical (or in-process) language course.

Activity 7.6

Given the following course learning outcome here, write three class-level learning outcomes that could help accomplish the course outcome.

> "By the end of this course, students will be able to use past tense and aspects (simple past, past perfect, and past progressive) in narrative speaking tasks with 70% accuracy."

References

Christison, M., & Murray, D. E. (2021). *What English language teachers need to know volume III: Designing curriculum* (2nd ed.). Routledge. http://dx.doi.org/10.4324/9780203072196

Graves, K. (2000). *Designing language courses: A guide for teachers*. Heinle & Heinle.

Tyler, R. W. (2013). *Basic principles of curriculum and instruction*. University of Chicago Press. http://dx.doi.org/10.7208/chicago/9780226086644.001.0001

8

Assessment and Feedback
Design, Develop, and Implement

Introduction

This chapter discusses designing, developing, and implementing assessment and feedback options within a curriculum. Although a curriculum has program, course, and class levels, the assessment and feedback component applies largely to courses and classes, although a program-level assessment program is not uncommon. Assessments are important because they measure whether a student has achieved the learning outcomes (as described in Chapter 7). The point of learning outcomes is to set forth what students should know by the end of a program, class, or course; assessments are there to determine whether students have achieved the outcomes. Assessment provides accountability for learning.

In this chapter, we focus heavily on the principles of effective assessments. Following this, we suggest ways in which assessments can be designed, developed, and implemented at the three curricular levels. Throughout, we also address the importance of utilizing assessment results to inform the critical feedback needed for ongoing language practice and development.

The House Metaphor

Assessment and feedback fit nicely into a house-building metaphor. After all, every action performed by a homeowner or a homebuilder can be assessed, as can the products of such actions. And feedback can easily be given on all of these actions and products as well. These actions and products are discussed more in Chapter 9, but for now, let's discuss what it means to have an assessment plan for building a house.

At the most basic level, a homeowner might have a very broad objective: to build a new house (or have one built). Often, the tacit assumption is that if a homeowner pays for that house to be built, it will indeed be built. But how will the homeowner assess whether the house was truly built? This seemingly naïve question has at least one obvious answer: the homeowner will see the house once it is built. But seeing a house is very different from really determining that the house was built to the desired specifications, and within budget, and on time, and with the right quality of materials. It is common for a homeowner to inspect the house before occupying it, and that inspection can be thought of as part of a larger assessment plan. If the inspection shows that the house is indeed in order according to the specifications established earlier, and the homeowner or some delegate is able to attest that the timeframe and cost corresponded to the original plan, then everyone can rest assured that the house passed its assessments. It really was built to the standards originally expected.

The same thought process can be applied to smaller sub-components of a house-building or remodeling project. For instance, if a laborer is hired to install an air conditioner, then the assessment comes when the unit is installed, looks good, and operates correctly. Along the way, the laborer's supervisor might come by to inspect certain aspects of the installation, and this is part of the assessment program, too, though these are formative rather than summative assessments.

The Nature of Assessment

The English word *assessment* originally referred to estimating the value of property for tax purposes. It is now used more broadly to include judgment about the nature, quality, or ability of a person or thing. However, the original notions of estimation and measurement are still very applicable in language learning assessment. Some educators use related terms, such as assessment, test, and evaluation interchangeably. While this may be appropriate in some cases, we clarify in Box 8.1 how we use these terms.

Tests

Tests often provide the most salient information used for the assessment and evaluation of student learning, especially at the class and course levels.

Box 8.1 Assessment, Testing, and Evaluation

In language learning contexts, assessment could be thought of as all of the tools and processes involved in gathering, scoring, recording, and interpreting important information about a learner's language development. The use of the term test, on the other hand, may be defined more narrowly. It is often used to describe specific kinds of measures used to estimate student knowledge or skill. Tests are usually limited to a single instrument or set of procedures but are an essential part of the broader notion of assessment. We define assessment to include additional elements, such as observation, interviews, surveys, or other techniques that help practitioners or program administrators better understand learning processes, attitudes, and beliefs, along with the specific adjustments to the classes, course, or program that may be necessary to optimize learning. Effective assessment facilitates the evaluation of student learning. Evaluation involves careful analysis that results in decisions based on data gleaned through the assessment process. Thus, one way to conceptualize the relationships among testing, assessment, and evaluation is captured in Figure 8.1, where testing helps inform assessment and assessment helps inform evaluation of student learning.

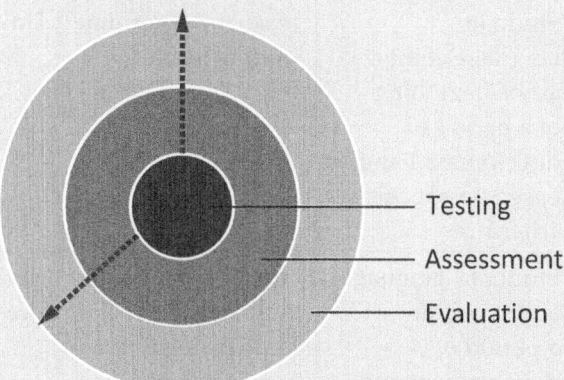

Figure 8.1 A conceptualization of the relationship among testing, assessment, and evaluation of student learning.

Quizzes, exams, writing samples, and oral interviews are common examples of tests. Yet, in language learning contexts, there may be different kinds of tests that are used in different ways. Test developers must understand how their tests will be used to ensure that they effectively fulfill their purpose. A test might be designed to determine admission into a program or proficiency level placement within a program, to diagnose what the learner still needs to learn within a particular proficiency level, to measure individual language development over time, or help determine whether a program is generally successful at fulfilling its mission. Some tests may be used for more than one purpose, while the application of other tests should be very limited. See Figure 8.2 for examples.

Type	What they measure	Who uses results and common uses	Examples
Proficiency	Students' language ability in general	Learners: determine their ability Admin: admissions decisions	TOEFL test, IELTS, Duolingo, Oral Proficiency Interviews
Placement	Students' language ability before a period of development and based on specific criteria	Admin: placement decisions	Final exam, Unit post-test (administered before placement)
Diagnostic	Students' language ability at the beginning of a period of development and based on specific criteria	Teachers: determine what to teach	Unit pre-test
Progress	Students' language ability within a period of development and based on specific criteria	Learners: evaluate improvements Teachers: evaluate improvements	Variation of a unit pre-test
Achievement	Students' language ability after a period of development and based on specific criteria	Learners: determine mastery Teachers: determine mastery Admin: measure class/course success	Final exam, Unit post-test

Figure 8.2 Various types and purposes of language tests.

Just as other components of a curriculum require careful planning, test construction is greatly strengthened when creators are thoughtful as they design, develop, implement, and evaluate their assessment tools. Those who develop tests for use within a curriculum need to ensure that their assessment tools are valid, reliable, and practical.

Validity

Validity means that the assessment measures what it purports to measure and does so fairly and accurately. A helpful metaphor is that of a fast-food restaurant chain. A violation of validity would be a restaurant chain advertising a plain hamburger on its menu, but then serving a cheeseburger with additional toppings. A valid restaurant advertisement must accurately represent what it claims to serve. Similarly, language tests need to accurately measure what they claim to measure. For example, if the intention is to test a student's ability to speak and interact in a given scenario, a written test would not be an accurate assessment, as it does not require speaking at all. Careful attention is needed throughout test development and evaluation in order to make the case that a test is valid for a particular purpose.

Reliability

Reliability is a necessary requirement for a test to be valid. It means that the assessment results are consistent. Returning to the fast-food metaphor, reliability asks if the food served is consistent across time and location. For example, if two customers order the same thing at different locations of the same chain restaurant, will they receive identical meals? If one customer receives a hamburger and the other receives a cheeseburger, then the restaurant does not provide a reliable meal. Part of the appeal of fast food is how reliable it tends to be. People like to know that the food they are served will be exactly the same every time and in various locations. In a similar vein, tests need to be reliable in order to be useful. If two students have the same language proficiency level, they both should receive very similar scores on a test designed to measure language proficiency. Or, if the same student took two versions or parallel forms of the same test, we would expect a very similar score if the tests were reliable. Tests that are confusing, poorly worded, or that attempt to measure a number of constructs all at once tend to be less reliable because a student might answer a question in a particular way given his or her interpretation of the question one day and respond differently on another day with a different interpretation of the same question.

Practicality

Practicality means that assessment can be designed, developed, and implemented in such a way that the time, effort, and resources needed are not unrealistic. There often is some tension between validity and reliability on one hand and practicality on the other. Usually, the more time and energy that is expended to ensure validity and reliability, the less practical the test development or implementation may be. While it would be inappropriate for practicality to infringe on the reliability or validity of an assessment, test developers need to consider ways to make the development or implementation of a test as practical as possible.

Other Factors to Consider in Test Development

Tests may differ in other important ways that may impact how they are constructed and used and how the data they produce should be interpreted. Thus, test developers should consider a wide variety of factors before they begin to develop a test. The following frames of reference may be helpful. While some scholars may appropriately see some of the distinctions listed here as overly simplistic, we believe they can be useful for test developers as they carefully weigh the functions, applications, and interpretations of the tests they develop.

Direct vs. Indirect

Direct testing requires learners to successfully demonstrate their language by actually doing what the outcomes specify. For example, learning outcomes might include using English to shop at the grocery store, asking for and following directions, or negotiating the terms of a business contract. In such cases, direct testing would involve the direct observation of the student in meeting the specific requirements. This might require students and teacher to go to a grocery store. Perhaps the greatest advantage of such testing is that it is likely to be authentic and valid. However, direct testing may not always be practical or possible. Rather than directly observe students shopping at the store, test developers may opt for a slightly less direct scenario such as a role-play that merely simulates the shopping experience. If a role-play scenario is not possible, test developers may choose other less direct methods, such as having students indicate on paper how they might respond to various shopping situations. Thus, testing approaches could range from highly authentic direct measures to a variety of increasingly less direct measures that may only suggest characteristics of the learner's language skill. Test developers will need to carefully weigh the advantages and disadvantages of using direct and indirect measures for language testing.

Knowledge vs. Skill

This framework is closely related to the previous framework. Knowledge represents what one knows and skill represents what one can do. While knowledge of language components, such as vocabulary and grammar, may be essential, they may not tell us much about the language skill of the learner in applying that knowledge in a variety of contexts. Ideally, testing would focus on the demonstration of what one can do rather than what one knows about the language. However, since certain kinds of knowledge are prerequisites to skill performance, there may be contexts in which testing the development of knowledge may be appropriate. This might be useful to determine whether students are adequately prepared with the vocabulary or grammar they may need to perform certain tasks. Test developers will need to carefully weigh the extent to which their tests should be designed to target skill performance vs. knowledge of particular language components.

Subjective vs. Objective

Subjective test items are usually those scored by expert human raters. This is fairly common for productive language skills such as speaking and writing, where open-ended responses may vary widely and need to be evaluated for specific criteria. Often, carefully created rubrics are used for this type of test item that reflect aspects of the learning outcomes being targeted. In high-stakes testing, rubrics are often validated through qualitative and quantitative analysis, and multiple raters are used after achieving high levels of reliability. This kind of subjective testing can be time-consuming and expensive. This is in contrast with objective test items, where the correct response to a question is predetermined and often selected by the student from several options. These may take the form of items, such as multiple choice, true or false, matching, or even fill-in-the-blank. Scoring objective items is usually faster and easier than subjective items, and they are often scored by machine. However, effective objective items may also take a great deal of time and energy to develop and also require qualitative and quantitative analyses.

Discrete vs. Integrated

Discrete test items are those that focus on a single language element or skill at a time. For example, an entire test may be devoted just to reading, listening, vocabulary, or grammar. One advantage to this kind of testing is that it can provide very precise information to the stakeholders regarding student performance in specific areas. For example, a reading test might show that a particular student demonstrates a pattern of understanding main ideas but struggles to draw appropriate inferences. This may help the teacher to recognize specific adjustments in the curriculum that may be needed to help the student achieve learning outcomes. Although discrete testing can be informative, it may not be entirely authentic. Language is rarely used in ways that isolate discrete skills. Rather, language is usually dynamic and interactive. Thus, integrated test items usually bring multiple skills into play for a more authentic demonstration of language ability. For example, a test for students preparing for university study might have them listen to a brief lecture, read a brief passage, and then discuss or write about the content. Test developers will need to weigh the appropriateness of discrete or integrated items within their tests.

Timed vs. Untimed

Timed tests have some kind of time constraint. This might include the need to complete the entire test within a specified timeframe or the need to complete particular items within an allotted time. The decision of whether to place time constraints on test components should be considered carefully. Choosing to use or not use time constraints could have important implications for the reliability and validity of a test. While using time constraints for some types of tests may be inappropriate, it may help simulate the dynamic and unrehearsed nature of many kinds of language tasks and interactions.

Formative vs. Summative

This frame of reference relates primarily to the testing purpose. Formative assessments are used to inform instruction. This could include a lengthy midterm exam used to determine the teaching and learning focus for the second half of a course. It might also be as simple as a question posed by a teacher in class to determine whether the class needs more practice with a particular task before moving on to other material. Summative assessments are used to determine student learning at the completion of instruction such as at the end of a unit, a course, or the program. Sometimes a single test can be used for both formative and summative purposes, depending on how it was designed.

Criterion Referenced vs. Norm Referenced

Criterion referenced testing refers to tests that are designed to measure student mastery of specific criteria associated with learning outcomes. The results of the test suggest that student performance either achieved or did not meet the specified standards, or it may show the extent to which the criteria were met. The performance of other students is irrelevant to the performance of an individual student. An oral proficiency interview based on ACTFL guidelines is a common example of a criterion-referenced test. Norm-referenced testing, on the other hand, is designed to compare a student's performance in a particular area with the performance of others within the same population. This allows stakeholders to compare performance levels for purposes of ranking students. The TOEFL is a common example of a norm-referenced test. While norm-referenced tests can be very useful in some contexts, they don't tell stakeholders the extent to which students have mastered particular language skills. Most testing within a curriculum should be criterion-referenced testing that is well aligned with the learning outcomes.

The remainder of this chapter will focus primarily on criterion-based tests that are used to measure student performance against the intended outcomes designated for a program, course, or smaller unit of instruction.

Tests and Assessments: The Program Level

Measuring student performance with a single test at the top curricular level—that of the program—is relatively rare. And in fact, a single test at any curricular level is generally not sufficient to determine student achievement: multiple measures are needed to get a full picture of student ability. Nevertheless, some programs do have one-shot assessment systems for graduating students. One example is an essay assignment for a writing program. Students who earn a passing score on a single essay exam can exit the writing program, regardless of whether they have completed the courses in that program. On the other hand, students who fail the same essay test, no matter how many courses they have taken, must remain in the program until they can pass the test.

A more reasonable and humane program-wide assessment approach includes that of multiple measures or tests. For instance, a potential graduate might take a listening, speaking, reading, and writing test at the end of his or her time in a program. The resulting score of these combined tests is then used to determine if the student successfully passed the program.

Perhaps the most common program-wide assessment system is that of no assessment. Instead, the programs rely on course assessments to validate a students' ability. So long as a student passes all the required courses in a particular program or series, he or she automatically graduates.

Because the principles for designing a single, multi-measure, or course-level test are essentially the same, we will discuss the design, development, and implementation of these tests together in the next section.

Designing, Developing, and Implementing Tests and Assessments

Before a test can be used to measure student achievement, it must be designed; yet, we lament with many woebegone students that tests in education are often poorly designed and developed. Frequently time-strapped teachers produce quickly developed tests that their students view as confusing, complicated, or off-topic. Taking adequate time to design a test is therefore prudent for good student–teacher relations, but also necessary for effective assessment. Once it is designed, additional measures can be taken to ensure that the development honors the thoughtfulness of the design prior to implementation.

Design

During the design phase, we look at the constructs as indicated in the learning outcomes. This becomes the basis for test construction. Tables of specifications clearly articulate the language constructs to be assessed, the methods for assessing student mastery of those constructs, the number of items, and the item types. The following tables provide an example of test specifications for a lower-proficiency reading class. The first table (Figure 8.3) identifies the constructs to be assessed. The column on the left identifies the passages students will read. The top row has the constructs being tested. The numbers represent the number of questions from each passage that are intended to target one of these constructs.

The second table (Figure 8.4) indicates the types of questions that will be used to assess these constructs for each reading passage.

In addition to planning content and test item types, curriculum designers should also determine the feedback that will be provided to the students. The simplest form of feedback is a number grade, yet such limited feedback is relatively ineffective in most cases because it does little to help students progress. Alternatives (or additions) to a single grade include a personalized grade sheet that outlines weaknesses and strengths, an interview with the teacher regarding the assessment and accompanying feedback, a thoughtful rubric with indications of areas the student did well or could improve, or even a list of correct and incorrect responses with accompanying explanations.

	Previewing	Scanning	Main Idea	Major Details	Minor Details	Inferences	Vocabulary in Context	Relationships
Grocery Ad	3							
Sunshine Camp		5						
David Beckham (730L)			1	1	1	1	1	1
Benjamin Franklin (310L)			1	1	1	1	1	1

Figure 8.3 Table of Specifications.

	Short Answer	Multiple Choice
Grocery Ad	3	
Sunshine Camp	5	
David Beckham (730L)		6
Benjamin Franklin (310L)		6

Figure 8.4 Assessment question types.

In essay assessments, including multiple draft essays, teachers often give marginal and end comments. The marginal notes are intended to point out specific areas for praise or improvement, whereas the end comment articulates general sentiments about the essay as a whole and may further justify the grade given. Many teachers use the end comment like a letter to the author, including a salutation with the student's name at the top and a sign-off at the end that may include the teacher's signature. This especially personalized approach mimics a one-on-one interview to some extent.

Other feedback plans can be very elaborate; for example, portfolio systems allow students to receive formative feedback on even very summative assignments and then learn, improve, and retake tests throughout the semester, ultimately presenting a collection of their very best work and a narrative of their journal of improvement for final grading when the course has ended.

Develop

Developing an assessment involves finding or creating language content and then writing or selecting the actual test items. Designers have several options when developing a listening test item. For example, they can use a preexisting recording from a textbook or an authentic source. In the absence of a listening passage that meets the needs of their students, they may need to create their own recordings. Some textbooks may also provide test questions for assessment purposes, but when working with original recordings, these items must be developed from scratch.

When drafting assessments and actually writing test items, it can be difficult to ensure they are valid, reliable, and practical. In fact, it may not be possible to know the effectiveness of a given assessment until it is piloted or implemented. Data collected from implementation can lead back into the design and development phases for those assessments, which is a common, if not necessary, occurrence, since test development is a very iterative process. Thus, realizing that test development is a process that may involve revisiting other curricular components or test specifications can be reassuring.

Despite this positive opinion of recursive assessment development, planning carefully during the design phase and working thoroughly during the development phase can increase the likelihood of having an effective assessment at the outset. For program- or course-level assessments, assembling a team of teachers to work together and review items is helpful. Even larger programs with personnel dedicated to assessment creation can draw on experienced teachers and others to help construct test items. Often at the course level, and almost always at the class level, the teacher takes on most of the responsibility for creating assessments, but this doesn't mean teachers cannot ask other teachers or testing personnel to review test items.

Box 8.2 is an overview for writing multiple-choice (MC) test items. We offer this example, since MC tests are arguably the most common and perhaps the most difficult to write. We direct your attention to other test development resources for other test types (Brown, H. D., 2018; Brown, J. D., 2005; Fulcher, 2013; Hill & Parry, 2014).

Box 8.2 Writing Multiple-choice Items

These items can make testing quick and easy: students can answer them quickly, and teachers can score them even faster. The downside is that crafting them well in the first place requires skill and time. We introduce much of the conventional wisdom about how to write MC questions here. But first, a word about the surprising variety of MC question types.

In their review of MC item-writing guidelines, Haladyna et al. (2002) highlighted several formats for MC questions. The most common is the traditional form: a stem with one correct answer and one, two, or three distractors. Other variations include matching and true/false formats. There are also complex MC in which some or all of the distractors can be correct (i.e., A&B, A&C, or AB&C). Not all of these formats come well-recommended; the last one—that of complex MC—is commonly criticized for being inefficient for teachers to write and score, difficult for students to navigate, and no more effective than more practical MC items in validation tests.

When writing MC items, Haladyna, Downing, and Rodriquez further summarize 31 guidelines for writing effective MC items. While most guidelines are common sense (don't use trick questions, proofread all items, test only one construct at a time), it can still be valuable for test writers to review these sorts of lists. With that in mind, items 14–31 of the original list are reprinted here:

Writing the stem

14. Ensure that the directions in the stem are very clear.
15. Include the central idea in the stem instead of the choices.
16. Avoid window dressing (excessive verbiage).
17. Word the stem positively; avoid negatives such as NOT or EXCEPT. If negative words are used, use the word cautiously, and always ensure that the word appears capitalized and boldface.

Writing the choices

18. Develop as many effective choices as you can, but research suggests that three is adequate.
19. Make sure that only one of these choices is the right answer.
20. Vary the location of the right answer according to the number of choices.
21. Place choices in logical or numerical order.
22. Keep choices independent; choices should not overlap.
23. Keep choices homogeneous in content and grammatical structure.
24. Keep the length of choices about equal.
25. *None-of-the-above* should be used carefully.
26. Avoid *All-of-the-above*.
27. Phrase choices positively; avoid negatives such as NOT.
28. Avoid giving clues to the right answer, such as
    a. Specific determiners, including always, never, completely, and absolutely.

> b. Clang associations, choices identical to or resembling words in the stem.
> c. Grammatical inconsistencies that cue the test-taker to the correct choice.
> d. Conspicuous correct choice.
> e. Pairs or triplets of options that clue the test-taker to the correct choice.
> f. Blatantly absurd, ridiculous options.
> 29. Make all distractors plausible.
> 30. Use typical student errors to write your distractors.
> 31. Use humor if it is compatible with the teacher and the learning environment.

Implement

It is not reasonable to implement assessments and feedback mechanisms in isolation from the implementation of the learning outcomes and learning experiences. This is because learning outcomes inform the assessments, and generally, students engage with the learning experiences prior to engaging with assessments.

Once it is time to implement, though, the process can range from relatively easy to incredibly complex, depending on such things as the level of test security, proctoring requirements, accompanying materials, location, and scoring procedure. The cost of assessment can vary along these same lines as well.

Some of the easiest assessments include classroom-based tests. For instance, a quick and inexpensive test in a speaking class might involve asking students to orally produce some language or make a spontaneous presentation of some kind of material in class. In these situations, the teacher (and/or classroom peers) can proctor the test and provide immediate, oral feedback. There would be little need for copying off testing materials, moving to a secure testing location, or engaging multiple external reviewers. The implementation would really just come down to the teacher introducing the test and its procedures, selecting the order of students, referencing some form of scoring guideline, and then noting each student's score and entering it into his or her grade.

Although the speaking test described is easy to implement, the tradeoff is that it is also inefficient. For one thing, only one student can perform at a time, and without the use of a recording device, neither the teacher nor the student can return to the performance and judge it more carefully. And if it is a high-stakes exam requiring multiple trained raters—as might be expected at the course or program level—all those raters would ostensibly need to attend the performance. To balance these tradeoffs, the teacher could record the student's performance. The teacher could also have multiple students record themselves at a single time, perhaps in a computer lab or at home. Making these adjustments allows for increased efficiency, but it also introduces new implementation considerations. For instance, using a computer lab necessitates the *existence* of a computer lab and accompanying technical support and server space. Assigning students to record at home or even on their cell phones requires that the teacher develop detailed instructions for how, when, and what to record and then provides a means whereby those recordings can be collected and stored for later scoring (usually via a learning management system such as Canvas or Blackboard). Then there is the matter of scoring. If multiple raters are needed to evaluate each recording, then the implementation will involve rater training, norming, and ultimately the rating itself with mechanisms in place for resolving disagreements between raters.

The authors (and likely the readers themselves) have seen some even more elaborate assessment implementations. At many universities, for instance, a testing center is used to ensure test security and represents a third-party implementation system. These centers are usually most amenable to multiple-choice type tests, so using them for implementation seems easy enough, but it still involves producing, copying, and delivering a given test with its scoring key. The testing center itself is an implementation mega-center with storage space for all the tests as well as students' personal belongings while testing, physical space for students to test in, materials for test taking (like pencils, scratch paper, computers), trained proctors, and mechanisms for scoring (if this is done onsite) and returning tests and scores to the original teacher. See Box 8.3.

Box 8.3 Implementing Writing-Based Tests

Writing-based tests are among the most complicated to implement. On the one hand, writing tests can be very effective direct assessment measures because the student is performing the very skill meant to be measured. However, scoring essays is also very subjective, and high-stakes essay exams at the course or program level generally necessitate multiple raters, with all the attendant implementation concerns listed for a speaking test. In addition, assessors must be alert to prevent plagiarism, particularly if students use computers to type their essays and have access to the internet. In one mind-boggling implementation scenario with which one of the authors was involved, international students attended a placement essay exam just days after arriving in the US from their home countries. All students were asked to congregate in a huge lecture hall, prove that they had paid for the placement test, and sit with an empty seat between every student. Proctors then distributed a printed version of the prompt and sufficient paper for students to compose their essays. It was a timed test, so proctors had to alert students of the passing time and then collect all the paper at the end of the test, including all prompts (for security purposes). The students' essays, weighing more than 100 pounds in all, were then carted to a separate location where 12 raters were waiting. The raters were given sample essays from the newly written pile to train and calibrate with. They were then paired with each other, all given a rather large stack of essays, and asked to read each essay carefully in order to provide a score based on a complex holistic rubric. On top of all this work, lunch was provided so raters could stay on task for the 5 or so hours it took to complete the rating of all the essays. Placement decisions were then recorded on a master Excel sheet that was then distributed to numerous stakeholders so that students were placed in the right classes, the right number of teachers were hired to fill those classes, and students were informed of which classes they were required to complete.

At the end of the semester, the entire process was repeated in the form of a proficiency assessment, but in this case, students were asked to bring their own computer to the testing lecture hall, disable the internet during the test, and then re-enable the internet in order to send their finished essays to a central electronic location. Students were asked to bring a computer fully charged with a 3-hour battery since there were virtually no electrical outlets throughout the entire lecture hall. Not surprisingly, a handful of students came with unreliable computers that randomly shut off during the test or ran out of battery. Proctors were also busy looking for signs of cheating, internet use, and plagiarism, including self-plagiarism, wherein students drew from previously written essays to draft the present one. A single implementation with these problems convinced the program administrators to use designated computer labs in all subsequent years and a more manageable, electronic, and multi-measure placement assessment that could be taken offsite.

Regardless of whether a language program is brand new or well-established, assessment implementation can be quite similar. However, for established programs, sometimes what might appear to be a small change or development in assessment can actually require a large-scale re-thinking of the implementation structure. For this reason, we recommend that individuals who manage implementation develop a well-articulated plan in advance of administering a test.

Curricular Level

As mentioned earlier, there is little reason to differentiate the design, development, and implementation of assessments and feedback at different programmatic levels. Regardless of the level, developers should follow the same principles and processes. The individuals involved at each level may be different, though. For instance, teachers generally supervise the assessment practices at the class level by writing and administering tests in class or as take-home or testing-center assignments. Often, there is little oversight of class-level assessments. Course assessment is a little different, particularly if several sections of the same course are expected to take a standardized test. In this case, multiple teachers might give input on the assessment procedures, or a program administrator may assist and/or make final decisions about a given test. At the program level, where decisions about advancement are made, administrators have a heavy hand in determining the assessment program. Also, the nature and purpose of the test may vary among the three curricular levels. An assessment at the program level may be high-stakes, whereas a class assessment may be low-stakes and formative in nature. See Box 8.4.

Box 8.4   Evaluation of Learning Experiences

A final step in the ADDIE model, which will be covered in greater detail in Chapter 11, is that of evaluation. Assessments and feedback should be evaluated in terms of their design, development, and implementation. In Figure 8.5, we illustrate several evaluation questions that can be used to help determine the value and effectiveness of each step of the process.

Design	Develop
Are the test specifications based on learning outcomes? Are they complete? Do they address all the intended constructs?	Do the test items match those listed in the table of specifications? Have multiple people reviewed the assessments?
Are the item types effective for the constructs being assessed?	**Implement**
Can someone unfamiliar with your curriculum use the test specifications to create a valid, reliable, and practical test?	Given the learning outcomes, assessments, feedback, and learning experiences, can the program, course, or class be effectively implemented?

Figure 8.5   Questions that help evaluate the value and effectiveness of learning experiences.

Additional Considerations

There are a number of additional issues that should be taken into consideration as tests are being constructed, implemented, and evaluated, since these could impact how well the tests function. As noted in Chapter 3, curriculum development must account for *who* the learners are. An important factor is class size and the composition of the class. Many language teachers have multiple levels in the same class. In an ideal situation, students with the same proficiency level are placed in the same classroom. The lack of resources may necessitate a multilevel classroom. Curricular and test designs will have to be adapted to account for this.

Another situation that needs to be factored in the development process is students with special educational needs. As Harmer (2015) notes, "it is highly possible that teachers will find themselves teaching classes which include students with special educational needs (SENs)" (p. 148). SENs can result from a number of factors, such as dyslexia, attention deficit disorder or autism. Each of these will require careful consideration in the design and implementation of curriculum and tests.

Instructions and Prompts
Test developers need to be careful that instructions and test prompts are appropriate for the test and the level of the learner. For example, if a particular test is designed to target speaking skills, but the directions are beyond the reading comprehension of the student, it may impact the score of what was intended to reflect the student's speaking ability.

Format and Length
Most tests will need to include a sufficient number of items or tasks targeting a particular language ability before we can claim validity or reliability. However, an excessively long test might fatigue the learner and impact the results. This problem could adversely impact reliability and validity.

Item and Task Difficulty
It should go without saying that test items and tasks should stretch students but not demoralize them. This is easier said than done since it is difficult to create a test that has the right balance for every student. However, one principle that can be generalized for a large group of students is that of item placement. For instance, in a multiple-choice test, the first few test items on a larger test should be simpler to give students a sense of success early on. The last few items of the test should also be easier as well to help students end on a relatively peaceful note and to help students who are scrambling to finish

on time. The middle of the test can ramp up to some of the more challenging questions. The same is true for oral interviews, where the tester can use middle questions to probe students' upper proficiency limits before returning to less challenging questions. For essay exams, multiple short essay prompts are generally better than a single one, allowing for a range of easier and more difficult writing tasks. Similarly, tasks that allow for feedback and revision can mitigate the difficulty of especially challenging writing exams.

Chapter Summary

Assessments and feedback are necessary components of a curriculum since they measure whether learning has taken place. To be sure, assessments should be designed based on established learning objectives so that students are not subjected to assessments that have little to do with what they were taught. And by the same token, all objectives should be assessed in some way, whether formally or informally; otherwise, there is little point in having those objectives.

In this chapter, we distinguished a test as a single measure in a larger assessment program, and we offered principles of good test development in general. These included issues of validity, reliability, and practicality. We also contrasted a number of additional considerations, such as direct vs. indirect, subjective vs. objective, and criterion referenced vs. norm referenced testing. Because assessments do not change much at the program, course, or class level, these principles are applicable to assessments at all curricular levels.

As with objectives (discussed in Chapter 7) and learning experiences (as will be discussed in Chapter 9), assessments and feedback need to be carefully designed, developed, and implemented to be effective. Without this foresight, assessments can at best be aggravating to students and, at worst, absorb countless resources without providing any useful information on student performance. For these reasons, assessment and feedback programs should be carefully and thoughtfully assembled.

Activities

Activity 8.1

Reflect on a test you have written or taken recently. Consider its validity, reliability, and practicality. Did the test questions measure what they were intended to measure (or could you determine what they were intending to measure)? Were they free from ambiguity and confusion? Were they reasonably practical to complete?

Activity 8.2

Given the list of "other factors to consider in test development" earlier in this chapter, think back on some of the tests you have taken or written in your past. Try to identify an example test that corresponds to each factor listed. For instance, can you think of a direct language test and an indirect one? How about a knowledge-based assessment and skills-based one?

Activity 8.3

Consider a program you are or have been involved with. What is the assessment procedure associated with completion of the program? Is it a single, multi-measure, or course-level assessment program? Or is it something else altogether?

Activity 8.4

Using the learning outcomes from your own course or one you are familiar with, decide on a construct to test, some possible content to use, and one or two methods that would best assess student performance. Create a table that outlines these test specifications.

Activity 8.5

Given your specifications in Activity 8.4, choose an item from your design and brainstorm possible ways to provide feedback to students.

Activity 8.6

Dust off an old multiple-choice test you have used or have taken. You might need to find one online if you don't have one readily available. Examine the types of multiple-choice items used, as well as the structure of the stem and distractors. Do any items contradict the recommendations from the Haladyna et al. (2002) study in Box 8.2?

Activity 8.7

Think about an exam you have recently taken or administered. In your mind, rehearse all the steps necessary to implement the exam, and then write out that implementation plan or a more efficient version from start to finish.

References

Brown, H. D. (2018). *Language assessment: Principles and classroom practices* (2nd ed.). Pearson Education.

Brown, J. D. (2005). *Testing in language programs: A comprehensive guide to English language assessment.* McGraw-Hill College.

Fulcher, G. (2013). *Practical language testing*. Routledge. http://dx.doi.org/10.4324/980203767399

Haladyna, T. M., Downing, S. M., & Rodriguez, M. C. (2002). A review of multiple-choice item-writing guidelines for classroom assessment. *Applied Measurement in Education*, *15*(3), 309–334. http://dx.doi.org/10.1207/S15324818AME1503_5

Harmer, J. (2015). *The practice of English language teaching* (5th ed.). Pearson Education.

Hill, C., & Parry, K. (2014). *From testing to assessment: English as an international language*. Routledge.

9

Learning Experiences
Design, Develop, and Implement

Introduction

The final major component of any curriculum that we will address is that of learning experiences. These are the day-to-day activities that make up most class time, homework, group activities, and assignments that students complete. Although they generally have a physical form, such as a worksheet or assignment description, learning experiences are inherently nonphysical. They are actions, interactions, and conditions that support language learning in some way. Any accompanying physical instructions or worksheets are usually only meant to outline the activity, collect evidence that the student completed the learning task, or record the target language use for purposes of assessment or feedback. In this way, learning experiences can be thought of as any condition that is purposefully engineered to provide students with instructions or opportunities to use or interact with language. That being said, any accompanying physical representation must be thoughtfully constructed. Furthermore, nearly every class is made up of learning experiences, and so documents that outline and schedule course- and class-level learning activities are called calendars and lesson plans. These materials, including assignment sheets, calendars, and lesson plans, are described in more detail in this chapter about designing, developing, and implementing learning experiences.

Building a House

In the house-building metaphor, learning experiences can be seen as the individual tasks that laborers perform. They are things like building walls, installing carpet, connecting pipes, and so forth. All these tasks lead to a complete house; all of them require some level of instruction or expertise to accomplish. And while a seasoned professional may not learn anything new from installing one more water heater per se, a novice plumber may be able to hone his or her techniques and may indeed come away from the experience with increased professional skills.

In renovation projects, oftentimes the occupants of the house will do some of the work. In the case of repainting a wall, for example, the homeowners who do the work themselves have a number of smaller assignments to complete in a fairly standard sequence. They need to decide on a paint color and determine how much paint to purchase. They must also collect the needed tools for the job and then clear and prepare the area for painting. Then they paint, followed by cleanup. All along the way, they may be learning new skills, developing new or improved techniques, transferring knowledge from previous work, evaluating their decisions and actions, and revising as needed. At the end, their product is a finished, painted wall, but through the process, they have also developed proficiency in painting, which in curricular design is the real benefit students receive from so much hard work.

When homeowners without much experience set out to do a little do-it-yourself painting job, they need instructions and someone to offer the sequence described here. This kind of instruction might come via website posts or internet video tutorials on the topic of painting a house. They might also come from a friendly hardware store employee or a professional contractor or designer. In any event, a more experienced, more proficient individual often passes verbal or written instruction on to the laborer, along with suggestions for when to accomplish each task. These instructions and sequence plans, along with all the various building tasks, need to be designed and developed before they are implemented. The old adage of "measure twice, cut once" puts these principles into carpentry terms.

Learning Experiences: Design, Develop, and Implement

Learning experiences encompass much of what is at the heart of day-to-day curriculum. Because they are usually class-based, it is generally teachers, not program-level developers, who determine the kinds of learning experiences students will encounter. Tyler (2013) encouraged teachers to identify the educational experiences that students need, along with the best ways to organize them for the classroom. Of course, some experiences transcend multiple classes. In these cases, a curriculum coordinator or a group of teachers arranges for things such as a multi-class assignment, an integrated skills activity, a capstone project, and so on. Given that most learning experiences are class-based, however, we refer to teachers in this chapter as those who engineer and implement them.

As with other curricular components, learning experiences must likewise be designed, developed, and implemented as part of a contextualized curricular effort (see Figure 9.1). When teachers use a textbook, most learning activities are already scripted; they were designed and developed by the textbook author, and now it is up to the instructor to implement the activities. But even textbook experiences need to be carefully considered in the curricular process. Merely throwing activities at students in a random way contradicts the purpose of having a curriculum in the first place. Though capricious activities may provide some utility to students in the end, operating long-term in this manner may undermine students' achievement of critical outcomes. Only when activities are tied to student needs, lacks, or wants (Macalister & Nation, 2020) *and* a curricular purpose do those experiences become curricularized. This is why a program and its student needs must be analyzed prior to textbooks being adopted or learning experiences being designed, developed, and implemented. Additional analysis may be needed when new contextual constraints are introduced, such as online curricular components or special educational needs students.

Of course, there should be room in all curricula for spontaneity. Curricular components, especially at the level of learning experiences, need to

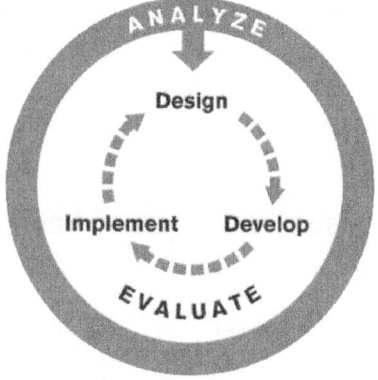

Figure 9.1 Principled Curriculum Approach.

be sensitive to the micro-context of individual classrooms and individual learners; spontaneous adaptations are essential. Anyone with even marginal experience teaching from a lesson plan knows, for instance, that a number of real-world factors can lead a lesson in an unexpected direction. Such variability may sound like an argument against carefully designing, developing, and implementing learning experiences. But we contend that careful planning and spontaneity are closely related. To adapt to the needs of learners in a given class period, a teacher must be attuned to his or her learners through micro-analysis of their needs, lacks, and wants. If a teacher switches tasks mid-lesson in order to address student concerns, the new task may be something the teacher has previously designed and developed. If a teacher tries something totally new and unplanned in class, he or she may be jumping directly to the implementation stage while designing and developing the experience along the way with the help of the students. Spontaneity in curriculum development, therefore, comes in the form of condensing the development process or rearranging the steps in order to react to micro-contexts.

Design

The design stage of the ADDIE model builds on the analysis and involves brainstorming, critical thinking, creativity, and planning (i.e., Palkova & Sapozhnikova, 2021). It includes determining *what* needs to be learned and *how* the students will learn it. Teachers should generate ideas as part of the design phase and write them down. Much of the process may be messy and may involve false starts and will almost always require some revising and refining. Where possible, teachers should invite input and critiques from other teachers and administrators who are familiar with the program, course objectives, and student needs. It may be necessary to balance theoretical ideals with what may be feasible in a given context. It may be appropriate to develop, implement, and evaluate prototypes with selected groups to determine the appropriateness of the design.

Designing learning experiences involves brainstorming and planning. Yet, much like assessment and feedback, the design of learning experiences must be based on the learning outcomes. Thus, teachers might ask the following questions as a guide when designing learning experiences:

- What *experiences* do students need in order to reach the desired outcome?
- What *materials* are needed to support these experiences and to attain the desired learning outcome?
- How should the experiences and materials be *sequenced* for maximum learning?

With these questions in mind, a teacher can begin envisioning ideal learning experiences and determining how they will fit together. If a teacher uses a pre-selected textbook, then envisioning the learning experiences is mostly a matter of selecting appropriate activities and then thinking through the sequencing and delivery of those experiences with perhaps a few supplemental activities or materials included. If a teacher is planning to select one or more textbooks, then the design process is a bit more complicated. A teacher might envision a number of exciting experiences and try to find a textbook that can match this vision. For teachers without a textbook, options for learning experiences are limited only by matters of practicality, but the subsequent development step will be longer and more involved (see Box 9.1).

Box 9.1 Learning Experiences and Pedagogy

Pedagogy can be thought of as the art and science of teaching, particularly at the class level. Learning experiences, therefore, are directly associated with pedagogical practice, and good pedagogy, one could argue, should lead to good learning. With this in mind, we introduce our own view of pedagogy by dividing it into what we feel are its four essential parts: objectives, learner backgrounds, methods, and materials. By considering these elements, teachers can design learning experiences that are pedagogically sound, meaning that materials and teaching methods are effectively chosen based upon students' backgrounds and the learning outcomes (see Figure 9.2).

To apply this notion of pedagogy, consider a group of very gregarious male and female students at an intermediate level of proficiency who need to develop improved conversation skills. Given their background and the objective, they might benefit from learning experiences that allow them to analyze a video. Or they might benefit from reading a passage on a controversial topic in small groups and then defending their opinions orally with another member of the class in mid-structured conversations.

If the student backgrounds were changed, then the materials and methods might change as well. For instance, if instead of being gregarious, the students were shy and retiring, then the videos or passages might need to highlight things that the students are comfortable speaking about, such as their hometown or topics of mutual interest. The methods might also favor more written preparation and highly structured conversations to ease students into the experience.

Student Backgrounds	Objectives	
Age, gender	Remember:	
Learning style, attention span	Recall facts, terms, basic concepts, answers	
Background knowledge	Understand:	
Sociability	Organize, compare, translate, interpret, describe, state main ideas	
Openness to new ideas/activities	Apply:	
Degree of introversion/extroversion	Apply knowledge, facts, techniques, and rules	
Accomplishments/strengths	Analyze:	
Concerns/worries/challenges	Examine, deconstruct, identify motives or causes, infer, find evidence	
Language proficiency	Evaluate:	
Prior language and literacy experience	Present and defend opinions, judge, validate ideas	
Educational background	Synthesize or create: Compile and combine information, propose solutions	
Materials	Methods	
Books, textbooks, or other texts	Brainstorming	Group work
Video, audio, podcasts, digital artifacts	Demonstrations	Guest speakers or lectures
Songs and music	Questions and discussions	Role playing
Pictures, infographics	Drawing activities and games	Worksheets
Stories or quotes	Conversations	Essays
Examples	Reflections	Field trips
Ideas or objects	Class discussions	Peer review
Historical information	Tutoring	One-on-one interactions
Memories or shared experiences		Student presentations

Figure 9.2 The four essential parts of pedagogy: objectives, learner backgrounds, methods, and materials.

Designing Learning Experiences

Designing pedagogically sound learning experiences is really a matter of brainstorming and outlining ideas. The design process later develops those plans into more tangible products, such as assignment sheets, syllabus and calendar items, instruction notes, and so on. Teachers are likely familiar with both the design and development processes and may in fact see no difference between the two because the two steps can be so iterative. A teacher will think of a terrific learning experience and jot down some notes (design). From those notes, he or she will craft an assignment sheet or series of instructions (develop), but in the process of writing this out, the teacher might decide to streamline or expand the activity (design) and modify the assignment or instructions accordingly (develop). A novice teacher might go through these steps deliberately and take some time to do it; an experienced teacher might spend just a few seconds on any given iteration of the design phase.

The point of designing learning experiences, therefore, is to systematically put thought into and plan out the things that students will experience. One helpful approach to doing this is the use of a table similar to Figure 9.3 that aligns outcomes with learning experiences and then necessary materials.

In Figure 9.3, the learning experience (going to the library) is not especially tangible and is only one of many that will be needed to accomplish the learning outcome. Another small part of the experience is learning how to locate academic sources. Maybe this will be done through examples, a short video, or a descriptive assignment sheet. The materials needed to facilitate the learning experience will vary depending on how the designers envision the learning experience being completed. In the case in Figure 9.3, the designers recognized the need for a library, some presentation materials (either in print or electronic), and a sheet for collecting source information. Other designers who envision this learning experience differently might have different materials listed. A benefit of this kind of table is that a teacher can readily see which materials need further design efforts. See Box 9.2.

Learning outcome	Learning experience	Necessary materials
Students can identify, summarize, and synthesize texts from various sources and incorporate them in their writing.	Students will go to the library and learn how to locate academic sources to include in a short research paper.	• Library • Presentation materials • Sheet to record source information (i.e., quotes, citations).

Figure 9.3 Aligning outcomes, experiences, and materials.

> **Box 9.2 Principles for Learning Experiences**
>
> The following principles can help guide curriculum designers when considering learning activities and materials.
>
> *Learning experiences and materials are connected to outcomes.* If experiences and resources are used without reference to the learning outcomes, they may serve no purpose. Every activity and every material must have a purpose provided by a learning outcome, or at the very least, by students' needs, lacks, or wants.
>
> *Learning experiences and materials are centered on stakeholders' assumptions about language learning.* From the analysis and the mission statement, hopefully we have a view of the stakeholders' values regarding language learning. As designers keep the vision and mission at the forefront of their minds, learning activities and resources will better match the values of the stakeholders.

Designing Learning Materials

Learning experiences almost universally have materials, though teachers do not always need to plan out these materials themselves. As discussed earlier, going to the library is a valid learning experience in which the library is the predominant material. But the teacher does not have to create the library, provided that one already exists nearby. The teacher is only responsible for designing the process for getting to the library and what will be done there. Will students walk there from class? Will they be responsible to meet at the library when class starts? How will students use library resources? Thinking this through represents the design step for learning materials.

Of course, some materials do require more teacher involvement. If a teacher wants students to write an essay, for instance, the essay needs a prompt, an assignment sheet, and a rubric. The teacher also needs to have a place to provide feedback and record a grade. In this case, designing the learning experience means thinking through these processes and envisioning what the prompt, assignment sheet, and rubric will look like. Some teachers design such materials during the development stage; they don't know what they want the assignment sheet to look like until they start developing it.

An important reminder for all teachers is that most students need and appreciate written instructions, especially for large, complex, or extended assignments. It is ineffective to merely state or explain a homework assignment and hope students remember the task and due date. Teachers should make time to design and then develop essential instructions.

Beyond assignment sheets, there are countless other materials that teachers might design. If a teacher plans to give a lecture, the teacher must envision the content of that lecture as part of the design process. In addition, the teacher must envision reading or listening passages, grammar instruction, classroom realia, conversation topics, definitions, record-keeping sheets, software, PowerPoint slides, informative handouts, and worksheets, however briefly, before they are developed or selected from existing resources.

Designing Learning Sequences

Just as important as designing materials is determining their intended sequence. An obvious principle in teaching is that students should be exposed to increasingly complex tasks so that the sequence of learning experiences progresses from easier to more difficult. Designing this sequence boils down to thinking it through, or trial and error. This is true for both calendaring (planning a course sequence) and lesson planning (planning a class sequence). When calendaring, a teacher should have a general sense of which learning experiences should go first, but other constraints, such as class breaks and programmatic due dates, may have some input on sequence too.

In some cases, a teacher might not realize the best sequence of activities. In one grammar class we observed, the major learning experiences were sequenced according to the textbook chapters, but after we examined the class more closely, it became obvious that the concepts in the textbook were not organized from easiest to hardest. So, at the end of the semester, a curriculum coordinator asked students from various sections of the course to rank each major chapter according to its perceived complexity. After aggregating this information (and consulting with the teacher), the course sequence was redesigned, and, unsurprisingly, student anxiety about the class declined.

A similar principle for sequencing should be observed within lesson plans. A teacher should try to envision the class moving from easier background information into more complex, new material. Thus, it is a good idea to design a brief review of previous information at the beginning of a lesson prior to moving into unfamiliar territory.

As mentioned, the design phase is largely one of brainstorming, making decisions, and jotting down notes. Those notes are then turned into polished documents for teacher and student use later in the development stage. Due to the recursive nature of curriculum development, though, the design step may precede development by just a few moments or may even overlap completely.

Develop

Developing learning experiences and accompanying materials is something most teachers feel comfortable with. In many ways, it is what teachers do every day in terms of calendaring out their course, generating assignment sheets, and planning their lessons. The distinguishing factor of development is that it brings the curricular designs to life; it is the point where the planner becomes the producer and documents are created.

In terms of production, teachers should draft, produce, and evaluate their designs and should do so with a quality standard in mind, whether that standard is self-imposed or fixed by an administrator. A teacher should also be conscientious both of deadlines and of audience needs. A course calendar, for instance, has students as its audience and therefore should be crafted for their ease of uptake. A lesson plan, on the other hand, is usually meant just for the teacher, so shorthanded scribbles with minimal instruction might be just fine.

Developing Learning Experiences

Earlier, we described the planning of learning experiences as a brainstorming or selection process of experiences that align with class objectives. In the development stage, those learning experiences are developed in several different ways. The most efficient way is to select a textbook that has a unified course and sequence table and several student activities that all align with the class objectives. A perfect match between textbook and objectives is rare, so teachers regularly have to develop specialized learning experiences. Such development might include writing out detailed notes of how a learning experience will take place or making the physical preparations for an activity. If a teacher has plans for his or her students to visit a museum to critique pieces of art in pairs, then the development stage may include checking on the museum's hours of operation, cost, and amenities for student discussion. It might also include placing the activity on the course calendar, writing up a short announcement to students, crafting an assignment sheet for the excursion, writing out step-by-step instructions for the instructor, and communicating with administrators about the experience beforehand. The end product of the development stage should be a working activity ready to be implemented.

Some learning experiences remain totally intangible throughout their entire development stage. For instance, a simple experience in which a teacher recounts a story from his or her own days as a student may not need to be written out. It may still need to be developed, though, which in this case would include the teacher having the actual experience in the first place and then rehearsing the retelling of it before class. But if it is a quick personal story, the teacher might not need to jot down notes or even mark it on the course calendar or lesson plan.

Developing Learning Materials

For most students, learning experiences are strongly tied to physical or electronic documents. These include course calendars, textbooks, PowerPoint presentations, and assignment sheets. These documents provide content or instruction that students can refer to repeatedly as they plan and manage their learning. Of course, not all learning experiences have associated materials; a lecture might have nothing more than a teacher's voice and actions associated with it. Nevertheless, when teachers plan to develop learning materials, they should do so with principles of quality, punctuality, and audience awareness in mind.

There are few universal standards for learning material quality. Perhaps one universal is that of accuracy:

- Calendars should accurately reflect the days of the semester.
- Textbooks should provide accurate and useful information.
- Presentations and assignment sheets should faithfully reflect class content and assignment criteria.

Beyond this, quality can be determined in myriad ways and at countless thresholds. A good principle is to seek input from other teachers, administrators, and students to ensure that learning materials make sense and are clear. Learning materials should also be developed with an eye to deadlines. Ideally, any supporting materials should be developed with sufficient lead time to ensure the quality standard associated with them. See Box 9.3.

Box 9.3 Assignment Sheets

Many minor assignments do not require full-blown assignment sheets. It is possible to explain something verbally in class and have students perform well. But when an assignment is large, complex, or extended, it requires an assignment sheet, whether that is paper-based or electronic. So what should go into an assignment sheet? Here are some vital components:

Title: The assignment title, including the class name and semester, if possible.
Identification: A place for students to write their identifying information, such as name or student number, if the assignment sheet will also be used to collect individual responses.
Instructions: Instructions written in simple language with enough detail to lead students through the entire assignment process yet not overwhelm them.
Due dates: A schedule, or list of deadlines or due dates that students must follow, along with instructions of where and how to submit the assignments.
Grading criteria: Information about how the assignment will be graded and how much it is worth. For discrete-point assignments, point values are usually sufficient; for essay assignments, a rubric is usually important.

It is worth reiterating that teachers should develop learning materials with a sensitivity to intended audiences. We have seen learning materials that seemed ill-suited to a particular audience, such as excessively long or unhelpfully short assignment sheets, syllabi that were demeaning to students, and course calendars meant for student use but full of parenthetical notes meant only for the teacher. Avoiding all confusion in a learning material is rarely possible, but with some audience awareness, input from others, and familiarity with the genre of the learning material, teachers can develop products that make sense to the right people.

Developing Learning Sequences

The two major learning sequences discussed earlier are those of calendaring and lesson planning. Calendaring involves establishing instructional activities and due dates for a given period and recording these either physically or electronically. We have seen a host of approaches to calendaring that span from the minimalist, in which only a few critical dates are listed in bullet format, to detailed calendaring, in which every day (including non-instruction days) is crammed with descriptions of learning activities and assignments due.

Calendaring choices are a matter of personal and institutional preferences, but the principles of quality, punctuality, and audience awareness still apply. The calendar should be accurate and useful for students. In terms of punctuality, it may be difficult to plan out an entire semester in advance. In fact, we have known some teachers who calendar one day at a time—though we highly advise against this. If calendaring the entire course ahead of time is not possible, we recommend that teachers calendar at least two weeks in advance and provide these chunks of developed calendar units to their students. Audience awareness means developing a student version of the calendar that is readable for them, in addition to a calendar with teacher notes if needed. We have seen effective electronic calendars in which all teaching notes, PowerPoint presentations, worksheets, quizzes, links, and so forth were integrated smoothly into each class day. This kind of calendaring straddles the line between calendaring and lesson planning. See Box 9.4.

While calendaring makes up the course-level sequence of learning experiences, lesson planning deals with the day-to-day curriculum. Novice teachers are advised to write out their lesson plans, which creates a tangible product for their own consumption. More experienced teachers may need little more than a few notes scrawled on a sticky note. Some teachers merely use the course syllabus as a reminder of what to cover in class each day. In all cases, the teacher develops a lesson plan, even though the last example illustrates a relatively intangible one.

Box 9.4 Calendaring Options

Teachers have come up with a bewildering assortment of calendaring options. Figures 9.4, 9.5, and 9.6 may be instructive for teachers seeking alternative methods for scheduling their course experiences.

Week	Day	Due Dates/Assignments
1	M	
	F	Speaking Report 1 due
2	F	Speaking Report 2 due
3	F	Speaking Report 3 due
4	F	Speaking Report 4 due
5	F	Reading Report 5 due
6	F	Reading Horizons Training Reading Report 6 due
7	F	Reading Report 7 due
8	F	Reading Report 8 due
9	F	Reading Report 9 due
10	F	Reading Report 10 due
11	F	Writing Report 11 due
12	F	Writing Report 12 due
13	F	Writing Report 13 due
14	F	Writing Report 14 due
	F	**Final Portfolio Due**

Figure 9.4 An option for formatting calendars.

Monday	Tuesday	Wednesday	Thursday	Friday
2/4	2/5	2/6	2/7 Introductions (30 min classes)	2/8 Pre-test Syllabus

Monday	Tuesday	Wednesday	Thursday	Friday
2/11 Conversations over Food	2/12 Advice for Staying Healthy	2/13 Nutrit **(30 min classes)**	2/14 Fruits VS Vegetables	2/15 American Food Recipes **Group Photo**
2/18 **No Class President's Day**	2/19 Fast Food Recipes	2/20 **Graduation**	2/21	2/22

Figure 9.5 Another option for formatting calendars.

Date	Description	Date	Description
M Jan 9	First day of class	F Mar 17	Spring break day—No Class
M Jan 16	MLK Day—No class	M Apr 3	Observation Reports due (on LS)
F Feb 10	Midterm on Reading begins (on LS)	F Apr 7	Midterm on Vocabulary opens (on LS)
M Feb 20	President's Day—No Class	F Apr 14	Portfolio Assignment due (on LS)
T Feb 21	Monday instruction— YES class	M Apr 19	Last day of class
M Mar 13	Midterm on Writing begins (on LS)	M Apr 24	Final Exam: 1119 JKB from 11 AM to 2 PM

Figure 9.6 Another option for formatting calendars.

Features of a lesson plan may differ from teacher to teacher and in different teaching guidebooks. One uncontroversial constant is that good lesson plans should be established on one or more learning objectives. These objectives should be measurable and realistic statements of what students should be able to accomplish by the end of the lesson. Here are three examples of such statements:

- ◆ By the end of this lesson, students should be able to use three new English phrases to create a dialogue which they can perform with a partner during the next class period.

- By the end of this lesson, students should be able to accurately form the past perfect tense of verbs in English in five novel sentences of their own creation.
- In this class, students will develop an increased awareness of three different genres of writing (writing in the humanities, in biological sciences, and in chemistry) by examining specific linguistic features which distinguish the genres.

Once the teacher has identified an objective, the rest of the lesson plan can be fleshed out to support that objective. For instance, the teacher may introduce some direct instruction or modeling of grammatical or lexical features that the students need to know. He or she may also provide time for students to manipulate those features as a group, in pairs, and/or alone until the students seem comfortable with the features. Then the teacher might supervise while having students work to accomplish the objective or to apply the instruction in a novel way. In this case, that might mean providing time for students to work in pairs to create a dialogue with target phrases, or giving students the time needed to work on creating spontaneous sentences with the past perfect tense. In the end, teachers should have some kind of accountability built into the lesson or into a homework assignment by which students can demonstrate that they have achieved the objective.

In addition to an objective and supporting instruction, teachers should leave room for announcements and other opening events, such as a warm-up activity to get students into a learning frame of mind or a discussion of previous homework or assignments. A teacher should also have one or more contingency plans in case of extra time at the end of the lesson or in case some part of the lesson plan doesn't work because of technology glitches or some other unforeseen situation.

In all, a general lesson plan has the following outline such as this one:

1) Objective
2) Materials needed
3) Business
   a. Announcements
   b. Check homework or previous assignments
4) Warm-up activity
5) Lesson instruction/activities
6) Display/collection of in-class work
7) Contingency plan
8) Homework assignments

Box 9.5 demonstrates a sample lesson plan, and Box 9.6 is an example of a handout that could be given to students. The lesson plan came from a very low-level ESL writing class in which students were beginning to write short, four- and five-paragraph style essays. Each class was 60 minutes long, and students met four times per week for a full semester.

Box 9.5   Sample Lesson Plan

Lesson Plan for Commentary in Writing: "For Example" Phrases and Fact or Story Phrases

Objective: Students should be able to add at least one "for example" statement or one fact or story statement to each body paragraph in the essays they are currently working on.

Background: Students spent Wednesday's class in the computer lab. We discussed simple thesis statements and topic sentences. Students learned that a thesis statement should contain an opinion on an issue and the main points of the paper. They then learned how topic sentences head each major paragraph and lead into commentary. I only mentioned that commentary can include quotes, stories, statistics, facts, and examples. They are now ready to learn how to use examples as commentary in their main paragraphs.

Materials needed:
1. Two pieces of candy
2. A fish bowl
3. The class handout with fish paragraphs and other items

Business (about 5 minutes)
1. Take roll.
2. Collect any "Perfect Sentences" assignments from last class.
3. Review the notion of thesis statements and topic sentences in American academic writing.

Warm-up activities (about 15 minutes)
1. Journal writing
   a. Have students write for 10 minutes on this topic—"What is the best job in the world?"
   b. After 10 minutes, choose two students to read their entries. Give them candy for participating.

Lesson Part I (about 5 minutes)
1. Read the following paragraph to students while displaying a fish bowl, and ask them to pay attention to the details of the paragraph.
   a. "Fish are good pets. They are small. Other animals are big. Fish can eat, sleep, swim, and exercise all in the same small place."

2. Explain to students that this is typical of their writing. Now, have them pay attention to details as you read the second paragraph:
   a. "Fish are good pets because they are small. For example, they can live in a tiny glass bowl. Other animals are big. For example, dogs need lots of space to run around and bark. And cats need a place to eat, a different place to sleep, and another place to use the restroom. But fish can eat, sleep, swim, and exercise all in the same small place."
3. Explain that they need to include more details as in the second paragraph. Now direct their attention to the words *for example* in the second paragraph. Explain that these words are one way to include more detail.

Lesson Part II (about 15 minutes): The second sentence of the paragraph—*Commentary*
1. Distribute the handout to students. Under the "For Example" heading, help them write a "for example" sentence after the first sentence, such as the following:
   a. "Hamburgers are unhealthy. For example, they are greasy and salty. Also, they are usually covered in ketchup and mustard, which can contain a lot of sugar."
2. Help students recognize that the words *for example* help make the writing longer, more thoughtful, more descriptive, and more complete.
3. Have them work alone to write "for example" phrases on several topic sentences.
4. Choose some students to read their sentences out loud.
5. Be sure to emphasize the importance that students remain on topic when finishing their sentences. New writers often place two or three different ideas into one paragraph because they struggle to control their essay in expected American academic style.
6. If there is time left over, encourage students to look at their own essays and begin adding commentary.

Lesson Part III (about 15 minutes): Other commentary
1. As students finish the "for example" sentences, help them understand that they can also tell stories and provide facts, quotes, and other commentary after the topic sentence. Provide one example on the spot, and write it on the chalkboard.
2. Tell students to turn to the "Other Commentary" section of the handout and write a story or other commentary after one or two of the topic sentences.
3. Have students share a few of the sentences out loud.

Contingency Plan
1. If there is extra time left over, have students apply this new technique to their own essays by writing topic sentences and fleshing the paragraph out with examples and commentary.

Homework
1. Students should add either one "for example" phrase or one fact or story to each body paragraph in their essay. I will check this when they turn in their drafts next week.

Box 9.6 Sample Handout

Handout: Commentary in Writing

Bad fish paragraph:

Fish are good pets. They are small. Other animals are big. Fish can eat, sleep, swim, and exercise all in the same place.

Better fish paragraph:

Fish are good pets because they are small. **For example**, they can live in a tiny glass bowl. Other animals are big and need more space. **For example**, dogs need lots of space to run around and bark. And cats need a place to eat, a different place to sleep, and another place to bury their feces. But fish can eat, sleep, swim, and exercise all in the same small place.

FOR EXAMPLE

1. Milk is good for your body.
2. Roosters are noisy.
3. Cell phones distract students in class.
4. Poverty contributes to many social problems.

OTHER COMMENTARY (stories, facts, etc.)

5. Homework helps students learn new things.
6. Learning another language allows people to enjoy new cultures.
7. Exercise makes people more fit.
8. TV keeps children from spending time with their parents.

One thing about lesson planning not mentioned already is that instructors should always take time to reflect on their lesson afterward and make observations or goals for improvement. They can gauge to what extent their materials and instructions met the needs of their learners and adjust if necessary for the next class. They might also consider issues of classroom management and think of ways to keep students engaged and on task or anticipate student concerns. Teachers can regularly solicit student feedback in formal or informal evaluations in order to get a fresh student perspective on their teaching, too. See Box 9.7.

Box 9.7 The ROPPES Approach to Lesson Planning

Consider the learning experience described earlier in this chapter. Students will go to the library and **learn** how to locate academic sources for inclusion in a short research paper.

At this point, we should be asking ourselves, "How will the student learn this?" The answer to that question may be developed into a lesson plan. While there are many ways to organize a lesson plan, let's look at the ROPPES approach—Review, Overview, Present, Practice, Evaluate, and Summarize.

Figure 9.7 is a very basic lesson plan. While formal lesson plans are usually much more detailed, the purpose of this chart is to provide a skeletal framework as an example of developing learning experiences.

With this basic outline, you can begin considering other necessary aspects of this learning experience. Do you need to reserve a room in the library to provide this instruction? Do you need to walk with students to make sure they can find the library? What does this information sheet look like? What should it include?

Review— 3–5 minutes	Review instruction from previous day on the contents of a short research paper.
Overview— 3–5 minutes	Focus on the use of academic sources. Explain why they are important and how they are used.
Present— 7–10 min.	Demonstrate how to find hard copies of academic sources in the university library by using the library's catalog. Show students the sheet they will be using to record the information they find.
Practice— 15–20 minutes	Help students use the library to locate academic sources on their own. Have them complete the information sheet with information from the sources they find.
Evaluate— 5–10 minutes	Have students provide evidence that they understand and can apply what they have learned. Provide feedback as needed.
Summary— 5 minutes	Debrief the students. Review the importance of using academic sources and answer any lingering questions.

Figure 9.7 A basic lesson plan outline.

Implement

In many ways, implementing learning experiences is what teachers do best. This is the stand-up-and-teach part of a curriculum. While it can be a time-consuming and challenging step, it can also be the most rewarding. And since learning experiences deliver the entire curriculum over the course of countless tiny installments, teaching really is where the curricular house we have been building becomes a reality.

Implementing Learning Experiences and Materials

Since the learning experiences and their accompanying materials are so intertwined, we see little reason to separate them here. In this stage of implementation, teachers teach and learners learn. The teacher follows his or her lesson plan, presenting materials as needed and managing the classroom atmosphere to ensure that learning can occur. Meanwhile, students interact with the learning experiences and make connections and develop new knowledge and skills along the way. Depending on the teacher's approach to education, he or she may be a facilitator in the classroom, quietly weaving students through a series of increasingly complex learning experiences. Or the teacher may be an expert, providing students with specialized information and learning opportunities.

Of course, instruction is only one part of implementation. Other elements include training the teachers and learners and delivering the learning products. Teachers themselves have to be trained on the learning experiences they are using, which seems absurd if teachers have designed and developed their own experiences. However, teachers often select rather than fully design materials, such as when adopting a textbook, a learning management system, or a new piece of software. In this sense, teachers need to become familiar enough with their method of delivery that they can present it to the class. They may also need to practice their delivery until they can effectively implement what they have designed. This is especially true when a teacher adopts assignments or learning experiences from another teacher. Even highly competent teachers can struggle to present someone else's lesson plan, so a bit of collaboration, adjustment, or practice may be in order.

Implementation also involves the training of learners so that they know how to use tools that are new to them. Students can be stupefied by what teachers assume are straightforward directions. In language classes, students may have such a limited grasp of the target language that instructions have to be accompanied by images or actions to get the point across. These considerations might be part of the design and development stages, but the true test of their effectiveness comes in the implementation stage.

Finally, implementation involves delivering the learning products, including storing textbooks, arranging for a classroom space, and photocopying materials. Generally, the concerns of product delivery are handled by program-level staff, since all courses will have similar needs for delivery resources, classroom scheduling needs, and so forth. But this does not mean that teachers have no part in this type of implementation. They need to request textbooks, make individual copies, and arrange the classroom to meet their needs. Additional information on program-wide implementation is presented in Chapter 10.

Implementing Learning Sequences

There is little to discuss in terms of implementing learning sequences beyond the advice to keep students apprised of the initial course calendar and any changes that may come up. Another recommendation is for teachers to build stability into their lesson plans by repeating predictable sequences of activities: start with opening announcements, move to a warm-up speaking activity, hold all tests on Fridays, and so on. See Box 9.8.

Box 9.8   Evaluation of Learning Experiences

A final step in the ADDIE model, which will be covered in greater detail in Chapter 11, is that of evaluation. Learning experiences should be evaluated

Design	Develop
Are the learning experiences based on learning outcomes?	Are the steps for implementing the learning experience clearly articulated?
Are the learning experiences based on the assumptions administrators, teachers, and students have regarding language learning?	Are the necessary materials created? Are the instructions clear for students?
	What method or approach did you use to develop the learning experience sequence (i.e., ROPES)?
Are the learning experiences feasible?	Implement
	How will the learning experiences be introduced and explained to learners?
	Where and when will they complete the learning experiences?
	How will they demonstrate completion of the learning experiences?

Figure 9.8 Questions that can help inform the design, development, and implementation of learning experiences.

> in terms of their design, development, and implementation. In Figure 9.8, we illustrate several evaluation questions that can be used to help determine the value and effectiveness of each step of the process.

Chapter Summary

This chapter has discussed the role of learning experiences, specifically how they should be designed, developed, and implemented. Learning experiences are day-to-day activities that make up the content of a course. They are tied to class objectives and are often supported by physical materials that tell students how to complete the experiences. In designing learning experiences, teachers brainstorm possible ways to connect learners to a desired objective. That brainstorming process should lead to experiences that can be developed into well thought-out activities that are complete with instructions, that support materials with a quality standard, that are punctual, and that are audience driven. The sequence of these activities should also be designed and developed to foster student learning. Once the learning experiences are designed and developed, implementation begins, which includes teaching the class and delivering materials. The end result, ideally, is the language development of learners such that they have increased linguistic ability that will always be theirs.

> ### Activities
>
> *Activity 9.1*
>
> Think about a class in which you were a teacher or student. Identify several learning experiences associated with that class. Describe their general characteristics and whether the associated materials were sufficient to make the experience useful.
>
> *Activity 9.2*
>
> Consider a class objective from a program you are aware of. What kind of learning experience(s) and materials might you design to fulfill the objective? Bear in mind that any given objective may require multiple experiences to accomplish it.
>
> *Activity 9.3*
>
> Given that learning experiences should be designed so that students encounter easier tasks before harder ones, reflect on a class you have taken as a student.

Did the learning experiences generally follow this pattern? Are there situations in which this type of progression is not ideal?

Activity 9.4

Locate an assignment sheet you have created or one that you worked on as a student. Based on the information in Box 9.3, determine whether the assignment met the minimum requirements. Are there additional details on your assignment sheet that do not appear in Box 9.3? Are there things not mentioned in Box 9.3 that you believe should be a part of every assignment sheet?

Activity 9.5

Locate a calendar for three courses not taught by you. Compare the calendars to determine similarities and differences. Which calendars were most user-friendly to you? Which seemed most efficient for the teacher? Are there features from the calendars you might adopt in your own calendaring?

Activity 9.6

Evaluate the lesson plan in Box 9.5. What features of this plan do you like or dislike? What features would you add or remove? Would you be able to teach this class based on the format and content of the lesson plan as printed? Why or why not?

Activity 9.7

Reflect on two different but effective teachers you have had in the past. What was their teaching and implementation style? Compare this style with the teaching and implementation styles of two ineffective teachers. What made the good teachers good and the ineffective ones ineffective?

References

Macalister, J., & Nation, I. P. (2020). *Language curriculum design* (2nd ed.). Routledge. http://dx.doi.org/10.4324/9780429203763

Palkova, A. V., & Sapozhnikova, L. M. (2021). Instructional design in foreign language teaching. In *SHS web of conferences* (Vol. 127, p. 03005). EDP Sciences.

Tyler, R. W. (2013). *Basic principles of curriculum and instruction*. University of Chicago Press. http://dx.doi.org/10.7208/chicago/9780226086644.001.0001

10
Program-Wide Implementation

Introduction

In the previous three chapters, we discussed learning outcomes, assessment and feedback, and learning experiences. These are core elements of any curriculum. In addition to explaining these features, we articulated ways to design, develop, and implement them. In this chapter, we revisit the last stage, that of implementation, in order to describe program-wide implementation. This is a consideration deserving of its own chapter, because effective implementation often comes only after thoughtful preparation and a view of the "big picture" in which program developers see how all curriculum components should work together—both old and new. Simply having a good curricular vision is insufficient, though. Research suggests that good ideas rarely lead to actual change because they evade implementation or the implementation approach is lacking (Allio, 2005; Pryor et al., 2007).

This chapter explains the implementation process by examining the major players involved in implementation: the facilitators, the learners, the product, and potential antagonistic stakeholders. We also discuss elements of strategic implementation (see Noble, 1999) by showing one way that curriculum designers can map out complex implementation processes.

The process of implementing a curriculum can be boiled down to two important concepts: competency and delivery. Competency refers to the buy-in and training of facilitators and learners—that is, making sure key individuals are supportive of curricular innovations, understand how the curriculum works, and know how to use it. Delivery of the product includes everything from acquiring textbooks for learners to passing out worksheet papers in a physical classroom. While there is certainly more nuance to competency and delivery, implementation is a step of curriculum design that teachers and administrators are likely already familiar with and yet may not always be prepared for.

Building a House

To use the analogy of building or renovating a home, implementation is the actual construction process that leads to a completed building project. Ideally, the construction takes place only after housing needs have been analyzed, the design has been conceptualized and approved by stakeholders for the new home or renovation with appropriate engineering specifications or blueprints, and finally the building materials have been selected—the lumber, stone, roofing supplies, paint, hardware, and so forth. All these materials have to be ordered and delivered to the home site at the right times, which is one part of the implementation process. And while the home designers (in our metaphor, the administrators) may choose to do most of the construction themselves, laborers—those with specific skills like knowing how to pour cement or paint walls—are usually hired to do the work because of their specialized skill sets and certifications. In curriculum implementation, the construction supervisors represent teachers who have the skills to manage a crew of laborers (or classroom of students) and deploy instruction so that learning occurs.

In the housing metaphor, construction supervisors (the teachers) are usually thought of as *cooperative* members of the team. After all, they are qualified professionals who are gainfully employed in their chosen profession and, as such, not only enjoy their work but are also able to look at a master blueprint and know exactly how to work in concert with their colleagues to produce a beautiful end product. Although this is the assumption, the reality can be messier. For instance, not all construction supervisors read the full technical engineering documents associated with construction or renovation, and some may be resistant to the design or may have valid insights into flaws of the design. They are also likely to encounter real-world problems that the building planners couldn't foresee, which may require innovative work-arounds or even complete redesigns. On top of all this, some construction supervisors may not have the specialized skills to complete a task called for in the design, so they may require some on-the-job skill training or may need support from specialist technicians.

Many of the limitations to effective construction can be paralleled with the limitations of teaching staff (see Box 10.1). For instance, although employed in their profession, some teachers may be stretched too thin, marginalized, or unsatisfied with their position and thus be uncommitted to curricular change. They may have aspirations for other work and, as a result, give only partial attention to their teaching. Moreover, individual teachers may not know how to interpret complex curriculum documents, and frequently teachers with considerable experience can be very resistant to curricular innovations or new ways of implementing a curriculum, particularly if they were not involved in developing those changes. Additionally, teachers can see design and practicality flaws that curriculum designers didn't anticipate, but they can also be unfamiliar with implementation procedures, which could hamper their ability to effectively deploy the curriculum. The implementation step, therefore, needs to account for all these and other potential limitations in order to give the best chances for a smooth curriculum transition.

Box 10.1   Curricular Construction Crew

It may be hard to follow parts of our house metaphor without a who's who guide to construction. This box should help to explain things.

Designers, Planners, Architects, Engineers, and Drafters

Construction: These professionals work with those who commission a project to analyze needs and then design and develop detailed plans to make the project a reality.

Teaching: These are program directors, coordinators, supervisors, and others involved in analyzing curricular needs and then designing and developing essential curricular documents. In some cases, a single teacher holds all of these roles at once, particularly when making a curricular change in a single course. Sometimes students are directly involved in (re)designing their own curriculum.

Construction Supervisors

Construction: These professionals have specialized training to read design plans and execute all or part of a construction project. They can do the work themselves or hire laborers, who they then manage.

Teaching: These are the teachers and facilitators who provide instruction to students based on the curricular documents. They are capable of doing all the tasks themselves (i.e., reading, writing, grammar, etc.), yet they work with one or more students to complete these tasks.

> **Laborers**
>
> *Construction*: These individuals do the physical labor on a house project. They hammer nails, set up drywall, cement the tile, install shingles on the roof, etc.
>
> *Teaching*: These are the students who do the work in the classroom and at home. They read books, write essays, learn new vocabulary items, practice grammar, etc.

Building Facilitator Competency

Facilitators are mainly instructors, but they might include others such as TAs, administrative staff, and service personnel. They should all develop a degree of competency according to their level of involvement in the curriculum as well as expected learning outcomes, the method of delivery, and the testing procedures. In some instances, they may have a high level of competency, particularly if they were involved with curricular design decisions, but in other instances, they may be very unfamiliar with new curricular processes. We will look at building their competency in the next section.

Instructors

The instructors are usually the most obvious agents of implementation. Ideally, they should be involved with planning curricular changes, and in some cases, they may even be the curriculum designers. To illustrate this in a small-scale curricular change, suppose a teacher of a beginning-level reading class was told of an increase in Iranian refugees who would be attending her class next semester (analysis) and therefore decided to include several short reading assignments that focused on Iranian and Middle Eastern cultural issues in order to bring cultural sensitivity to her non-Iranian students while making use of the Iranian students' cultural schemata for reading comprehension (design). She found several appropriate texts that fit her topic requirements, read them, and created study guides, vocabulary lists, and comprehension questions to accompany the readings (develop). She then ordered the texts or printed them and enthusiastically introduced both the texts and the support materials to her students, who were lukewarm to the texts at first, but came to enjoy them through the teacher's positive attitude and willingness to modify some of the support materials according to students' needs and requests (implementation).

In a scenario like this, where the curricular change is fairly minute and the teacher has a strong locus of curricular control, the curricular change can be very smooth. For instance, because she had selected them, the instructor was able to use the texts competently. This meant she read them, created support materials for them, and thought through how to present them to the students effectively. She even made modifications to alleviate concerns of antagonistic stakeholders (the students who were lukewarm at first). If the text selection had been imposed on her by a supervisor, things might have been different.

Other curricular changes are much broader and/or more complex and require more instructor support. An example of this is the migration of a writing class from a traditional classroom to an online setting. Such a shift has implications for teachers who will need to adapt to a new way of teaching that effectively utilizes technology. Even teachers who are familiar with teaching in a computer classroom might still encounter frequent curricular changes as they integrate new technological applications into their classes or encounter glitches in service. The international move to online instruction caused by the COVID-19 pandemic is an example of this. Teachers were obligated to quickly develop online teaching competencies, often with limited prior preparation.

When administrators impose large curricular changes, even when those changes are warmly embraced by the teachers, the administrators still have the onus to support instructors as they develop needed competency in certain materials or processes. This can be explained using the prior example of a writing teacher migrating from a traditional classroom to an online setting. Even if the administration made digital affordances available, such as a robust learning management system, a secure grading portal, and online proctoring services for tests, the instructors may still need orientation on how the new applications work. For instance, teachers may need help knowing what certain software applications do and developing approaches for effectively engaging students with computer-mediated instruction, such as how to make the most use of videos, chat functions, presentations, group work, class discussions, homework, assignment submissions, and so forth. Effective training can be done in multiple venues and at different times. A quick orientation to a new learning management system, for instance, could be done in a single, large-group presentation before classes begin. At other times, teachers can attend periodic workshops about principles of computer-mediated instruction or read literature on best practices. In other words, supporting facilitator competency generally happens in pre- and in-service trainings which the implementation team should schedule and arrange.

In addition to issues of physical and principled uses of curricular components, instructors also need to understand the blueprints or plans of the curriculum. They need to know what the expected learning outcomes are and the testing procedures for determining whether students meet those outcomes. In this way, students and teachers can use the curricular components to their intended end rather than in a random or misguided direction. The short message here is that instructors cannot simply be handed a new curricular component and be expected to know what to do with it. Instead, any top-down administrative curricular changes should be accompanied with appropriate pre-, in-, and/or post-service training so that teachers know what to do with new components and, ideally, how their use will contribute to student and curricular success.

In thinking through the support of teacher competence, it might be helpful to consider answers to the following questions:

1. What new materials or techniques am I asking facilitators to use?
2. How do those materials or techniques differ from what they are already familiar with?
3. What are the two or three most important things facilitators must know in order to start using those materials or techniques?
4. Who can best provide training on the new materials or techniques? A fellow teacher, a supervisor, a curriculum developer, or a specialized trainer?
5. When will that training be most useful? Before instruction starts, during instruction, after instruction (such as a reflection activity), or a combination of before, during, and after?
6. In what size group should that training be conducted? Whole group, small group, one-on-one, or some combination?
7. What kind of questions or concerns are facilitators likely to have that should be addressed during or after training?

Administrative Staff and Service Personnel

The role of administrative staff in implementation is often behind the scenes, but their support is invaluable in ordering, storing, maintaining, and servicing curricular components. For instance, staff members may provide access to funds for purchasing books, computers, copy machines and paper, or other materials. Think of a university bookstore as an example of this (at least before Amazon). If teachers wanted to use a new textbook in their class, that book needed to be ordered, shipped to the school, stored as inventory until students purchased it, exchanged for money, potentially re-purchased, and eventually discarded or donated elsewhere. Traditionally, all of these steps were carried out by administrative staff and service personnel. However, as texts become more accessible online and in digital formats, instructors and students are taking on some of these administrative and service roles. For instance, a teacher might list a new textbook on his or her syllabus and instruct students to purchase it online. Thus, the students become purchasing agents and become responsible for storing the book and ultimately returning, donating, or discarding it when done.

Just because the administrative and service personnel roles may shift to students or instructors does not mean that curriculum designers can overlook these duties when planning for implementation. A common reality of asking students to order their own textbooks is that delivery times can vary widely. Students often have timely access to books when teachers order them through the school bookstore well in advance of the first day of class. However, if students process their own purchases online, they may wait a week or more before the texts arrive. Similarly, if instructors are left to their own devices to order and distribute textbooks for the class, they might also run into text delivery problems. Fully digital textbooks alleviate some of these issues but present their own problems with internet/computer access, copyright limitations, student familiarity with and willingness to use digital books, and so on.

The example of a new textbook is fairly simplistic, and the role of administrative staff is still evolving, but bigger changes, such as the purchase and service of computer equipment generally still fit under the purview of administrative staff and service personnel who purchase, install, troubleshoot, maintain, repair, and ultimately discard hardware and software. Curricular designers must be aware of the implementation costs of their curricular changes so that their plans don't break down in the face of practicality issues, such as budgetary constraints.

Administrative staff and service personnel also tend to interact with students in key roles: advising them in their class options, offering tutoring services, answering questions, providing student support services, maintaining physical spaces, and so on. Again, these are sometimes absorbed by instructors, but still, administrative staff must be apprised of all curricular changes, learning outcomes, delivery methods, and testing procedures so that they can provide the most up-to-date guidance and support possible to students and help coordinate among teachers and between teachers and upper administration.

Supporting administrative staff and service personnel can be accomplished in administrative training sessions, unless costly and complex administrative changes are needed. Still, one-on-one or small group sessions with administrators are usually sufficient for training, and if a particular administrative assistant leads the language program, that individual could do most of the training.

Building Learner Competency

Just as facilitators need to become familiar with and competent with new curricular components, so do students. And just as teachers might be resistant to curricular change, students are sometimes even more resistant because simple things like the change of a textbook can end up being an unexpected and unpleasant expense for cash-strapped students. Also, new ways of teaching can cut against the grain of students' expectations for effective instruction, particularly if students are used to lecture-style classes and are now being asked to engage in group conversations or vice versa. Perhaps the most disruptive curricular change for both teachers and students is the introduction of new technologies or software, since these often present a steep learning curve, which the COVID-19 pandemic put into sharp relief for educators and students. This all being said, there are certainly curricular changes that can be well received by both facilitators and students. But generally, the designers who introduce a curricular change often need to help students see the value of new curricular changes.

When it comes to building learner competency, usually it is their instructors who introduce the new curricular methods or materials. Teachers, of course, need to be familiar with the new curricular elements so they can transfer this familiarity on to their students. And this serves to emphasize the importance of teacher and facilitator support: expecting teachers to explain a complex new website or sell their students on purchasing an expensive new textbook without providing adequate rationale for those elements can spell disaster or revolt. Sometimes it's fine for teachers to learn the utility of a new material alongside their students, but even in these cases, the teachers should at least be apprised of the curricular change long enough in advance to allow them time to review the new material on their own if they would like.

Once teachers are prepared to introduce the new material to their students, they can do so in a traditional way (i.e., during class time), or they can do it through other innovative approaches, such as self-study, homework assignments, outside-of-class group work, or a variety of other methods. For instance, when teachers introduce a new textbook, they might lead students through the first few introductory pages, the table of contents, key parts of several chapters, and so on. Doing this in class ensures that all present students receive the same instruction. But a teacher might also assign the same instruction as homework or create a worksheet that requires students to answer questions only after scanning each section mentioned earlier. All this can be part of the learner training component of implementation.

With technology, learner competency might happen as described previously, through in-class or homework-based activities. But it is probably more likely that after a brief introduction by the teacher, students will continue to learn about a particular website or electronic application on their own. In this scenario, the competency component might last the entire semester as students figure out new ways to use the application. And because of the natural proficiency of younger learners with technology, many experienced teachers might find it more productive to have students show them how a particular device, website, or internet application works. In this way, students and teachers become competent through a reversal in the teaching roles. This role reversal might not be feasible or even beneficial in every instance, but it should at least be considered as a possible way to support learners once in a while.

The previous paragraphs have dealt mostly with new curricular materials in which a sales pitch is often needed. However, sometimes new curricular materials or methods can require teachers to establish and maintain very specific rules, and the articulation and enforcing of these rules is part of the implementation step. Take as an example of these kinds of rules a situation we were familiar with, in which a school required students to write an essay as part of their final exam. Students were given the topic of the essay in advance and were required to bring their own laptops to class on the final exam day in order to write the essay within a specific timeframe. This was a new approach to the final exam, which was historically handwritten on paper, and students were unfamiliar with it, but many could immediately see ways to cheat. They could pre-type the essay (although they didn't know the exact prompt, they at least knew the general topic, which might have been good enough). They could also potentially use the internet to search for pre-written essays on the specific topic once they got it during the final. They could also use grammar- and spell-checking software and potentially email or e-chat with one another to discuss their answers to the essay or to brainstorm what to write. If the essay prompt was posted electronically, they might be able to stay home and write their essay remotely, perhaps with the help of friends or roommates.

Of course, the curriculum designers had thought through some of these issues and partially used some to their advantage: they wanted students to use grammar- and spell-checking software, and they were supportive of students using an online dictionary. But as students brought up questions about pre-writing their essays and writing those essays from home, the teachers and curriculum designers had to consult together in order to establish set rules. These included things like students had to be physically present to take the final exam, and all students had to sit in a formation where the teacher could monitor what was on their screens. Also, students were told that they could bring an outline of an essay on the general topic, but not a full essay. Most of the students followed these rules as a matter of personal integrity, but if that had not been the case, then teachers and curriculum designers would have had to radically redesign their implementation so as to prevent cheating. In fact, the sheer requirement for surveillance and the cumbersome nature of having every student take a laptop to the final eventually pushed curriculum designers to find another approach, which was to hold each final exam in a computer lab and then eventually to use a fully online system. This required some reworking of schedules, which they were able to accomplish with the help of service personnel, and the final exams became much easier to implement and administer.

In this example, we can see how implementation can often include strict rules. The example also illustrates the give-and-take nature of implementation: sometimes student questions and approaches to using material require that curriculum designers, instructors, facilitators, and learners work together and react to each other to find the most productive and efficient implementation method.

One important note about building learner competency is that writing down specific instructions is often very helpful. A written record of how to use a new material or how to access a website, for instance, can help those learners who prefer visual instructions, and it can be helpful for learners who wish to return to the instructions again later. Whenever possible, accompany learner support with a written copy of instructions.

In thinking through building learner competency, it might be helpful to consider answers to the following questions:

1. What new materials or techniques am I asking learners to use?
2. Who will train learners to use these materials or techniques? The curriculum designers, a supervising instructor, their instructor, individual learning, online tutorials, etc.?
3. When should that training occur and how long/extensive should it be? Who will create a written version of the training?
4. What rules must learners obey in order to make the materials or techniques useable for their intended purpose? If there are too many rules, how might the methods or materials be redesigned or implemented in a more efficient way?
5. What kind of questions or concerns are students likely to have that should be addressed during or after training?

Delivery of the Product

The third component of implementation is the actual delivery of the product, which covers a wide variety of considerations. For instance, delivery includes establishing an actual learning space, making sure the learning space is adequate for the curriculum tools, and storing all books, manipulative kits, CD-ROMs, and software. It also means putting these materials in place for student and facilitator use and making sure any external internet links are live. But delivery also includes inventory maintenance, building upkeep, computer support and troubleshooting, divvying up of and tracking limited resources, assigning teacher office space, and the actual teaching of classes where teachers deliver the instruction.

In online instruction, many of these considerations are digital, so physical space is less of a concern, but electronic materials must still be distributed and stored in an electronic space, such as a learning management system, as well as a repository that teachers and/or administrators can also access, such as in Box, Google Docs, or Dropbox. In addition, even with online instruction, teachers need a place to store their computers and maintain teaching supplies. Also, technical support and physical servers need upkeep that must be considered.

Figure 10.1 contains an uncomprehensive list of questions to help new or experienced directors of a curriculum sort out issues of product delivery.[1] Anyone can benefit from scanning the list and quickly answering each question to determine how much they know about their program's delivery mechanisms. It is unlikely that a single person will be responsible for all of these tasks, although that does occasionally happen, as may be the case with individual tutoring situations. But usually in an English language program, the work is divided among a relatively large number of people.

An especially relevant and visible part of product delivery happens in the classroom on a daily basis in the form of teaching. When teachers introduce the class, assign a textbook, pass out homework sheets, arrange conversation pairs, and do any number of other classroom activities, whether in person or through online instruction, they are in fact implementing the curriculum. Thus, a major element of implementation is day-to-day teaching. A brief discussion of lesson planning and delivering learning activities was covered in Chapter 7. It may be helpful to review that chapter again in light of its relevance to implementation.

Strategic Implementation

So far, this chapter has emphasized class-level implementation since it is more tidy and easier to conceptualize than programmatic implementation or even course-level implementation. After all, class-level implementation can usually be done by a single teacher with very little coordination among

Where will physical classroom instruction take place?
- What are the physical characteristics of the classrooms?
  - Size and shape
  - Lighting sources
  - Heating and cooling sources
  - Seating capacity and arrangement
  - Presentation features (chalkboard, whiteboard, projector, microphone, speakers)
  - Technology (computers, internet access, cell phone service, etc.)
- What is the proximity of classrooms to other locations?
  - Water fountains
  - Bathrooms
  - Teacher and administrative offices
  - Areas of noise or high traffic
  - Cafeteria space or restaurants
  - Parking spaces

How will digital instruction be given?
- Platform for learning
- Synchronous or asynchronous delivery
- Accommodation for access to and familiarity with technology
- Time zone considerations

Where will offices be located?
- The office of the director
- The offices of assistants, advisors, administrators, supervisors, support services and staff
- The offices of teachers

Where will products be stored, and who will have access to them?
- Textbooks and resource books (physical or electronic)
- Computer hardware
- Copy machines and copy paper
- Student files (paper or electronic)

How will instruction be delivered?
- Traditional whole-class instruction (face-to-face)
- One-on-one instruction (e.g., tutoring)
- Online instruction
- Hybrid online and traditional instruction
- Distance instruction

Who will deliver instruction?
- Certified, credentialed, or experienced instructors
- New, inexperienced instructors
- Graduate students
- Teaching assistants
- More advanced learners
- Experts in content (but not necessarily pedagogy)

Who will manage teaching, teacher training, student needs, scheduling, recruitment, discipline, finances, and janitorial work?
- The director
- Supervisors
- The teachers themselves
- Administrative assistants
- An external agency

Figure 10.1 Product delivery questions.

other stakeholders. But in this section, we will take a look at messier large-scale implementation efforts. By large-scale implementation, we mean implementing multiple major curricular components, often in stages, across several dates while involving several groups of stakeholders. An example of this might be the revision of an entire language program in which several class levels are changed, new course material is added, and additional placement/proficiency assessment procedures are adopted. Accomplishing all this in one huge overhaul could significantly destabilize a program. Furthermore, accomplishing all this alone is almost impossible, and working in a team to accomplish it can be extremely taxing. In other words, there is no easy way to implement large-scale curricular changes. However, utilizing a strategic approach can substantially clarify and streamline the process.

A strategic approach to implementation requires curriculum developers and implementers to coordinate their efforts and draft an implementation plan in advance of any implementation. In fact, some components of the curriculum might still be in the design or development stages as other components advance to implementation. A strategic implementation plan should include at least the following five steps, which are then covered in more detail:

1. Create a project timeline
2. Analyze stakeholders—persuade and engage them
3. Delegate tasks to appropriate individuals
4. Communicate in multiple ways, tailoring to different audiences
5. Evaluate the results of your implementation and adjust as necessary

Create a Project Timeline

To begin a strategic plan, create a project timeline by listing out the curricular components that need to be implemented, prioritizing them, and then dividing the list into logical units of time, such as materials or methods to be adopted in fall semester, spring semester, and over summer. Ideally, such a list already exists from the design or development phase and includes projects that are still in those stages as well, but if not, now is the time to create a working document as described for implementation purposes. In fact, many upper administrators are more likely to respond to a well-crafted project timeline when deciding how to allocate funds, so it might be helpful to create a project timeline in advance of any program analysis, design, or development so the people with the funding can see how implementation might take place. This approach requires some guesswork and possibly some re-working of the plan once data are collected and the development and design steps have begun. The point here is that an attractive, thoughtful project timeline can sometimes be a very good ally in winning funds for an expensive curriculum overhaul, and a timeline like this is usually a requirement in formal grant applications.

Figure 10.1 is an example of such a document. It comes from a program that had been operating with a weak assessment plan. As can be seen, the project timeline includes replacing the placement instrument, creating formative and end-of-semester assessments, and holding norming sessions at the end of the semester. In addition, the timeline includes the adoption of an extra level of classes with attendant teacher training to use the new materials, substantial teacher training on the other three levels as well, and new integrated vocabulary and grammar mini-lessons. This is certainly an ambitious plan that needs to be carefully timed, planned, coordinated, and executed.

A project timeline like this is an important planning tool in that it focuses on just the essential and novel implementation projects that are coming up, but it can be modified to meet the needs of any program. Some programs, for instance, will want to include many more items on their list, such as hiring teachers for the upcoming semester and holding regular in-service training. Also, many programs will need to flesh out the details of each item with specific dates and specifications for how and where to implement. This might be done on separate files and/or in prose form. It is a good idea to review this timeline in pertinent meetings or hold extra meetings to coordinate efforts, keep people apprised of upcoming changes, or receive reports on what has been accomplished.

Analyze Stakeholders

As part of the strategic implementation plan, planners should carefully consider all the people who will be affected by those things that will be implemented. These include:

- funding bodies who will support implementation with money
- administrators who will support the implementation with approvals and time
- staff members who will support implementation with physical and human resources
- teachers who will support the implementation with their time and human resources
- students who will support the implementation with their money and attitudes toward the new method and materials

Each stakeholder is important, and ignoring any could halt or imperil the implementation, so it is best to engage each stakeholder early and persuade them to support the implementation vision.

To persuade stakeholders, planners should determine what benefit(s) the stakeholders will derive from the new methods or materials and identify what is needed from them to accomplish the implementation goals. Unfortunately, it is misguided to expect that all stakeholders hold their students' intellectual development as their highest concern, and appealing only to this ethic will almost guarantee a futile ending. Funding agencies, for example, usually must pick among multiple competing proposals that all promise to improve student learning. So to persuade them, implementers may need to show how their plan is cost effective, promises to be successful, is better than alternatives, and is likely to improve the agency's standing as a funding agency within whatever context is important to them (e.g., it will raise their profile through publications and presentations or improved relationships with another, more powerful department, college, program, or institution on campus). It is possible to counterbalance financial needs with these benefits so as to show exactly what their funding is expected to buy. Planners should be careful not to pander or come across as overtly complimentary, as these can be seen as schmooze tactics. Instead, they should get to know the funding agency well, cultivate relationships if possible, develop some effective messaging, and then state their case factually (see Karsh & Fox, 2019).

Of course, funding agencies are just one example of stakeholders who need to be persuaded. Administrators are another (though sometimes they are the funding agencies), and they often give the needed permissions and approvals to move forward. There may be many of them, and they may have built small kingdoms, so that even if a plan has funding, they may be reluctant to implement what they see as a threat to their kingdom or a redundancy or a bad idea. And they may be right: if an idea is a legitimate threat or redundancy or a bad idea, administrators should be thanked for stopping it. However, it is generally the case that such administrators need to be worked with rather than worked against. It may be possible to use funding or other approvals to help them accomplish something they have wanted to do if it can still accomplish what curriculum developers have planned. An example of this might be offering to run training workshops for TAs in the education department (something they have wanted to do but lack the expertise) in exchange for their support in establishing an ESL minor in their college with some of your teachers (something you want but that they have been lukewarm about).

With staff members, teachers, and students, the politics can be a bit simpler, but they should not be ignored. Just because someone *can* order an assistant, a teacher, or a student to adopt a particular method or material doesn't mean they *should*. Again, implementers should engage these stakeholders early by providing a vision of the plan and how it will benefit them. This will also help them to feel part of a progressive and exciting team. In some cases, very experienced teachers may have strong opposition to a particular vision, and they should be handled with extreme care. They should be allowed to voice their concerns in appropriate forums and to be taken seriously. Implementers should make improvements and adjustments based upon their well-founded suggestions and ensure that they are truly valued, not just appeased. Doing so will often make them strong allies to a cause.

Delegate Tasks to Appropriate Individuals

The next step is to delegate tasks, since there is likely to be more to accomplish than can be done alone. Where possible, people should be paid to accomplish their tasks, or their tasks should be made a condition of their contract so that a certain level of performance can be expected. For instance, if a teacher is hired to spend 20 hours creating orientation packets for all levels of instruction, and what they deliver fails to meet expectations, they can be asked to account for their time. If they indeed spent all 20 hours, then it might be that the task legitimately required more time. If they spent just 10 hours, they can be asked to spend more time and make the materials better.

When delegating, supervisors should set explicit deadlines and follow-up to ensure the task gets done. Follow-up can be done in formal ways by holding a regular meeting or asking for regular written reports (through email, even), or it can be done in informal conversations at convenient times. Also, supervisors should take note of who will lead every major implementation project. As seen in Figure 10.2, this information can be included in the project timeline so that everyone in the implementation process knows who is accountable for each project.

Communicate in Multiple Ways, Tailoring to Different Audiences

During implementation, or even in preparation stages, implementers should take time to keep stakeholders appraised of their progress, particularly of their successes. This may include circulating a quarterly report among high-level administrators or catching colleagues up during hallway conversations. They should use multiple methods and always be on the lookout for ways to send positive news about what the implementation is accomplishing. It may be productive to send out a short email after a particularly successful implementation to generate interest in the project or remain near the forefront of stakeholders' minds.

When sending out updates, it is ill-advised to give the exact same bit of communication to all stakeholders. What is said, written, or presented should

Semester	Completion Date	Items	Project lead
Fall	ASAP	Order new books and materials for levels 1–3 for use at the beginning of fall	Teachers and staff
	August	Implement new placement instrument and assess its effectiveness throughout the year	Program director
	Begin in August	Implement new formative and summative proficiency assessments throughout fall semester	Testing coordinator (with help from assessment committee and teachers)
	September	Write and submit course proposal for new level 4 classes & submit curricular revisions for levels 1–3	Program director
	November	Create a scope and sequence, sample syllabi, and first-week lesson plans for levels 1–4 that teachers can follow in spring semester	Curriculum coordinator (with help from teachers)
Winter	January	Train teachers on the new level 4 materials and objectives; distribute sample syllabi and first-week lesson plans and train teachers to use the scope and sequence for levels 1–3	Content supervisors
	February	Research and purchase more appropriate books/materials for use in levels 2 & 3	Content supervisors (with input from teachers)
	March	Begin developing integrated vocabulary and grammar mini-lessons for levels 1–4	Content supervisors (with help from curriculum committee)

Figure 10.2 Sample project timeline: revising levels 1–3 and adding 4.

Semester	Completion Date	Items	Project lead
	April	Create rubrics and hold norming sessions for final assessments in levels 1–4	Testing coordinator (with help from content supervisors)
	April	Create orientation packets for new teachers with objectives, sample syllabus, lesson plans, assignments, assessments, and sample student work that is superior, moderate, and lacking	Content supervisors
Summer	May	Train teachers on integrated vocabulary and grammar mini-lessons for levels 1–4; distribute orientation packets	Content supervisors
	May–August	Pilot writing lab program with tutors	Writing coordinator (with help from tutors)

Figure 10.2 (Continued)

be tailored based upon the amount of time and the specific interests of each group of stakeholders. For instance, when updating students on an implementation process, it may be best to omit details about resource management and instead focus on telling students how much the new methods or materials are improving their test scores. When talking to administrators, however, implementers might still mention the increase in test scores but also add in some information about how the methods are using fewer resources than expected.

It is also a very good idea to have a 30-second "elevator speech" prepared in order to succinctly explain an implementation vision to any given stakeholder and to enumerate the benefits that are already being seen (or the additional support that is needed) (see Sjodin, 2012). Whenever possible, use a PAR story in this kind of speech. This approach is described in Box 10.2.

Box 10.2   PAR Stories

A PAR story is a rhetorical device that allows someone to highlight actions he or she took using a captivating and efficient approach. The point is to tell a story that has a *problem*, an *action*, and a *resolution* (PAR), in which the teller is the protagonist.

P—Stands for a Problem that you've encountered
A—Stands for an Action that you've implemented to overcome the problem
R—Stands for the Result you got or thing you will get with their support. Use data to back up your claim if possible
Here is an example of a PAR story as part of a larger pitch:

"Over the last three years, our students' reading scores have been dropping, which has led to lower levels of advancement (this is the problem). My team and I analyzed the problem and realized that many of our students struggle with simple phonics and decoding skills. I've begun piloting a couple of phonics lessons in the lowest beginning classes (these were the actions). Students have been very receptive to the lessons, and their reading scores are showing signs of improvement. Ten of my fifteen students jumped a grade level in the last reading test (these are the results). I'd like to do a little more analysis of this program, but if it is successful, I'd like your permission to implement it in all of our beginning-level classes. It's very possible that this little change will put our students' reading scores back on par with their other classes and alleviate the advancement problem. Do you think a wider implementation might be feasible?"

Evaluate the Results of Your Implementation and Adjust as Necessary

Ideally, evaluation will take place all throughout the implementation process in informal ways. This might include watching how instruction is delivered or examining books as they go out to students. In any event, implementers should monitor the implementation of new methods and materials and take action if something goes awry. If a particular test turns out to be too difficult to implement the way it was envisioned, then its implementation should be revised. In some cases, this cannot be done immediately, so it is wise for implementers to write down their reflections on features of the implementation that didn't work in order to improve the process in the future. In other cases, the implementation will be basically effective but might seem to be missing a few small steps, so of course, resources should be devoted to filling in those steps. If students are required to take a laptop to the final exam, but then the teacher realizes that there are too few electrical outlets for students to keep their computers charged, then something must be done. Perhaps consider changing rooms or supplying extension cords and extra power strips until a more permanent solution can be found or turn to online testing with appropriate digital proctoring.

Understanding Personal Strengths and Weakness as an Implementer

There is no question that implementation can be very difficult, particularly with large-scale projects. However, there are ways to make the process easier. One way is to have a solid implementation plan, as was discussed and outlined above. Another is for implementers to know their own strengths and weaknesses so that they can capitalize on what they do well and compensate for what is harder for them. In this section, we introduce three concepts associated with personality that can affect the performance of an implementer. These concepts have been researched and studied in organizational behavior literature, which is a subfield of applied psychology.

Leader vs. Manager

The first concept is the distinction between a *leader* and a *manager* (Zaleznik, 2004). This is important to implementation because an implementer needs to be part leader and part manager in order to both inspire others and get the work done. Leaders have vision and are able to persuade others to follow that vision. They encourage trust among colleagues and followers and delegate responsibilities to capable people. Meanwhile, managers take the vision, create a plan for execution, and carefully enact it until the vision is realized. Managers assign tasks to others and innovate if necessary, but are otherwise focused on doing or delegating the grinding, day-to-day work that leads to final project success.

When implementing a curricular change, someone needs to act as the leader by holding up the vision and inspiring others to see the new curriculum through that perspective. Such leadership and vision can get people to rally behind even difficult projects. But leadership is not sufficient; in fact, it is common for good ideas to be persuasively suggested in faculty meetings and then stall out in execution and implementation because the leader who suggested the idea doesn't have the management skills to transform the vision into reality. The leader may see the vision but then is unable to carry out all the small parts. Likewise, there may be very good managers who make their own small, private plans for improvement and then dutifully fulfill them because they are managers at heart. A program filled with managers and no leaders will accomplish a lot, but most of it will be done without much coordination, which can pull a language program in many different directions.

The key here is to know where individuals in a language program lie on the leader/manager spectrum. Let's turn to you as the reader as an example, assuming that you are part of the implementation team in your language program. If you are a good balance of leader and manager, the odds are you are already very successful at getting others to listen to your ideas and then assigning tasks to make those ideas a reality. If you are more leader than manager, you have probably come up with many great ideas but seen few of them result in final products. If you are more of a manager, you may be craving a larger, more unified purpose for your hard work. Once you identify what combination of leader and manager you are, you should capitalize and compensate appropriately by developing more skills or partnering with someone who has complementary skills. For instance, if you are more of a leader, then you could cultivate working relationships with a manager who can help you execute your vision. If you are more of a manager, the inverse is true: find an inspiring, charismatic leader in the program who you could support. Together, you can implement change in ways that are far more successful than if either of you worked alone. Of course, it is always a good idea to work on your own leadership and management abilities so that you can, to some extent, be both.

Thinker vs. Doer

The next concept distinguishes what might be called *thinkers* and *doers*. This idea comes from Kolb's (1984) experiential learning and learning style theories. Some individuals learn through abstract conceptualization, or deep *thinking* about an issue; others learn through active experimentation, or what might be thought of as *doing* or acting on ideas. As a result of their learning styles, individuals often react to problems in ways that mirror their learning styles. Thinkers are the people who take time to think through multiple angles on an issue; they consider all of the implications of a decision before agreeing on a direction. They temper the impulsive action of doers so as to reduce the possibility of making simple mistakes or taking action on something that will ultimately be regrettable. Doers, on the other hand, rarely deliberate for long. They are more eager to make a decision and then determine the extent to which that decision was right or wrong after the fact. To borrow a cliché, thinkers look before leaping, while doers leap and then look. Both thinkers and doers are critical to implementation, since the thinkers provide reasoning and thoughtfulness that doers tend to overlook. The benefit of doers, however, is that they fight to get the work done. They are eager and have a passion for accomplishing things. So, while thinkers provide good cerebral judgment, they may continue thinking indefinitely or may put off deciding on a plan of action without the help of doers who are naturally restless until things start getting done.

Turning to you as the reader again, the key here is not to covet being a thinker or a doer per se but to recognize where you are on the spectrum and capitalize or compensate. If you are a doer, you should definitely team up with a thinker who will provide stability to your decision-making. If you are a thinker, team up with a doer in order to get your good decisions actualized. Working across the spectrum like this is often not easy, because thinkers can get frustrated with the impulsiveness of doers who seem to make decisions too early, and doers can get frustrated with thinkers who "overthink" everything. But if you are able to appreciate and value one another's strengths, then the implementation process will be more robust (thanks to the thinkers) and will move forward productively (thanks to the doers).

Task vs. Relationship

The final concept is a distinction between task orientation and relationship orientation (Bass, 2008). Individuals who are task-oriented often view a project or task as their most important concern. They view other people as a means of accomplishing those tasks and value efficient performance highly. They might sometimes seem cold and uncaring toward other employees and might take credit for the work of the people they supervise. Relationship-oriented people, on the other hand, generally view individuals and relationships as more important than projects. They value harmony and goodwill over performance because, to their thinking, harmony will foster an atmosphere where workers are more productive. People who value relationships will inquire about non-work relationships and therefore seem warm and caring.

The distinction between task and relationship orientation is important in implementation because the people who do the implementing may sometimes respond better to task masters and sometimes to relationship masters. Further, implementation is both a task and a relationship in that the implementation of a curricular change is a *bona fide* task, but it is people and their relationship to other people that ultimately make up curricular change at the individual level. Given this complex dynamic, implementers need to be focused on the task sometimes and on relationships at other times. If you know yourself to be either task- or relationship-oriented, it is possible to compensate by learning about the other orientation or helping those you work with expect certain traits from you. But a good working alternative is to pair up with someone who has the opposite orientation so as to benefit from both.

Chapter Summary

This chapter has been focused on implementing curricular changes that have been designed and developed after a process of environmental and learner analysis. The implementation stage is where curriculum design meets actual students, and in order for that transition to be effective, implementers must prepare carefully for success.

Ultimately, we boiled implementation down to three major principles: build facilitator competence, build learner competence, and deliver the product. Facilitator competence often comes in pre- or in-service training, where a supervisor meets with teachers or administrators to instruct them on curricular changes. Learner competence occurs in the classroom, where teachers are the trainers. Product delivery happens when teachers use the new methods or materials; it includes lesson planning and teaching.

Coordinating implementation efforts is a big project, so a strategic plan is generally needed. This plan helps implementers keep track of what needs to be done, when, and by whom so that the whole implementation process is mapped out in advance. This isn't all, though, since implementing a large-scale curricular change requires the help of multiple people. Thus, an implementer should also be aware of the strengths and weaknesses of his or her personality traits along at least three constructs: leader/manager, thinker/doer, and task/relationship orientation.

The concept of implementation follows the metaphor of building a house to a large degree. Once builders have analyzed the location of a proposed home, identified the needs of the future residents, and then designed and developed the plans, it becomes the duty of contractors and subcontractors to make the plan a physical reality by purchasing the materials and assembling the home. Ideally, the contractors and subcontractors come prepared for the task, but even if this is true, they may need a little bit of training on the particular specifications of their current project. So it is with curriculum implementation: the curricular needs should have been analyzed and filled with a design and the development of certain components. Then it is up to administrators and teachers to provide necessary parts and assemble the curriculum into a cohesive whole while receiving some localized training as necessary. From here, students can work with the curricular material to generate learning. Once the work of implementation is underway, the curriculum as a whole can be evaluated summatively, which is the topic of the next chapter.

Activities

Activity 10.1

Given the three levels of construction and curricular roles as described in Box 10.1 (designers/administrators, contractors/teachers, workers/students), think about your language program or one you are familiar with. Categorize individuals in your program according to these roles. Who are the designers, planners, architects, engineers, and drafters? Who are the contractors and subcontractors? Who are the construction workers? Do any of these roles overlap or conflict?

Activity 10.2

Take a moment to think through the questions at the end of the "Instructors" section of this chapter. Apply them to a curricular component you could (or need to) implement soon. If you have no such component, then think about a recent curricular change you experienced and reflect on the implementation you observed. Write down and justify your answers as you envision an implementation plan that involves instructors.

Activity 10.3

Given the curricular change you identified in Activity 10.2, apply the questions at the end of the "Building learner competence" section. How would you answer these questions in order to implement an effective curricular change among learners?

Activity 10.4

The sections on "Facilitators and learners" implicitly focused on implementing new materials or methods within an otherwise stable curriculum. But starting up a new curriculum from scratch also requires extensive facilitator and learner support. Imagine you were to start a new class within an existing program, a new program, or even a new school for language learning. What kind of competence would facilitators need in order to be successful in the new curriculum? What kind of general support or orientation would learners benefit from at the programmatic level or class level in order to be successful?

Activity 10.5

Assess a language course you are familiar with or have recently taken based on the product delivery questions in Figure 10.1. Consider the physical facilities and the human resources that make the delivery of the instruction possible. What additional delivery considerations exist or existed in your course that are not listed?

Activity 10.6

Imagine that you were planning to implement a small curricular change, such as introducing a new textbook in your class or enforcing a no-cellphone-in-class rule. Go through the five steps of strategic implementation to create a small project timeline, analyze at least one stakeholder (e.g., the students), consider one person to whom you would delegate a task (even if it's just yourself), decide who you would communicate progress to and how, and finally identify how you might evaluate the success of the implementation.

Activity 10.7

Think about a curricular innovation (or group project) you have worked on in the past. Try to identify how you approached it in terms of the three behavioral concepts discussed at the end of this chapter. Were you more of a leader or a manager on the project? Did you perform the function of a thinker or a doer? Did you focus more on the task or more on relationships?

It might be difficult to adequately assess your own personality traits based upon just one curricular implementation or project, so think back on multiple occasions in which you have had to work with others and try to place yourself on each behavioral spectrum in this chapter. Write a paragraph describing your implementation approach, as well as some thoughts about how you might compensate for any limitations you see.

Note

1 A more comprehensive list might be found in guides for language program administration. While the scope of this book does not provide for a section on how to effectively run an English language program, full books have been dedicated to this topic, including the following

- *A Handbook for Language Program Administrators* (2016) by MaryAnne Christison and Fredricka Stoller (Ed.)
- *From Teacher to Manager* (2008) by Ron White, Andrew Hockley, Melissa Laughner, and Julie van der Horst Jansen.

References

Allio, M. K. (2005). A short, practical guide to implementing strategy. *The Journal of Business Strategy, 26*(4), 12–19. http://dx.doi.org/10.1108/02756660510608512

Bass, B. M. (2008). *Bass & Stogdill's handbook of leadership: Theory, research, and managerial applications* (4th ed.). Free Press.

Christison, M., & Stoller, F. (Eds.). (2016). *A handbook for language program administrators* (2nd ed.). ALTA English Publishers.

Karsh, E., & Fox, A. S. (2019). *The only grant-writing book you'll ever need* (4th ed.). Basic Books.

Kolb, D. (1984). *Experiential learning: Experience as the source of learning and development*. Prentice Hall.

Noble, C. H. (1999). The eclectic roots of strategy implementation research. *Journal of Business Research, 45*(2), 119–134. https://doi.org/10.1016/S0148-2963(97)00231-2

Pryor, M. G., Anderson, D., Toombs, L. A., & Humphreys, J. H. (2007). Strategic implementation as a core competency: The 5P's model. *Journal of Management Research, 7*(1), 3–17.

Sjodin, T. L. (2012). *Small message, big impact: The elevator speech effect*. The Penguin Group.

White, R., Hockley, A., Laughner, M. S., & Jansen, A. H. (2008). *From teacher to manager: Managing language teaching organizations*. Cambridge University Press.

Zaleznik, A. (2004). Managers and leaders: Are they different? *Harvard Business Review, 82*(6), 74–81.

11

Evaluation of Process and Product

Introduction

The fact that this chapter comes at the end of the book is unfortunate because, for example, as curriculum designers plan out their mission statements, goals, and objectives, they should simultaneously evaluate those documents to ensure they reflect the context of the program. The same goes for other components of curriculum: learning outcomes, assessment, and learning experiences. Designers should evaluate their analyses of the program as well as their designs, outputs, and implementations of curricular change. The point is to evaluate everything along the way, not just (but certainly including) the final curriculum.

However, the notion of evaluation brings with it a lot of negative connotations. It can feel rigid, artificial, clinical, and oppressive. Teachers "in the trenches" may view evaluation as an attack on the value of their class or their own jobs as teachers. Meanwhile, administrators may not know how to measure the successes and liabilities of their programs, which can lead to poor, inconsistent, or unpopular evaluation processes. On the other hand, if it is done effectively and compassionately, evaluation can be a powerful tool for both teachers and administrators. It can help both groups secure funding, capture resources, and ensure curricular and pedagogical effectiveness. Most importantly, an effective evaluation mindset can lead to sustained student success.

In this chapter, we address evaluation by discussing simple and manageable ways to engage in it and reap the benefits explained above. We further distinguish between two focuses of evaluation: evaluation of the *process* by which curricular decisions are made and evaluation of the *product* of curricular decision-making.

Building a House

The building metaphor is straightforward when it comes to evaluation. Nearly every step of a construction project is double-checked by a host of formal and informal evaluators. For example, if a family is planning to build their own home, they might begin the process by thinking about their needs and wants in a house. At first, they may want a large home with multiple garages, lots of yard space outside, and a guesthouse for when relatives come to visit. Then, after thinking about their real needs and constraints (including their budget), they may trim down their design a little: maybe a two-car garage, a modest yard size, and a spare bedroom instead of a guesthouse. The process of thinking through their needs and constraints is part of the evaluation process.

More formal evaluation processes are sure to follow. After developing plans for a house, those plans should be reviewed and approved by a professional architect to ensure structural integrity. The ground on which the house will eventually stand must be inspected; the cement work, framing, plumbing, and electrical lines all get inspections either from official government workers or from tradesmen with sufficient experience evaluating each job. The same is true when renovating; even if the renovation is small (painting a wall, for instance), someone still needs to take a step back and decide whether the job looks right. In some countries, many of these steps require building permits issued through the local government. The point is that evaluation is a constant, repetitive process. When done correctly, it is just as much a preventative measure (reducing future building problems) as it is a snapshot of current work.

A critical feature of evaluation is that it should be tied to set criteria. When craftsmen, tradesmen, or official inspectors are qualified to evaluate a part of the building process, their evaluation is often tied to their knowledge of good construction. This is especially true if they take measurements or make critical observations to inform their evaluations. In some cases, such as choosing paint colors for a wall, the opinion of just one person might be sufficient to make an informed decision. In any case, a set of stable criteria should be used during the evaluation process so that even subjective opinions can be properly vetted and interpreted. More will come in this chapter about creating effective evaluations.

What Is Evaluation?

In very simple terms, evaluation can be described as looking at what something *is* compared to what it *should be* along certain criteria. Stake and Schwandt (2006) give a very broad yet clear definition. "The evaluation of programs and projects is premised on the common idea that quality is discernible and capable of representation. To distinguish quality, one must be able to discriminate—to tell the difference between the absence and presence of quality. . . . Discerning quality is always a matter of expectation and comparison."

When students fill out end-of-semester teacher evaluations, they are comparing the teacher's job to a fairly subjective image of what a good teacher should do along with criteria such as thoroughness, rigor, approachability, and so on. When teachers evaluate a textbook during the adoption process, they look at features of the textbook in comparison to preferences for textbook design and coverage, the needs of students, the purpose of a course, and so forth.

Evaluation, then, is a comparison based on criteria. Ideally, the point of evaluation is not merely to check off that something does or will work well, though this is certainly one point. Evaluation should also be used to improve a product or process, as well as to ascertain and compensate for weaknesses in a process or product. After evaluating a textbook, for instance, a teacher might need to supplement instruction for topics the textbook doesn't cover.

Types

There are multiple types of and reasons for evaluation. The four main types of evaluation are formal, informal, formative, and summative (see Figure 11.1 or more details). Formal and informal evaluations exist on opposite poles along a continuum. Formal evaluations are highly structured measurements that are generally very rigorous and sometimes intrusive to the curriculum. The informal variety, however, is less structured and less intrusive. They often have a small scope and a much simpler design. The terms formative and summative for evaluations refer to the use of the evaluation. Formative evaluations are used to inform and improve. Summative evaluation results are often used as a final indication of the success of whatever person or object is being evaluated. It's important to realize that the same evaluation can be used for both formative and summative purposes. Evaluations can exist on any point along either continuum, depending on the design and purpose of the evaluation.

There are several reasons for conducting evaluations. Most of them can be categorized as developmental, mandated, routine, or reactionary impetuses.

	Formal	Informal
Formative	**HIGHLY STRUCTURED EVALUATIONS OF WORK IN PROGRESS** • Pilot testing new curriculum components with robust measurements and analysis • Conducting mid-quarter teacher evaluations using a rigorous survey • Comparing several dictionaries in order to determine which one to recommend to students in a vocabulary class	**LESS STRUCTURED EVALUATIONS OF WORK IN PROGRESS** • Collecting students' spontaneous impressions of the new lecture material they are using • Asking for a colleague's opinion on a lesson plan • Monitoring students' reactions to a newly hired teacher
Summative	**HIGHLY STRUCTURED EVALUATIONS AT THE END OF A CURRICULUM CHANGE** • Collecting multiple perspectives on the effectiveness of a new pronunciation software tool after a semester of use • Holding teacher and student focus groups to discuss the strengths and weaknesses of a pilot GRE preparation course • Conducting an accreditation review of a language program	**LESS STRUCTURED EVALUATIONS AT THE END OF A CURRICULUM CHANGE** • Asking students at the end of a course to jot down a few thoughts about what they learned in the class • Overhearing several students complain about a textbook they finished that repeated things they learned last year • Receiving an email from a former student who got a management position thanks to a speaking class she took at your institution

Figure 11.1 Types of evaluations.

Developmental

Developmental evaluations consider curriculum design, development, and implementation. As curriculum components are created, they should also be evaluated for their merit and worth.

Example: The director of an IEP has allocated funds to purchase a subscription to a new electronic grammar resource. But before making the purchase, the grammar coordinator examines the functions of the new resource carefully (and perhaps pilot tests the program with a group of students) to determine if the resource meets the needs of the students better than other alternatives, including remaining with the status quo.

Mandated

Mandated evaluations are required by a supervising or authorizing entity. While they are imposed by an external group of stakeholders, they may or may not be carried out by representatives of that external group.

Example: Many institutions are required to be evaluated by an accreditation organization or another outside entity. In many instances, the purposes of these evaluations are to safeguard time and resources devoted to a particular institution. The Commission on English Language Accreditation regularly evaluates the programs that it accredits and promotes.

Routine

In addition to evaluations that are externally mandated, institutions may have a regular evaluation plan that includes recurring formal evaluations. This may be decided by one group of stakeholders, such as the administrators, or it may be the decision of multiple groups (i.e., administrators and teachers).

Example: Student evaluations and teacher self-evaluations are routine evaluations that are institutionally initiated by administrators and sometimes conducted by the teachers themselves.

Reactionary

Evaluations that become necessary because of a crisis, an incident, or an observation are reactionary. Reactionary evaluations often occur when a stakeholder makes an informal evaluation that leads to further discussion and potentially a formal evaluation.

Example: A group of students who typically have very good grades all fail a reading test. Upon inspection, it appears that the book they were assigned dealt with themes they were uncomfortable reading, and so they all chose not to finish the book. The book was subsequently replaced with a less offensive option.

See Box 11.1 for additional exploration of evaluation.

Box 11.1   A More Technical Definition of Evaluation

Evaluation

Although evaluation is well described as a comparison based on criteria, a more sophisticated definition is this: a methodic, criterion-based process of gathering information used to determine the merit and worth of an evaluand in order for stakeholders to make defensible decisions about aspects of a curriculum.

To break this definition down, examine the meaning of these relevant words:

Evaluand: This is the object of evaluation, whether tangible (e.g., a textbook) or intangible (e.g., a body of knowledge students should possess).

Criteria: Predetermined aspects by which the evaluand is measured or judged

Merit: A quality by which an evaluand does what it was constructed to do

Worth: A quality by which an evaluand fulfills its purpose in a way that is superior to alternative means

Consider This Example

After receiving a large number of requests, a language program finally added an elective pronunciation course to its class offerings. It was taught by a teacher trained in TESOL who had about 10 years of experience as a speaking teacher but no dedicated experience as a pronunciation instructor. Armed with a simple "English Pronunciation" textbook, a familiarity with the International Phonetic Alphabet, and computers for students to record their own speech, the teacher began the course. At first, the students were horrified to hear their own voices and to receive critical comments on their pronunciation, but by mid-term, students were happily making several recordings each week and were using a number of feedback approaches to help them improve their English pronunciation. By the end of the semester, the students and teacher were ecstatic about all the great work they had done during the semester. But after the final pronunciation exam, it turned out that only 25% of the students had made any measurable progress in their pronunciation. That meant 75% of the students had remained at their pre-semester level. While an improvement of 25% seemed good to the teacher, the administration wasn't nearly as impressed, so they decided to eliminate the class.

Now Let's Examine the Story in Terms of Evaluation

The major evaluand in this story is the pronunciation course. It was meant to improve students' pronunciation, which was the criterion by which success would be determined. However, according to the administration, the course appeared to lack merit, since only 25% of the students passed. And considering the low pass rate, it was obvious to the administrators that the pronunciation course had little actual worth. And they were probably right: if the majority of students aren't passing, then something is going wrong.

The criteria could change, and in so doing, change the relative amount of merit and worth ascribed to the pronunciation course. What if, for instance, curriculum planners wanted the course to help students lower their affective filters and overcome fears of listening to their own voices? In this case, the pronunciation course was full of merit and worth. Obviously, the criteria of an evaluation matter.

Instead of changing the criteria, though, the evaluand could change. For instance, let's consider the pronunciation textbook as the evaluand. To what degree does that particular book effectively teach pronunciation? The teacher could also be the evaluand: a background in TESOL and experience as a speaking teacher do not equate to a pronunciation specialist. Course activities, strategies, and assessments could all be potential evaluands. Whatever is chosen as an evaluand, along with the criteria, will shape the outcome of the evaluation and the ultimate decision of policymakers.

Evaluating the Product

Curricular evaluation should be applied to both the products and process of curriculum design. The products include anything tangible or semi-permanent in the curriculum, especially the governing documents, assessments and feedback, and learning experiences. The process refers to the stages of development used to create these products, including analysis, design, development, and implementation.

Usually, the ultimate point of evaluation is to improve things, so it should come as no surprise that every curricular product will show weaknesses that could be improved. What to do about these weaknesses is a matter of institutional prerogative. For example, a website adopted for a listening class might have a lot of on-site advertisements. Students and teachers are likely to see this as a weakness, but as long as the ads don't distract students from their work, this may not be worth resolving immediately. Bigger concerns, such as an ineffective proficiency exam, might take priority.

Of course, some evaluations do have major implications. Such is the case with accreditation visits. To maintain accreditation status, many language programs are obligated to undergo periodic review in which they assemble massive amounts of documentation on their program and then receive a formal, outside evaluation of their entire curriculum. In these cases, accrediting bodies may have a list of action items that program directors are obligated to address. If a program does sufficient self-evaluation, it can address major curricular concerns before they become targets of a formal accreditation visit. Consider the evaluation of the products here in terms of programmatic self-evaluation.

Governing Documents

The governing documents, which provide vision and direction at all levels of the curriculum, deserve to be evaluated on a regular basis. These include the program mission, course goals, class objectives, and outcome statements at all levels. Some thought should be given regarding who evaluates the documents. While it is a good idea for a program director to be involved in the evaluation of course goals, individual class objectives probably don't need to concern him or her. Instead, teachers and area supervisors can probably evaluate class objectives well enough. There is one governing document, however, that all stakeholders should weigh in on during evaluation, and that is the mission statement, because of its impact on all subordinate governing documents.

Program Mission

Evaluation should be applied to the mission statement to determine whether the curriculum really has the right purpose. This is tantamount to evaluating the *why* of curriculum design. It is a good idea to evaluate the mission of the program periodically (e.g., routinely) to ensure that a program's reason for existence hasn't changed, or to likewise ensure that a program can adapt to changing purposes. In this case, evaluators can ask questions such as these: How well does the mission statement describe who and what the program teaches? Are there elements of the mission statement that are no longer relevant to the population or content of instruction? Are there population considerations or instructional elements that are missing from the mission? In this sense, the existing mission statement is compared to what it should be on the criteria of its effectiveness in describing the purpose and aims of the language program.

Additionally, the mission statement can be evaluated as a document for communication. For this purpose, evaluators should decide on criteria by which the mission statement should be evaluated. These might include simple things like length and readability, or they might encompass more abstract criteria, such as correlation to the needs and wants of the learners. If brevity and readability are important, evaluators should determine whether the document is too long or unnecessarily difficult to understand. They might also find ways to trim the statement or translate it into plain writing. If it needs to be correlated to student needs and wants, then evaluators could read through the mission statement themselves to evaluate that correlation, or they might ask students and teachers to comment on that fit and provide suggestions for improvement.

An evaluation of the mission statement can be done in several ways, including by committee in a meeting, individual input through questionnaires, or a series of smaller conversations and meetings. The most elaborate evaluation we have seen involved tiers of meetings in which the top administrators met first to evaluate the mission, then invited program supervisors to a retreat for further discussion and input, and then asked all teachers to attend a meeting where they were placed in teams to offer feedback on specific pieces of the statement. In the end, the preexisting mission statement was reduced and streamlined substantially, resulting in a very focused, half-page document in which every single word was carefully evaluated to ensure that the most precise meaning was conveyed.

Course Goals

Course goals should also be evaluated periodically to ensure that they are serving the program mission, thus creating an overarching evaluation of the *what* of a curriculum. The same is true for course outcomes. The evaluation of goals may be a large undertaking at any instructional level. Therefore, a curriculum evaluator may need to carefully select which goals to evaluate at a given time, rather than evaluating all goals simultaneously. Perhaps one course can be highlighted and evaluated each semester in a faculty meeting. Another option is to have teachers regularly evaluate their own courses and present recommendations for change whenever they feel compelled to do so. If the entire curriculum is being built from scratch or is being totally renovated, then it may be prudent to evaluate all courses simultaneously in one giant curricular evaluation. Small curriculum committees often conduct these evaluations. In one meeting, committee members printed all course objectives for the entire program and arranged them on a conference table. This allowed everyone to see the whole curriculum at once, and it ensured that the objectives were aligned across skills and that they demonstrated continuity and sequence across skill levels (see Chapter 4 for details of these concepts).

Objectives

Finally, class objectives and outcomes should be evaluated to determine whether the *how* of the program is successfully leading to the fulfillment of the goals and mission above them. Because each lesson should ideally have one or more objectives, and because there are so many lessons in a given curriculum, it is usually the teacher's job to self-evaluate his or her own class objectives by examining the teaching materials, procedures, and student behavior relative to those objectives. If the teacher feels that an objective was too hard for a set of students, he or she could remove it or reduce expectations in order for students to succeed. Most teachers are naturally sensitive to this kind of process and adjust their class objectives almost automatically. Thus, the evaluation of class objectives is usually informal, formative, and reactionary. Sometimes, a more formal evaluation of class objectives occurs. This might include, for instance, when a teacher trainer looks over a new teacher's list of class objectives and offers feedback.

Assessments and Feedback

Every language program needs tests to ensure that learning occurs. Furthermore, these tests need to accomplish what they are designed to do, so they should be evaluated with that in mind. For instance, most language programs give students placement tests when they are admitted to the program. This might take the form of an oral interview, a battery of skills tests, or something more standardized, such as a score on the TOEFL exam or something similar. Whether such placement tests successfully place students (and whether they are humane, ethical, and practical) is a matter of assessment evaluation. Are oral examiners really qualified to place students at an appropriate level, for instance? Are the various skills tests reasonably paced and written in such a way that even low-proficiency learners can at least understand the instructions? Can scores from the TOEFL exam really be used to accurately place students in a reading class? If an assessment is not performing its intended purpose, it should be rethought and redesigned until the intended purpose is attained. This might mean simplifying the language in a test, adding additional components or evidence to an existing assessment, or discarding an assessment altogether and developing something new.

Beyond placement tests, programs are virtually all required to give proficiency tests as well as numerous formative assessments that in some cases may not even resemble typical tests. For example, in a conversation class, the teacher may simply observe student interactions and thus evaluate their performance by walking around the room and listening in on student conversations. Or writing classes may utilize a portfolio system in which student writing is only formally evaluated at the end of a course even though students receive feedback all along the way. Ultimately, every assessment should be evaluated to make sure it is accomplishing its intended purpose adequately.

Assessments are universally evaluated using at least three major criteria, that of reliability, validity, and practicality. These three concepts were described in Chapter 8 and form the essential elements of assessment, but there are other important considerations as well. For instance, is a given test too difficult or easy? Is it a fair and ethical assessment experience? Is the right kind of test or combination of tests being used? Does the test have an acceptable and accurate rubric and answer key? Is the test helping students learn? Ideally, assessments will be evaluated throughout their design, development, and implementation phases, but just about every language learner has at some point been a victim to a language assessment that seemed to be poorly constructed, unfair, or focused on measuring something totally different from language ability. For this reason, assessments should be evaluated both formatively and summatively.

Feedback procedures should also regularly be subjected to evaluation. The first and most critical question is whether students receive feedback. In an ideal world, all assessments would ultimately result in students learning from the assessment. Assessment evaluators try to make this happen by ensuring that feedback is proffered and that it is manageable, timely, relevant, accurate, meaningful, and consistent.

Traditional feedback methods include teacher comments, notes on a rubric, and in-person response, though feedback can come in a variety of other creative and time-saving ways. These might include group-feedback, peer-feedback, self-feedback, computer-programed feedback, and so forth. Assessment designers and evaluators should work together to ensure that feedback is given, that the process for generating feedback makes sense in general, and that students have an opportunity to learn from the feedback. See Box 11.2.

Box 11.2   Criteria for Evaluating Assessments and Feedback

Assessments

When evaluating assessments, consider these major criteria in addition to other characteristics that may be important.

Reliable: A test yields consistent results each time it is used.
Valid: A test measures the constructs it is intended to measure.
Practical: A test uses student and teacher resources (time, money, energy) well and is not burdening to either party.
Humane: A test is designed to be fair, equitable, and considerate of the general needs and abilities of test takers (e.g., tests are kept to a reasonable length and skill level/area; students with special needs are accommodated, etc.).
Ethical: Test responses are kept confidential and used for their intended purpose (e.g., placement exams are not also used for advancement decisions unless this dual purpose was worked into the test design).

Feedback

When evaluating feedback, consider these major criteria.

Manageable: The amount of feedback does not overwhelm the student.
Timely: Feedback is provided soon after an assessment is completed.

> **Relevant**: The feedback relates to the material in the assessment; superfluous or extraneous feedback is limited.
> **Accurate**: The feedback (including answer keys and automated responses) contains correct information.
> **Meaningful**: The feedback is clear, interpretable, and useful for the student; it responds to the students' context and needs.
> **Consistent**: The feedback is logically ordered and remains stable across numerous instances of feedback.

Learning Experiences

Learning experiences is a broad category used to describe things like class instruction and activities, worksheets, homework assignments, lesson plans, and so forth. These day-to-day experiences should be evaluated, although the evaluation process is likely to be rather informal and reflective most of the time. Sample evaluative questions might include the following: Are the learning activities contributing to a specific learning outcome? Are the students engaged with the class materials? Is the homework easy to understand? Are the class activities paced well, easy to execute, and relevant to student learning? These evaluations might take place when developing or designing the experiences, when implementing them in class, or after class in a moment of reflection.

In addition to these typical evaluations, micro-evaluations go on all the time during instruction and might involve reading the expressions on students' faces or asking students if they understand a particular assignment. Additionally, more formal evaluations of multi-day or course-long experiences (such as term paper assignments or group projects) might be evaluated summatively once the semester is over or as the teacher is preparing his or her materials for an upcoming semester. This is also true of the sequencing of learning experiences; a teacher often needs to evaluate the calendaring of assignments so that students work on more complex and demanding tasks as the instruction continues. See Box 11.3.

Some criteria for evaluating learning experiences include their relevance, applicability, engagement, and practicality. Learning experiences should be *relevant* to something, whether that be a learning outcome from the governing documents, an upcoming test, or a broader social objective, such as awareness of cultural norms within a language community. Learning experiences are *applicable* when they foster the kind of learning expected of them. In one college-level oral communication class, a teacher screened an entire animated musical movie to his class. His intention was for students to hear extensive

> **Box 11.3 Linking Learning Experiences to a Standardized Test or to Students' Actual Needs?**
>
> There are countless teachers, administrators, and curriculum designers who express frustration that they can't just help students learn a language. Instead, they are obligated to teach to objectives that they disagree with or, perhaps worse, to a specific test they can't control.
>
> Naturally, this brings up the question of whether it is okay to teach to a test. Our answer is yes. When the test is well-constructed and reflects the kinds of language skills and abilities that students need, then teaching to a test can be a very efficient way to run a language course.
>
> If the test is only concerned with one kind of communication, for instance, a high-stakes oral proficiency interview, then teaching to that test will naturally result in selective instruction. Students probably won't get much writing experience. But again, this might be fine, especially if students enter the program expecting a selective type of language instruction.
>
> *Washback* is the term given to the phenomenon in which a test influences the kind of instruction offered. In the case of well-designed tests, the washback effect can be very positive. But what about situations in which a test fails to reflect student language needs and is unnecessarily biased in favor of one or two limited language skills? In that case, the washback may be negative. In these cases, teachers or administrators might try to change the test. They might also over-teach by covering the material that will be on the test in addition to things that won't be tested directly. Another option is to prepare learning experiences that creatively get at the test material while also exposing students to other instruction they are sure to need in the future.

target English pronunciation with the hope that perception would lead to improved production. His students weren't convinced, nor were they happy with the learning experience. This is a situation in which the lesson was relevant to an outcome (improve pronunciation), but not very applicable because the learning activity did not really contribute to improved pronunciation.

Learning experiences should also be engaging and practical. An engaging experience is one that relates to the interests of the learners and requires them to perform slightly beyond their capabilities, but not so far that they are overwhelmed. Practical learning experiences are *feasible* in that they do not overly tax teacher or student resources and are physically possible. A learning experience that requires extensive teacher preparation may need to be cut based on this criteria alone, even if it is otherwise relevant, applicable, and engaging.

Other Product Evaluation

Outside of the three major curricular components already listed, there are still numerous products in a language program that can and should be evaluated. These include, for example, the physical space of the program, the teachers and administrators who work in a program, the students who are admitted to the program, and the culture of the program. These all deserve sufficient evaluative scrutiny, although evaluators will need to determine the criteria to apply. Where any one of these curricular components is performing at the level they should along the criteria established, then no follow-up action is needed. But where reality falls behind the ideal, then curriculum officials may need to intervene for the benefit of the program and ultimately the students.

Evaluating the Process

As was mentioned earlier, curricular evaluation can be used to examine the *process* of curriculum design as well as the product. In terms of the curricular development process, the way the curriculum is designed will partially determine its final outcome. The five essential processes of curriculum design that should be evaluated are 1) analysis, 2) design, 3) development, 4) implementation, and 5) evaluation.

Analysis

Any time a curricular product is scheduled to be created or improved; an analysis should be performed in advance. The analysis identifies the context, purpose, and need of that product, whether that is a governing document, assessment, or learning experience. In some cases, the analysis is laborious and highly involved, but in other cases, it might simply be a matter of observing a problem in class that can be addressed with minimal effort. In any event, the process used to analyze a curricular change should be evaluated.

Look back at the analysis process to ensure that stakeholders were adequately involved and that essential insights were accurately captured from the critical questions: why, who, what, how, where, and when. This is especially important when analyzing the entire program. It is possible that one or more stakeholders were overlooked or misrepresented when analyzing the program. Furthermore, when collecting insights from students, administrators, or teachers, the questions used to solicit their thoughts should also be subjected to evaluation. Were questions worded clearly? Were they comprehensive? Did they lead people to answer in an unbiased way? Ideally, the data collection tools were rigorously evaluated and appropriately modified prior to being used in the analysis. The data collected from various analyses might also be hard to interpret, so part of evaluating the analysis is determining whether additional people should be involved with interpreting the data.

Some of the journalistic questions highlighted in the analysis stage are thought questions, or questions that a single person could answer on his or her own. This should also be evaluated; perhaps more people should be involved in determining a mission statement or other curricular products. Maybe one or more of the questions were overlooked or superficially answered. Finally, evaluators should always ask whether anything is missing from the analysis process that should be included because of its potential to impact the curriculum. Thinking through these types of questions collectively constitutes the evaluation of the analysis process. See Box 11.4.

Box 11.4   Evaluating the Analysis of a New Curriculum

During the writing of this book, a local entrepreneur approached us because he wanted to create a new language program for international and immigrant students. He had developed a loose business plan and had something of a vision for his school. Several months after consulting with him, the entrepreneur had taken our suggestions to create governing documents. We asked about that process as a means of informal evaluation. It turns out that he had started by using his own impressions and vision for the school to drive the governing documents. He hired a young intern with some TESOL experience to turn that vision into reality. As part of her responsibilities, the intern contacted directors at other English language programs in order to help solidify the niche the new program was trying to fill. As prospective students began inquiring about the new program, the intern took note of their interests and needs.

We were duly impressed that the director had arranged for so many stakeholders to be involved in shaping the curriculum. The method for collecting their input, however, was more haphazard. In most cases, the director or his intern had merely conversed with stakeholders in incidental conversations. There were few written notes, emails, or other forms of stable data to which they could return for clarification. This exposed one weakness of the analysis, and we recommended that the director keep better notes and develop a curricular synthesis that would help catalogue the decisions he was making. In this way, the evaluation allowed us to highlight a weakness that a relatively small adjustment in procedures could help resolve.

Design

Following analysis is the design phase, where curricular components are planned out and thought through. Ultimately, documents and products should be designed in ways that respond to stakeholder needs, so the evaluation should determine to what degree this was done and whether more should be done to improve the decision-making process. For instance, if the analysis showed that students needed more opportunities to practice speaking but revised curricular designs do not reflect this, then the process by which that decision was made should be evaluated. Remember that the evaluation of the product was described earlier in this chapter, although it is obviously common to evaluate the product and the design process simultaneously.

To evaluate the design process, look back at decisions that were made regarding governing documents, learning outcomes, assessments and feedback, learning experiences as well as other curricular components, resources, and materials. Were those decisions based on the most important information from the analysis, or were they made capriciously? Was input on the design of all documents and materials adequately gathered from a broad range of stakeholders with diverse perspectives, or were decisions made by an insular group of administrators? Were design decisions made quickly and effectively, or did they drag on for weeks, months, or semesters? Conversely, were design decisions made hastily or without deference to weighty considerations that could destabilize the curriculum?

Development

The development process breathes life into the curricular designs. This is the phase where textbooks are selected, in-house materials are generated, purchasing decisions are made, and so on. These decisions should reflect criteria identified in the design phase. Therefore, the obvious first evaluation step for development is to ensure that curricular components, materials, resources, and assessments are well aligned with the curricular design. The process by which these decisions were made should be evaluated as well. How, for instance, were textbooks chosen? How were in-house materials created? Were results from the analysis and design phases effectively communicated to the developers? Were the developers qualified to produce final products for the curriculum? Were resources developed efficiently, as opposed to being rushed or taking too long to produce? Were stakeholders adequately involved in development? Were materials and resources piloted with teachers and students? Where piloting of curriculum components or resources occurred, were appropriate refinements made in the development phase?

Implementation
The implementation phase is inherently one of process, so it may be easier to evaluate than some of the previous steps. To evaluate implementation, consider how well the teachers and students adopted the new curricular material. There are bound to be areas where things could have gone smoother. Were there challenges with teachers, students, or other stakeholders that should be kept in mind for the implementation of subsequent iterations of curricular components? Can adjustments be made now to ameliorate any problems? Are the curricular materials, resources, and assessments functioning as envisioned in the design and development phases? Have needed adjustments been identified?

Evaluation
Evaluating the process of evaluation means looking for weaknesses in the evaluation method. It may sound circular, but this type of meta-evaluation is useful in making sure that the evaluation process itself is not biased or capricious. Thus, questions to ask may include the following. Were reasonable evaluands examined at each step? Were stable criteria used to evaluate each process and product? Was the evaluation sufficiently comprehensive and yet still practical? Did the methods of evaluation make sense and produce interpretable results? More will be discussed later in this chapter about selecting various methods for evaluation.

Evaluation standards can be useful when conducting a meta-evaluation (Yarbrough et al., 2011). The evaluators will undoubtedly find flaws or mistakes that may or may not affect the overall outcome of the initial evaluation. The purpose of meta-evaluation is not to nullify the initial evaluation. Instead, by looking back at the evaluation, limitations and strengths that may enhance the overall quality of the program can be identified. As a side effect, evaluators can also learn and enhance their skills to become better evaluators. See Box 11.5.

> **Box 11.5 A Quick Guide to Evaluating Product and Process**
> There is a lot to keep in mind when evaluating a language curriculum. Figure11.2 can keep all of these elements in perspective.

	PRODUCT	PROCESS
ANALYZE	Review the analysis documents to ensure that they are complete. Do they adequately describe answers to the critical questions: why, who, what, how, where, and when? Is there enough detail to guide the developer in designing the curriculum? Are the documents written so they can be easily understood and applied?	Look back at the analysis process to ensure that stakeholders were adequately involved and that essential insights were accurately captured from the critical questions, why, who, what, how, where, and when. Is anything missing from the process that should be included because of its potential to impact the curriculum?
DESIGN	Review design documents to ensure that they are complete. These may include descriptions of objectives, syllabi, various course materials, and resources, as well as test specifications for assessments. Also, see that they are clear enough to guide the developer in designing curricular components, materials, resources, assessments, and so on.	Look back at the design process to ensure that decisions regarding curricular components, resources, materials, and assessments were based on the most important information from the analysis. Determine whether input on the design was adequately gathered from a broad range of stakeholders with diverse perspectives. Is anything missing from the process that should be included because of its potential to impact the curriculum?
DEVELOP	Review curricular components, materials, resources, and assessments that have been developed to ensure that they are well aligned with the curricular design. See that the content is well written. Ensure that formatting is aesthetically pleasing and that it facilitates clarity and access by prospective teachers and students. See that materials and their accompanying instructions and activities are easily understood by those within and those outside the program.	Look back at the development process to ensure that curricular components, materials, resources, and assessments are well aligned with the curricular design. Were stakeholders adequately involved in development? Were materials and resources piloted with teachers and students? Where piloting of curriculum components or resources occurred, were appropriate refinements made in the development?

	PRODUCT	PROCESS
IMPLEMENT	Create and review an implementation document that describes challenges with implementation that need to be refined in future implementation. Also include a description of how well the materials seem to function in accordance with their design and development. Describe possible adjustments that may need to be made.	Look back on the implementation process. Were there challenges with teachers, students, or other stakeholders that should be kept in mind for the implementation of subsequent iterations of curricular components? Are the curricular materials, resources, and assessments functioning as envisioned in the design and development phases? Have needed adjustments been identified?

Figure 11.2 Elements for evaluating a language curriculum.

Process of Evaluation

The prospect of evaluating so many parts of a curriculum can seem daunting. Some evaluations are more formal and larger in scope. In reality, teachers and administrators are constantly evaluating informally. Smaller formal evaluations also occur regularly. This seven-step evaluation model proposed by Teraoka (2010) is a simplified yet complete step-by-step process for conducting formal and informal evaluations that can be applied to any evaluation, regardless of its scope or size. The seven steps are listed here and followed with broader descriptions of each step.

Step 1: Select an Evaluand
Step 2: Establish Evaluation Criteria
Step 3: Determine Evaluation Methods
Step 4: Collect Data to Answer Evaluation Questions
Step 5: Analyze and Interpret Results
Step 6: Present Results and Implications to Stakeholders
Step 7: Implement Change

Step 1: Select an Evaluand

Initially, an evaluand is easy to identify. It is a curricular product or process, as described earlier in this chapter. However, it does not have to be limited to just the listed products and processes; it could also be a person, activity, or other construct. Given these parameters, consider these major categories of evaluands that regularly impact curriculum development:

Learning—What is being learned by students?
Methods of Learning—How are students learning?
Teacher Performance—How are teachers helping learning?
Supporting Materials & Resources—What materials and resources are being used by students to learn?
Assessments—How effectively is learning being assessed?
Facilities—What impact do facilities have in the learning process?

Some example evaluands include a textbook, a new teacher, a placement procedure, or student engagement during class. Video conference software and other distance learning tools would be appropriate evaluands in online learning contexts. After selecting an evaluand, an evaluator must identify the purpose for the evaluation, such as responding to student needs, increasing the stability of a program, or improving cohesion among curricular components. If a convincing rationale cannot be presented, the evaluation is not likely to yield useful data or inform appropriate change and could be a waste of resources.

Step 2: Establish Evaluation Criteria
Establishing evaluation criteria is a matter of determining the important features of the curricular component under scrutiny and prioritizing them. A new textbook, for instance, might need to be interesting to students first and comprehensive in regard to course objectives second. A new test might need to be valid and reliable but also easy to grade and short enough to prevent test fatigue among the students. A learning management system might need to be user-friendly, inexpensive, and easily managed on multiple electronic devices. A mission statement might need to be inspiring, informative, and yet easy for teachers and students to understand.

Deciding upon relevant criteria does not need to be a difficult and time-consuming experience, although a little bit of research can help identify important features to consider. Take as an example the decision to adopt a new textbook. Evaluators might look through multiple textbook options to get an idea of features that are important in their final decision. They might also speak with publishers and teachers who can offer their own perspectives on criteria. Some teacher training manuals might also highlight elements of a textbook worth evaluating. And, of course, evaluators will have their own opinions. The point is not necessarily to have the perfect set of criteria; rather, the point is to have criteria that are relevant for the context in which the curricular component will be used. For instance, online, hybrid, and distance learning programs should have different criteria for evaluation than traditional programs. See Box 11.6.

Box 11.6   Evaluation Questions

Evaluation is a lot like research; both rely on the identification of a problem, an appropriate methodology, and the interpretation of results. And like scientific-based research, which is focused on answering a specific research question, evaluation should also be focused on answering specific *evaluation questions*. An evaluation question places the evaluand and criteria together in a single, measurement-oriented question. Here are some examples to illustrate such questions.

New Textbook

Context: A grammar class is in need of a new textbook, and curriculum designers have identified three potential candidates. Now they must narrow their selection to just one book. They have two major criteria: they want the book to address all the grammar points listed in the course objectives (coverage), and they want the book to be interesting and engaging to students (interest).

Evaluation question: Which book will offer the most grammar coverage and be of most interest to students?

Methodology: The evaluation question suggests that both teachers and students will need to be involved during the data collection process since teachers can evaluate the coverage and both teachers and students can provide insight into the textbook interest measure.

Revised Vocabulary Tests

Context: In an effort to increase language proficiency, a reading curriculum has revised a set of vocabulary tests. The tests were recently implemented, and evaluators want to determine whether the tests are helping students read better (Criterion 1) and are easy for the teachers and students to administer and take (Criterion 2).

Evaluation questions: To what extent do the revised vocabulary tests result in higher reading comprehension scores compared to the old vocabulary tests? Are the revised vocabulary tests easier for students and teachers to administer and take compared to the old tests?

Methodology: The evaluation questions require a comparison between old and new test administration. For the first question, quantitative scores on reading comprehension quizzes could be used, as well as some

> self-response questions asked of students to determine whether they feel like they are better at reading because of these tests. The second question also requires comparison, so evaluators and participants should, at a minimum, have some experience with both test types in order to offer comparative insights. Also, the criterion of "easy" in Question 2 might need to be unpacked with terms such as *quicker, more intuitive, simpler in design,* etc.

Step 3: Determine Evaluation Methods

In major evaluation tasks, an evaluand should ideally be measured using multiple triangulated approaches. These may include a combination of *qualitative methods*, such as observations, interviews, focus groups, open-ended questionnaires, and *quantitative methods* like achievement/experimental test data, grades, and checklists. Lynch (1996) delves into data collection more deeply and addresses positivistic and naturalistic approaches to evaluation methods and data collection.

Some evaluations require sophisticated and precise measurements of data, but others occur so quickly and have such local implications that there is no time or reason to design a complex evaluation methodology. An example may be evaluating one's speaking voice in a lecture hall, where the methodology is to say something out loud and see if students can hear. Often, evaluations with simplistic methodologies can become one piece of evidence in a larger evaluation. For instance, if students regularly find it difficult to hear in various lecture halls, additional qualitative methods could be employed to get a bigger picture of the problem (repeated observations or student input), as well as some quantitative methods (testing lecture hall acoustics, counting how many or which students are having trouble hearing).

Step 4: Collect Data

Once methods and instruments are designed, evaluators can then collect data from appropriate sources. For instance, sources may include any of the following:

1. Existing data
2. Program administrators (e.g., interviews, conversations, focus groups, etc.)
3. Individuals or groups affected by the curricular component being evaluated
4. Persons who planned, initiated, or funded curricular components

5. Persons with special expertise related to the curricular component
6. Curricular activities that can be directly observed

In collecting data, evaluators should consider who will participate in and who will make the evaluation. In the example of a lecture hall sound problem, participants minimally include the students (to listen) and the teacher (to perform a volume check). In survey, interview, and questionnaire methods, human beings are needed to serve as participants, and they should obviously have some experience with the evaluand in question. Methodologies that do not directly involve humans must still be executed or interpreted by a human, so identifying who will be involved in these processes is also vital.

Step 5: Analyze and Interpret Results

After collecting the data, evaluators should organize and interpret the results in a way that is useful for answering the evaluation question. In some cases, although not always, this may require specialized knowledge of analysis methodologies, such as statistical analysis. For instance, a language program director might want to evaluate student placement procedures by comparing students' scores on an entrance test with final class grades at the end of the first semester. A statistical test could reveal insights that even a careful look at the raw data might miss. However, a statistical analysis might be wasteful and even inappropriate if a program director were asking a handful of teachers to give feedback on a new attendance procedure, since it is hard to quantify a small number of verbal responses. Thus, keeping the evaluation questions and guiding purposes present will help evaluators remain neutral as they organize and interpret data in an appropriate way. See Box 11.7.

Box 11.7   More on Data Collection

Data collection involves more than just determining what to measure and who will take measurements. Other concerns of logistics, training, ethics, and pragmatics are similarly important.

Logistics	Assigning who will be involved in collection; scheduling where and when data collection should occur to produce the most representative sample
Training	Training data collectors to ensure that collected data is valid and reliable
Ethics	Protecting the confidentiality of participants
Pragmatics	Executing data collection within the institution's budget, time, and human resources constraints

The analysis phase of evaluation may also require evaluators to look for explanations of their findings in new ways by collecting follow-up data. For instance, if a teacher is evaluating a new online assignment and finds that most of his or her students failed the task, it might be easy to assume that the new online assignment was ineffective. But the teacher might ask the students about their experiences with the online assignment to learn why it broke down. If the students report they have no access to a computer, they are uncomfortable typing, or they couldn't get the internet to work, then the assignment's failure may have been strongly influenced by other factors that must be addressed before a new assignment can be properly evaluated.

Analysis of data should be sensitive to any limitations of the methods used. These limitations may include a small sample size, lack of triangulation, insufficient data, bias in how information was elicited or provided, or limited access to information and inexperience of data collectors. Knowing an evaluation's limitations will help others determine whether the data are *valid* (it reflects what it is intended to reflect) and *reliable* (similar results would be obtained if data were gathered again).

Step 6: Present Results and Implications to Stakeholders

An evaluation is not complete until its results have been shared with appropriate stakeholders. The primary stakeholder of an evaluation is generally the person or group who commissioned the evaluation and supplied funding or resources for the evaluation. However, not all evaluations are commissioned or funded by external groups; in fact, sometimes evaluations are done to prove a point to an otherwise unresponsive or unaware administrator, as might be the case when documenting expensive deficiencies in a curricular product. In this case, reporting the results to a director, a dean, a chair, or other official may be both important and politically difficult.

Before deciding what to say about evaluation results and how to say it, evaluators should first consider who their target audience is by answering these questions:

Interest: Who would be most interested in the findings?
Influence: Who has the most influence in initiating changes related to the findings?
Authority: Who is in the chain of command leading to the individual with the most influence?

How the results are reported will depend on the audience. A director, dean, or chair may have a busy schedule, so a report may need to be just a few key points in a five-minute "elevator talk," and such a speech should be prepared and rehearsed in advance. If reporting to students, evaluation results could be a simple in-class discussion of findings where the teacher initiates the presentation and interpretation of results; this kind of response to evaluation should happen after mid-term evaluations, for instance, so that students know that their evaluation responses matter. See Box 11.8.

In terms of reporting results, there are a number of venues that each serve a different purpose. For instance, results can be reported through an informal briefing, a class discussion, an elevator speech, a faculty meeting, a press conference, a government report, a scholarly presentation or publication, and so on. In some cases, only one of these venues is necessary for reporting results, but generally, disseminating information in multiple venues could be beneficial.

Box 11.8   Rhetoric and the Delivery of Results

Three principles of rhetoric can help build a solid foundation as evaluators plan to share their results with others.

Exigency

The first is *exigency*, or the catalyst for evaluation. When reporting evaluation results, you should clarify what exactly caused you to start the evaluation in the first place. Was it low test scores? Confusion on the part of students or teachers? A request from an administrator? A nagging feeling that finally led to an evaluative action?

Purpose

The second rhetorical principle is *purpose*—what is your purpose in sharing your evaluation results? Are you hoping to make a change, keep things the same, or just make others more aware of an ongoing situation? Understanding your purpose for sharing results will ensure that you and the audience are moving in the same direction.

Audience

The last principle is *audience*—you must know who you will be reporting your results to and what they value. If your audience values educational reform for the sake of better educational practices, you should discuss your results in terms of how a change will facilitate this objective. If your audience is a group of stockholders or financial sponsors, your results should help them understand the financial implications of your findings. Take the time to research the interests, preferences, political alliances, and pet projects of those members in your audience.

Step 7: Implement Change

In the graphical representation of the evaluation model, the box surrounding the last step is intentionally dashed. This is because the evaluator often will not have control over when results are perceived and acted upon. Evaluators may suggest implications based on the evaluation results, but these, too, may be ignored or modified by the stakeholders with control of change. Being aware of and even expecting this can prepare evaluators to pitch their results and their accompanying implications in a way that excites administrators or managers to action. But even if an evaluator will have a limited voice in an implementation discussion, it is helpful for the evaluator to consider possible implementation methods so they can provide recommendations, give an opinion on likely outcomes for proposed changes, or encourage stakeholders as they implement changes to their program based on evaluation results.

Of course, if an evaluator is in a position to implement his or her own changes, implementing them may still require some thoughtful planning and perhaps a return to previous principles in this book of designing, developing, and implementing a curriculum or curricular component.

Chapter Summary

In this chapter, the broad concept of evaluation was introduced, which is an activity that should accompany every stage of the curriculum design process. The house metaphor offers a strong connection to evaluation. Just as every part of home construction is scrutinized and evaluated, from the initial plan to on-site building work to final inspection, a curriculum needs constant and vigilant evaluation.

A simplistic definition of evaluation that compares a curriculum product or process to its ideal version along a set of established criteria was presented. Curricular evaluation may come as a reaction to a problem or a systematic checkup and may be formal, informal, formative, or summative. Evaluation can be applied to curricular products, such as learning outcomes, assessments, or learning experiences. It can also be applied to the processes involved in creating those products, which include the analysis, design, development, implementation, and even the evaluation steps.

We also proposed a seven-step process for evaluation that leads evaluators from selecting an evaluand to determining appropriate criteria and methods for the evaluation, collecting and analyzing data, and, finally, communicating findings and implementing changes. The point of evaluation is not just to take measurements; it is a tool to make methodic, rational decisions that will improve the curriculum. In every step of the curriculum change process, evaluation should be used to confirm that the whole process is moving toward a better curriculum, not just a different one.

Activities

Activity 11.1

Consider an evaluand of interest to you or your language program and prepare it for evaluation based on our simple definition by describing what the evaluand is or how it works now, what the idea would be, and two or three criteria that would help you evaluate the evaluand.

Activity 11.2

Think of three or four recent evaluations you have been involved in, whether as a participant, a developer, a facilitator, or an administrator. What types of evaluations were they? Options include formal/informal, formative/summative, and developmental/mandated/routine/reactionary.

Activity 11.3

Think through the major curricular products that can be evaluated and apply them to a language program you are familiar with. What governing documents can or should be evaluated? What assessments or feedback processes are in need of evaluation? What learning experiences are due for evaluation?

Activity 11.4

Imagine that, after years of waiting, your language program is finally being moved to a beautiful new building. Consider how you might evaluate the strengths and weaknesses of the new facility in terms of helping students learn. What criteria would you use to determine its strengths and weaknesses?

Activity 11.5

Reflect on a curricular product you were recently involved in changing or creating. Think back to the part(s) you were involved with and evaluate the process you used to reach your decisions. How did you analyze the context and student needs surrounding the product? What about the design, development, or implementation? Were your process evaluations sufficiently comprehensive, or did you make decisions on limited data, perhaps for practicality reasons? How would you approach the evaluation process differently next time?

Activity 11.6

Pretend that a colleague has contacted you to help him improve his teaching. He is worried because attendance at his class has gone down substantially in the last two weeks, but he doesn't know why. What evaluand makes sense to focus on given the limited context in this activity, and what types of evaluation (formal/informal and formative/summative) and specific methods would you use to evaluate that particular evaluand?

Activity 11.7

A reading teacher has purchased a class set of novels that students are expected to take home and read in preparation for daily comprehension checks each morning in class. Despite free access to the books, the students are consistently failing to achieve passing scores on their reading comprehension tests. What are some potential evaluands to examine in this situation? What kind of criteria and methods would you use when investigating those evaluands?

Activity 11.8

A program director is worried about grade inflation, since teachers have a lot of freedom to design and grade their own tests, quizzes, and assignments. To confirm or allay her fears, she has contacted you to perform a comprehensive evaluation of the assessment products and procedures in the program. What kinds of methods and data collection procedures could be used to perform such a large-scope analysis?

Activity 11.9

A teacher has given the following homework assignment to a group of low-proficiency ESL grammar students and explained the assignment carefully: "With a partner, please write and then produce a standard TV commercial (30 seconds long) encouraging people with your similar backgrounds to attend this language program. Your commercial should include at least four imperative phrases, since we have been learning about these types of statements in class. The due date is next Monday. Bring your videos to class on a laptop, so we can show them on the LCD projector." On the assignment due date, a couple of students came with very nice-looking video presentations, but the majority of students came unprepared, didn't have videos to show, or were absent altogether. The assignment appeared to be a disaster. Following the seven-step evaluation model, determine what you think the major problems with the assignment were. Obviously, Step 5 (analyze and interpret results) will not be possible, so make up a set of possible results and interpretations and continue with the model.

Activity 11.10

Think of a material, procedure, or component you have recently evaluated in your institution. Describe the evaluation process for your context, especially considering the seven-step evaluation model.

References

Lynch, B. K. (1996). *Language program evaluation: Theory and practice*. Cambridge University Press. http://dx.doi.org/10.1017/CBO9781139524629

Stake, R. E., & Schwandt, T. A. (2006). On discerning quality in evaluation. In I. Shaw, J. C. Greene, & M. M. Mark (Eds.), *The Sage handbook of evaluation* (pp. 404–418). Sage.

Teraoka, R. (2010). *Developing a curriculum evaluation model for the English language center at Brigham Young University* [Unpublished master's thesis, Brigham Young University].

Yarbrough, D. B., Shulha, L. M., Hopson, R. K., & Caruthers, F. A. (2011). *The program evaluation standards: A guide for evaluators and evaluation users* (3rd ed.). Sage.

Index

Note: Page numbers in *italics* indicate a figure and page numbers in **bold** indicate a table on the corresponding page.

AB Community College 62
ACTFL 134, 161
ADDIE model 2, *8*, *169*, 175–178, *194*
   graphic representation *5*, *13*, *43*, *128*
administrators 1, 35, 108, 202, 211
assessments 11–12, 153–154, 170–171
   difference between tests 155
   evaluating 232–234, 242
   traits of 157–161, 163–164, 233–234
      formative 11, 160
      summative 11–12, 160
   see also evaluation; tests

Backward Design 2
bottom-up approach 46
Brigham Young University *61*, *66*

class level development 8–10, *88*
   assessments 11, 171
   contextual analysis 40–41, 86
   learning outcomes 11, 26, *27–28*,
      74–75, *128–129*, 149–150
   mission statement 20–21, 23–24,
      27–28, 73–74, 231–232 (*see also*
      governing documents)
co-constructed model 29–31, 44
committees 118, 140–141, 231
Common European Framework of
   Reference (CEFR) 134
community college 7, 61–62, 116–117
concurrent university work 3, 68,
   105, 117
contextual analysis 4, 41–42, 52–53, 63
Contextualized Curriculum Model
   12–13; *see also* ADDIE model
contextual synthesis 102–103, 120–122
course level development 8–10, 12,
   20, *88*
   assessments 11, 171
   contextual analysis 40, 86

goal statements 20, 23, *27–28*, 67–70,
   71–72, 231 (*see also* governing
   documents)
learning outcomes 11, 26, 25, *27–28*,
   71, *128–129*, 144–148
COVID-19, 49, 201, 204
culture 6, 39, 46–47, 82, 200
curricular control 29–30, 201
curriculum
   constraints of 19, 36–38, 131
      cultural 7, *16*, 397
      governmental 38, 51
   definition of 18–19
   delivery of 197–198
   development of
      authority to develop 29 (*see also*
      curricular control)
      in context 4, 6–7, *13*, 35–37 (*see also*
      contextual analysis)
      revision 120, *147*
   etymology of 19
   impact of 1, 19
   traits of 75–76

Defense Language Institute 44
Design Layers 2
diagnostic tests 89, 92, 156; *see also*
   placement tests; proficiency tests;
   tests
distance learning 41, 51, 130, 243; *see also*
   online instruction
Dynamic Written Corrective Feedback
   (DWCF) 69

elevator speech 215, 246
English Foreign Language teaching
   (EFL) 6–7, 10
English Second Language teaching
   (ESL) 6–7, 49, 83–84
   in examples 23, *27–28*, *61*, *68–69*, *110–117*

evaluand *228–229*, 241–242
evaluation 139, *169*, *194*, 225, 227–228
  process of 241–248
  self-evaluation 227, 229
  types of 225–227
exams *see* tests

feedback 11–12, 63, 139, 162–163
  evaluating 233–234
First Year Composition program (FYC) 116
focus groups 63, 120, *226*, 244
funding 35, 51, 209–211, 246
  self-funding 38–39

Generation 1.5 *48*, 117
goal *see* course level development
Google Docs 207
governing documents 21–22, 27, *104–105*, *119*
  evaluating 230
  levels of
    goal statements 20, 23, 26, 67–71, 231
    learning objectives 20–21, 23–24, 26, 73–74, 231–232
    mission statements 20, 22, 25, 59–64, 230–231)
  process of writing 63–64, 69–70, 74
  traits of 75–76
group activities *22–23*, *74*, *179*, 188

hidden curriculum 35–36
hybrid learning 51, 130, 243; *see also* online instruction

IEP 9–10, 42, 124, 145–147
Interagency Language Roundtable (ILR) 134

Jackson, Phillip 35

lacks 89, *90*, 92, 175
learning experiences 12
learning outcomes 11, *22–23*, 24–26, 73–74, 130–132, 231
  types of 145
  see also governing documents
lesson plans 73–74, 182, 188–189, *192*, 194; *see also* class level development
linguistic diversity 113

mind documentation 24
mission *see* program level development
multiple choice questions 164–166, 170–171

Northshore Community College 61

objective *see* class level development
online instruction 39–41, 49–51, 201, 207, 243; *see also* distance learning; hybrid learning
oral proficiency interviews 161, 166

PAR story *215*
pedagogy *178*
placement tests 156, 232; *see also* diagnostic tests; proficiency tests; tests
process-oriented curriculum design 2; *see also* ADDIE model
product-oriented curriculum design 2
proficiency levels 135
proficiency tests 9–10, 156; *see also* diagnostic tests; placement tests; tests
program level development 8–10, 19–20, *88*, 94–96, 209
  assessments 9–11, 161
  contextual analysis 42–51, 86, 134
  learning outcomes 11, 20, 25, *27–28*, 65–67, *128–129*, 133
  mission statements 11, 20, 22, *27–28*, 87–88, 230 (*see also* governing documents)
  program-wide activities 10, 12
project timeline 120, 209, 213–214
prototyping *138*, 139–140, *147–148*

quizzes 11, 155; *see also* tests

racism 35–36

SAM 2
sexism 35–36
special education needs 47, 170, *233*
stakeholders 210
surveys 52–53, *119*, 245
  examples 56–57
  see also assessments; feedback

teacher-student relationship 177, 188, 200, 204
teaching assistants (TAs) 200, 211
testing center 166–167
tests 10, 11, 154–157
   online proctoring 201, 205–206
   test development 155, 162
   traits of 157–161
   types of 160
   writing based tests 166–167
   see also assessments
textbooks 19, 40, 69, 176, 202
   online 203

TOEFL 11, 86, 156, 161, 232; *see also* proficiency tests
top-down approach 31, 46
Trickle-Down Curricular Governance *24*
tutoring *179*, 203

virtual learning *see* online instruction

washback 89, 235

zoning laws 38; *see also* curriculum, constraints of